Kelly's
Financial Planning
for the Individual

(7th Edition)

A guide to investment and personal finance

SIMON PHILIP FIFP, CFP
Arthur Andersen

Published by
GEE Publishing Ltd

Previous editions published in 1986, 1987, 1989, 1994, 1996 and 1998.

7th edition published by GEE Publishing Ltd 2000.

ISBN 1 86089 915 3

GEE Publishing Ltd
100 Avenue Road
Swiss Cottage
London NW3 3PG
tel: 020 7393 7400
www.gee.co.uk

Typeset by
Multiplex Medway Ltd, Walderslade, Kent.

Printed by Bell and Bain Ltd, Glasgow.

Contents

| *Chapter* | *Page no.* |

Biography of Simon Philip

Simon Philip is a Private Client Services Partner in Arthur Andersen. He is a Fellow of the Institute of Financial Planning, Chairman of its Technical Committee, and is a Certified Financial Planner. He writes regularly for newspapers and magazines on various personal finance matters and is regularly quoted in the financial press. He advises a large number of private and corporate clients.

Preface

Regular readers of *Kelly's Financial Planning for the Individual* will be aware that its main purpose is to state, in concise and easily readable terms, the main aspects involved in financial planning for individuals. This edition is no different. It is aimed primarily at professional advisers and individuals wishing to make maximum use of their money.

Since the sixth edition was published in 1998, there have been a substantial number of changes in legislation and the investment product marketplace and these have been incorporated in the text. We have added a significant amount of new content, particularly in new chapters called 'Land and property investments' and 'Higher risk and alternative investments'. These new chapters, as well as dealing with mainstream issues, have allowed us to spread into such exotica as spread betting, woodlands and racehorses. Finally, there has been an update of tax rates and allowances, savings rates and life assurance rates.

As ever, there are a number of people to whom I would like to pay tribute for their contribution to the preparation of this edition. For the last three editions, David Wells has shouldered a significant part of the burden of getting the book to print. On this occasion, he has borne virtually the whole burden, thus enabling me to focus on client commitments. I am aware that the book provided an interest for him whilst convalescing at home after repairs, however I owe him my deepest gratitude for the many hours he has invested.

I would also like to pay special thanks to Patricia Mock and Ian Luder who have allowed me to incorporate significant amounts of their Arthur Andersen text *Personal Tax and Investment Planning* and this has added greatly to the book.

In addition, I would like to thank my colleagues in the Private Client Services team at Arthur Andersen. They are a fantastic team to work with, and many of the issues that this book seeks to capture have arisen from work done for our clients. I would particularly like to thank Orlando Harvey Wood, Jon Preston, Charlotte Philpott and Clair James. I would also like to thank Michael Voller of the Michael Voller Tax Consultancy and Ann Whitfield of Macfarlanes who provided their specialist advice.

Finally, I would like to thank the Kelly family whose enthusiasm continues to make this book possible and, most importantly, my wife Alison and daughters Annabel and Georgina who always provide me with unfailing support and encouragement.

Simon Philip
London
August 2000

1   Introduction to Financial Planning

A definition of financial planning for the individual could be: 'finding the best ways of utilising the financial facilities that exist in order to maximise personal wealth and minimise personal taxation'. This book is concerned with achieving that optimum state.

The range of knowledge required to manage one's own financial affairs successfully can be very wide, covering the whole field of savings, investments, pension arrangements, life assurance policies, mortgages, provision for school fees and tax avoidance measures. Under the heading 'investment' alone, the opportunities extend from the traditional areas of unit trusts, single premium life assurance investment bonds and stocks and shares to specialist investments such as works of art, stamps, forestry and even bloodstock. However, while many individuals will have little cause to venture into the less traditional fields, they will still be faced with a myriad of options in every aspect of financial planning.

The key to successful planning lies not just in making the right selection, but making the decision that best suits one's personal requirements. This involves striking the correct balance between savings and investments, ensuring one has sufficient liquidity, and establishing that investments are tax efficient and provide the return at the right time, at an acceptable level of risk.

The benefits of thorough forward planning of financial matters, both in the long and the short term, cannot be over emphasised. To this end, this first chapter includes a comprehensive examination of how to recognise indicators which signal the need for financial action and how to establish the requirements of any individual.

For the purpose of convenience, the male gender has been generally used throughout the book. However, unless otherwise stated, the information applies equally to females.

1:1   Signposts for action

There are a number of circumstances that should signal that appropriate action may be necessary, including

(a) substantial unearned income by way of interest received from cash deposits;

(b) no life assurance premiums paid, indicating that life cover may be required;

(c) the payment of income tax at the higher rate;

(d) investment portfolio shows very small holdings in many individual companies, with the resultant copious paperwork;

(e) substantial proportion of an estate in a marriage being in one spouse's name;

(f) a higher rate taxpayer with large holdings in loan stocks or high yielding gilts;

(g) substantial cash deposits being held, whilst a mortgage is outstanding;

(h) income-producing assets being held by a higher rate taxpayer, when a spouse is taxed at lower rates;

(i) credit balances on directors' current accounts in private companies while the companies have substantial cash balances at the bank;

(j) no pension scheme contributions in the accounts of companies;

(k) no pension contributions paid where the individual is self employed or in non-pensionable employment;

(l) the imminent acquisition of a capital sum, for example, from the sale of a business or property or other asset or an inheritance;

(m) no capital funding arrangements for share purchase or partnership purchase on death or retirement;

(n) an income which just exceeds the maximum for age allowance purposes;

(o) no will;

(p) no provision for income in the event of ill-health;

(q) an elderly person with grandchildren or nieces and nephews;

(r) the prospect of retirement within the next five to ten years.

The types of action which may be taken in all of these circumstances are dealt with in depth in the subsequent chapters.

1:2   Financial services legislation

A particular problem for both the individual and the professional adviser is the constantly changing financial environment resulting from new legislation and changes in economic and market conditions. The last 14 years have seen substantial financial services legislation implemented, and this has had a considerable impact on investment providers and intermediaries and on their dealings with clients. Further reforms are on the way following the passing of the Financial Services and Markets Act 2000.

Regrettably, financial scandals have also been a feature of recent years and investors are now more aware of the need to obtain advice from competent and honest independent advisers and to examine that advice critically before investing.

1:2.1 The legislation

The Financial Services Act 1986 (the Act) replaced the Prevention of Fraud (Investments) Act 1958 in order to provide more effective protection for investors. The Financial Services and Markets Act 2000 has a wider scope and brings all regulation under the control of the Financial Services Authority (the FSA). It is expected to be implemented in the summer of 2001.

1:2.2 Authorisation

In order to carry on investment business, it is necessary for a person to be authorised to do so, unless specifically exempted (conducting investment business without authorisation is a criminal offence). Previously, a professional adviser could obtain authorisation:

(a) by being a member of a self-regulatory organisation (SRO);

(b) by being a member of a recognised professional body (RPB); or

(c) by direct authorisation by the Financial Services Authority (formerly the Securities and Investments Board (SIB)).

In future, authorisation will be granted to advisers by the Financial Services Authority.

Someone offering investment advice has a choice of two basic options. They can either choose total independence (an independent intermediary) or to be tied to one organisation (a tied agent or appointed representative). A high proportion of independent intermediaries have chosen to join 'networks' – organisations which regulate them as appointed representatives and provide research and support to all their members. All advisers are obliged to make their status clear to members of the public.

An independent intermediary is a person (or firm or company) authorised by an SRO, RPB or the FSA to advise on and/or arrange investments. Where advice is being given, he is required to have knowledge of the investment market and the range of products available, and to recommend those best suited to the particular individual. He is the agent of his client.

Appointed representatives are the responsibility of the authorised business which appoints them. Those employed by insurance and investment companies are permitted to advise on and arrange only investment products provided by their companies.

A further choice is available to those involved in arranging investment business and that is to be merely an introducer. Introducers must decide whether they will refer clients to one appointed representative or to independent intermediaries. Introducing investment business to independent intermediaries is not 'investment business' under the Act.

1:2.3 Investment business

The five broad categories of investment business defined in the Act are as follows

(a) dealing in investments;

(b) arranging deals in investments through others;

(c) safeguarding and administering investment assets;

(d) managing investments belonging to others;

(e) advising others on their investments (both general advice and in relation to specific investments);

(f) establishing, operating or winding up a collective investment scheme, such as a unit trust.

The adviser will have to comply with strict rules as regards investment work. The following requirements are of particular relevance.

1:2.3.1 Client agreement

An adviser may not enter into a transaction with a client unless it is in accordance with the terms of a written agreement. Although the format for the agreement is not laid down, the regulatory bodies do list a substantial number of items to which it must refer. These include a statement of the basis on which the adviser is to be paid, a statement of the client's objectives and risk profile and any restrictions on the type of investments which he or she wishes to make, details of termination procedures and of the client's cancellation rights, if any.

1:2.3.2 Know your client

This requirement includes a general provision that an adviser must take reasonable steps to ascertain details of the client's financial and personal situation which are relevant to the investment services to be provided. The adviser should also have reasonable grounds to assume that the client can meet the financial liabilities of the transaction and, most importantly, that he understands the risks involved.

1:2.3.3 Best advice

The best advice requirement follows on from the need to know the client. An adviser must not make a specific recommendation to the client unless he knows it is suitable for him. Where a client requests a specific investment which the adviser believes is unsuitable, he must make his view known (preferably in writing) to the client and only proceed if the client still insists; alternatively, the adviser may decline to act. Independent advisers are required to consider all the different types of investments available which meet the client's particular requirements.

Having chosen the most suitable type of contract, the adviser must then select the one which he believes to be the best of that type. He has therefore to keep himself informed as to the current terms in the market for each particular product; there are electronic networks and regular publications which enable him to do this. In some cases, for example annuities and term assurance, cost will be the principal factor.

For others, advisers should take into account such factors as underwriting requirements, likely future investment performance, standards of service, policy charges and the financial strength of each company. In assessing the products available, they must include those of non-commission-paying offices.

1:2.3.4 Best execution

This requirement involves the adviser in ensuring that the transaction is carried out on the best terms available. This will include price, charges and any other advantages to the client.

1:2.3.5 Cancellation rules

The cancellation rules of the FSA apply to investment agreements in respect of regular premium life assurance policies and personal pension contracts. Subject to certain exceptions, where the rights of investors are already adequately safeguarded, these rules also apply to single premium life assurance policies and unit trusts and OEICs (whether bought directly or through ISAs).

1:2.3.6 Record keeping

In order for the best advice and best execution rules to be adequately policed, there are strict requirements for the adviser's records to show the reasons for any particular recommendation. Accordingly, all instructions received from a client should be fully recorded. After the instructions have been carried out, the adviser must see that the client is sent a statement giving full details of the transaction.

1:2.3.7 Clients' money

This must be held on trust for the client and held in a separate bank account from the adviser's own monies.

1:2.3.8 Financial resources

These rules lay down the financial resources that must be maintained at all times and vary according to the size, nature and type of investment business and the associated risks involved.

1:3 Professional advice

For some individuals, impartial professional advice will be essential at the outset, often because they do not have the time to devote to assessing their best course of action. However, those who undertake their own financial planning should have an approach as thorough as a professional adviser's. Despite this, it is almost inevitable that at some stage specialist advice will be required.

Obtaining professional advice involves its own selection process. Apart from the requirements of the legislation, it is useful to examine the main criteria which should indicate that the professional adviser is providing a thorough and competent service

(a) the adviser must be regulated and authorised by one of the bodies that regulate investment business (see **Appendix 1**);

(b) the adviser should consider all aspects of the client's affairs without restricting himself to particular areas;

(c) a positive service should be provided, with the adviser approaching the client where appropriate;

(d) regular reviews of the client's affairs should be carried out;

(e) the adviser should recommend non-commission paying contracts and investments if they are most suitable for the client;

(f) where a fee basis operates, any commissions received should be declared and taken into account against the fee or used to obtain better terms for the client;

(g) the adviser should have a good technical knowledge and, ideally, should have appropriate professional qualifications;

(h) the adviser should carry an appropriate level of professional indemnity insurance.

An investor intending to appoint a financial adviser should question potential candidates on these points. If the adviser has been recommended by a person who has already used his or her services, this is clearly advantageous.

1:4   Ascertaining client requirements

In order to meet the 'know your client' requirements, it is essential for the adviser to ascertain the circumstances of the client, together with their personal and financial requirements. To do this, the adviser should normally meet the client at least once and perhaps several times before final advice can be given. At the first meeting, the adviser will need to obtain the necessary information. **Appendix 2** is an in-depth questionnaire of a type which a professional adviser might employ and will additionally provide a guide as to where action needs to be taken.

1:5   Reports

Once the requirements are established, the adviser will usually make a report summarising the present position and making proposals for a course of action to be taken. It will be up to the client to decide whether to proceed with them or not. It is preferable that the proposals are made in writing to avoid any misunderstandings that could subsequently arise.

There is no set form of report, as this will mainly depend upon the particular case as well as personal style. Where investment planning is being undertaken, it is often useful for supporting statements to be prepared showing the capital and net spendable income position both in the present situation and that immediately afterwards if the proposed course of action is taken.

1:6 Reviews

Even after a client has acted upon the adviser's proposals, he or she will still need an ongoing service through regular reviews. In most cases, an annual review should be sufficient but this will depend on whether the client's own circumstances have changed, for example, as the result of the inheritance of a capital sum or a change of job, or because of external factors, such as new products or major changes in legislation or economic and market conditions. The management of personal finances can only benefit from regular dialogue between adviser and client. Without this dialogue, opportunities will be missed and the benefits of past advice will be dissipated.

2 Investment planning

Once the individual's personal circumstances and financial requirements have been established as outlined in the previous chapter, consideration can be given to appropriate investment planning.

2:1 Investment considerations

The following specific information should be settled at the outset before a decision is taken on particular investments

(a) the amount of capital available for investment;

(b) precise details of existing investments;

(c) the ages of the individual and his or her dependants;

(d) the degree of risk the individual is prepared to take, bearing in mind there is often a close correlation between risk and reward;

(e) the period of time for which the investments can be made before access to the capital is required;

(f) whether or not some investments can be subject to a period of notice;

(g) the current and likely future tax position of the individual;

(h) the income required from the investments;

(i) whether the main requirement is capital growth, income, or a combination of the two;

(j) whether the investments are to be made within any particular constraints, such as trustee investments or ethical considerations;

(k) the degree of involvement which the individual may wish to have in arranging and managing the investments;

(l) details of any anticipated capital receivable in the short term, such as proceeds from a life policy or an inheritance;

(m) details of any significant liabilities or personal expenses likely to arise in the near future, for example, tax liabilities or the purchase of a new car;

(n) whether there are any personal priorities or objectives, such as the provision of school fees;

(o) whether adequate arrangements have already been made in respect of the following

    (i)   pension provision;

    (ii)   life assurance cover to protect the family in the event of early death;

    (iii)   house purchase (consideration should be given to repaying any mortgage or loan);

    (iv)   wills and inheritance tax planning;

    (v)   permanent health insurance.

Having ascertained the above information, it should be possible to prepare a broad investment structure. For this purpose, capital should normally be invested in three categories in the following order, with the exact proportion in each category based on the individual circumstances

(a) The first part of the capital should be in an emergency fund for complete security and immediate access, for example a bank or building society deposit account.

(b) The second part of the capital should be in low risk investments with guaranteed returns, like short-dated gilt-edged securities. Such investments can usually be realised at short notice. A higher net investment return (capital growth plus income) can often be provided from this part of the capital than from the emergency fund. This part of the capital can also be used for the purposes of imminent house purchase or annual tax liabilities.

(c) The third part of the capital should be in higher risk/higher reward investments with the aim of providing a higher net return than both the rate of inflation and the rate obtainable from fixed interest investments. The usual assets are carefully selected shares, investment trusts, unit trusts or OEICs. The investments in this category should normally be considered as longer-term investments, with a view to being held for a minimum period of four to five years.

Notes

1. For people who have retired or who will retire shortly, a greater proportion of capital should normally be invested in the first and second parts since they would usually be less able to make good any capital loss out of their future income.

2. In considering the proportion of capital to be invested in the third part, the effect of inflation and normal life expectancy should be borne in mind. These are illustrated in the following tables.

The effect of inflation is such that £1,000 in today's money will be worth the amount stated at the end of the period shown if the annual rate of inflation over the period is as indicated.

End of Year	2¹/2% inflation	5% inflation	7¹/2% inflation
1	976	952	930
2	952	907	865
3	929	864	805
4	906	823	749
5	884	784	697
10	781	614	485
15	690	481	338
20	610	377	235
25	539	295	164
30	477	231	114
35	421	181	80
40	372	142	55
45	329	111	39
50	291	87	27

The normal life expectancy of a person is as shown below

Present age	Male – years	Female – years
50	33.1	36.1
55	28.3	31.3
60	23.5	26.5
65	19.0	21.9
70	14.9	17.7
75	11.3	14.0
80	8.4	10.7
85	6.1	8.1
90	4.4	6.0
95	3.3	4.5

When the general structure for the capital has been decided, the various types of investments can then be considered. These may be divided into the two main categories of

● fixed investments; and

● variable investments.

11

2:2   Fixed investments

The principal feature of fixed investments is that either the capital or the income arising (and sometimes both) is determined from the outset and is guaranteed (or is at least relatively certain) as long as the investment is held. These investments will form the first and second parts of capital (in some cases, they may also be included within the third part).

The specific choice of investment will depend on the exact circumstances of the individual and on the returns available from the various investments at the particular time together with the current and prospective levels of interest rates in general. The investment yields mentioned in this chapter are those available in September 2000 and are shown gross unless otherwise stated.

The more usual types of fixed investments are as follows

(a) cash accounts;

(b) money market funds;

(c) cash unit trusts;

(d) Tax Exempt Special Savings Accounts (TESSAs);

(e) National Savings investments;

(f) instant access insurance bonds;

(g) guaranteed income and guaranteed growth bonds;

(h) high income insurance bonds;

(i) gilt-edged securities;

(j) eurobonds;

(k) local authority loans;

(l) company debentures and unsecured loan stocks;

(m) permanent interest-bearing shares;

(n) preference shares;

(o) zero dividend preference shares of investment trusts; and

(p) purchased life annuities.

2:2.1   Cash accounts

The range of interest-bearing cash accounts has developed significantly in recent years. There is no longer either a concentration on branch-based accounts (of both banks and building societies) or a clear distinction between current and deposit accounts. New banks have come into being, owned by supermarkets and life assurance companies, and building societies have shed their mutual status and become banks with a Stock Exchange listing.

The main types of cash account available and the rates of interest being paid at September 2000 were

(a) branch current (cheque) accounts paying no interest;

(b) branch current (cheque) accounts paying a low rate of interest (0.1%–2.0% p.a.);

(c) telephone operated current accounts paying tiered rates of interest; payments may be made by cheque or by telephoned instructions (0.25%–1.0% p.a.);

(d) high interest cheque accounts paying 3.0%–6.0% p.a.; the rates on some of these are directly linked to the bank's base rate;

(e) branch based deposit accounts (0.2%–7.0% p.a.);

(f) postal deposit accounts, paying higher rates than branch based accounts and operated by post from a central office (1.4%–7.0% p.a.);

(g) telephone operated deposit accounts, with transfers made between the account and the investor's current account (1.0%–7.0% p.a.); and

(h) Internet accounts (paying 4.5%–7.0% p.a.).

Accounts operated electronically, by telephone or post require one to four days for money to be available, and so are not strictly 'instant access'. Some deposit accounts require a period of notice for withdrawals or restrict the number of withdrawals which may be made in a specified period. Deposits may sometimes be placed for a fixed period and/or at a fixed rate of interest.

In selecting a deposit account the investor will take into account

(a) the interest rate offered, in relation to those of other accounts;

(b) the financial strength of the deposit-taker;

(c) convenience; and

(d) any conditions imposed and their impact on his likely use of the account.

Interest is paid under deduction of income tax at the lower rate. This can be reclaimed by non-taxpayers, who can also apply on form R85 to have their interest paid without deduction of tax. This form is obtainable from banks and building societies.

In the unlikely event of a bank or building society becoming insolvent, investors will receive statutory protection. Under these arrangements, 90% of the deposit (subject to a maximum balance of £20,000) will be repaid.

2:2.2 Money market deposit accounts

Money market deposits are usually for a fixed term and are usually subject to a minimum investment of £10,000.

'Fixed term' means investments are for a fixed period, during which time investors cannot have access to the money invested. This term can vary from overnight to five years.

The interest paid is calculated on a daily basis and credited at regular intervals, or at the end of the investment period. The rate payable reflects current money market interest rates and varies according to the amount invested and either the investment period or notice required on withdrawal. Like traditional bank deposit accounts, interest is normally paid net of lower rate tax (the main exception to this is for investments of £50,000 or more for a fixed period of at least seven days where the interest is paid gross; these are known as time deposits).

For fixed terms, the following rates were payable at the time of writing (September 2000) by one of the major banks for amounts exceeding £50,000

one month	– 6.06%
three months	– 6.19%
six months	– 6.28%
one year	– 6.38%

These rates indicate that the bank believes that interest rates are currently on an upward trend.

Money market deposit accounts may be suitable for individuals with very large amounts as a short-term home until they commit their money on a longer-term basis. An example of this could be where someone intends to invest on the stock market when they consider the time is opportune. For smaller amounts, it is likely that an ordinary deposit account would be more suitable.

2:2.3 Cash unit trusts

Cash unit trusts are managed money funds, investing in a variety of instruments, which are commensurate with a proper degree of security. These investments can include bank deposits, short-dated gilt-edged securities, Treasury Bills and local authority bonds. Some cash unit trusts offer a cheque book facility, making them a very useful way of holding funds needed for occasional substantial payments.

2:2.4 Tax Exempt Special Savings Accounts (TESSAs)

The object of TESSAs was to encourage savers by enabling the accumulation of up to £9,000 of capital over five years in a tax-exempt deposit account. They were available only from banks, building societies and similar European institutions until 5 April 1999, when individual savings accounts (ISAs) were introduced. The capital of TESSAs maturing after 5 April 1999 may be reinvested either in the cash component of a max-ISA, or in a cash mini-ISA (see **Chapter 4**), or in a 'TESSA-only' ISA. The amount transferred does not count towards the ISA subscription limits.

The ISA must be opened within six months of the maturity of the TESSA. It does not have to be with the same bank or building society. If it is not, the provider of the TESSA must give the investor a certificate confirming the entitlement to the ISA, to be submitted with the application.

Providing the TESSA is kept open for five years, the interest credited is exempt from income tax.

Investments into a TESSA could not exceed £9,000 and could either be made by lump sums, not exceeding £3,000 in the first year and £1,800 in each of the next four years, or by regular savings up to £150 per month. If less than the maximum was invested in any year, the shortfall could not be carried forward to be used in subsequent years.

Interest was fixed at the outset or variable, and credited without deduction of income tax. It can be withdrawn, subject to retention within the TESSA of an amount equal to tax at the lower rate. The net interest is tax free at the time of withdrawal, and the retention is paid out tax free at maturity. At the present time (September 2000), TESSAs generally offer rates of up to 7.2% p.a.

If the investor withdraws more than the net interest, that is, some or all of the retained interest or the capital, the TESSA is automatically closed. Lower rate tax on all the interest earned will be deducted. Even if the interest has accrued over more than one year, it will all be taxable in the year of closure. It will also be subject to higher rate tax, if applicable.

2:2.5 National Savings investments

There are various types of National Savings investments available with the purpose of appealing to investors with different requirements and tax rates. The following National Savings investments were available in September 2000

(a) Fixed Interest Savings Certificates;

(b) Index-Linked Savings Certificates;

(c) National Savings Bank Ordinary Account;

(d) National Savings Bank Investment Account;

(e) Income Bonds;

(f) Pensioners' Guaranteed Income Bonds;

(g) Fixed Rate Savings Bonds;

(h) Capital Bonds (Series V);

(i) Children's Bonus Bonds (Issue S);

(j) Premium Bonds; and

(k) Individual Savings Account.

2:2.5.1 Fixed Interest Savings Certificates

Fixed interest certificates offer a guaranteed tax-free return if held to maturity. The minimum holding per individual is £100 and the normal maximum holding is £10,000, but husbands and wives can effectively double their maximum holdings by each holding certificates on trust for the other, in addition to their personal holdings. Holders of maturing issues of certificates may use the proceeds to purchase 'reinvestment certificates', for which there is no limit. If the certificates are encashed before maturity, the return provided is lower and depends on the length of time that they have been held. Certificates held beyond their maturity date continue to earn interest but only at the 'General Extension Rate'. This rate is normally unattractive (it is currently 3.09% per annum) to encourage investors to buy the current issue. National Savings now writes to holders of certificates to advise them of the maturity of their holdings.

At September 2000, National Savings offered two fixed-interest certificates

55th issue five-year certificates – interest: 4.15% per annum compound

4th issue two-year certificates – interest: 4.5% per annum compound

As these returns are tax free, the interest on the five-year certificates is equivalent to 5.19% per annum gross to a basic rate taxpayer and 6.92% per annum gross to a higher rate taxpayer. For the two-year certificates, the equivalent gross returns are 5.63% and 7.5% per annum, respectively.

2:2.5.2 Index-Linked Savings Certificates

The return offered by these certificates is tax-free and based on the change in the Retail Price Index (RPI) over the investment period together with extra interest at a fixed rate. Index-linking and interest are capitalised on each anniversary so that subsequent growth is based on the value at the beginning of the year. Early encashment, after the first year, will provide index-linking and interest additions (at varying rates) up to the month of withdrawal. The minimum individual holding is £100 and the maximum £10,000, but husbands and wives can effectively double their maximum holdings by each holding certificates on trust for the other, in addition to their personal holdings. As with fixed interest certificates, the proceeds of matured certificates can be invested (without limit) in reinvestment certificates. Certificates held beyond the maturity date will continue to be index-linked and to earn interest (at a rate to be determined).

Whether Index-Linked Certificates prove to be a worthwhile investment will mainly depend on the future level of inflation. In general, for investors who require a guaranteed real return and are unlikely to require access to their capital during the investment period, National Savings Index-Linked Certificates have definite attractions. The choice between Index-Linked Certificates and Index-Linked Gilts will depend on whether an income is required, the amount to be invested and the investment timescale.

At September 2000, National Savings offered two index-linked certificates

17th issue five-year certificates – interest: 2.0% per annum, plus RPI compound

4th issue two-year certificates – interest: 3.0% per annum, plus RPI compound

As these returns are tax free, the interest on the five-year certificates (assuming inflation at 2.5% per annum) is equivalent to 5.63% per annum gross to a basic rate taxpayer and 7.5% per annum gross to a higher rate taxpayer. For the two-year certificates the equivalent gross returns are 6.88% and 9.17% per annum, respectively.

2:2.5.3   National Savings Bank Ordinary Account

The rate of interest offered on this account at September 2000 is 1.85% per annum for each complete calendar month where the balance is £500 or more, provided the account is open for the whole of a calendar year. The rate received on other balances is 1.75% per annum. The minimum deposit per individual is £10 and the maximum deposit £10,000. Interest of up to £70 per annum (£140 per annum if the account is held jointly by two individuals) can be received tax free. Even for higher rate taxpayers, the National Savings Ordinary Account is unlikely to be attractive compared to other investments available.

2:2.5.4   National Savings Bank Investment Account

This account credits interest at the following rates (as at September 2000)

Under £500	4.5%
£500 – £2,499	4.6%
£2,500 – £4,999	4.7%
£5,000 – £9,999	4.8%
£10,000 – £24,999	5.0%
£25,000 – £49,999	5.3%
£50,000+	5.7%

The interest is taxable, but is credited without any deduction being made at source. Although the maximum deposit per account is £100,000, a higher balance is permitted if it results from interest credited to the account. Withdrawals are subject to one month's notice or, if the money is required immediately, a 30-day interest penalty.

A deposit in the National Savings Investment Account can be a worthwhile investment for an individual not liable to tax, particularly as there is no need for a tax repayment claim or a form R85 to be completed.

2:2.5.5   Income Bonds

The interest rate on Income Bonds at September 2000 is 6.0% per annum payable on the fifth day of each month for investments below £25,000. The rate increases to 6.25% per annum for investments of £25,000 and over. The minimum holding per individual is £500 and the maximum holding £1 million. Although the interest is paid gross, it is subject to tax.

The main disadvantage with National Savings Income Bonds is that if the interest is to be paid in full, three months' notice of withdrawal is required and the bonds must be held for a minimum period of one year (if the bonds are encashed earlier, half the normal rate of interest is payable). Instant encashments can be made, but are subject to a 90-day interest penalty. Consequently, this investment is likely to be more attractive to non-taxpayers who require a monthly income and are in a position to give the required period of notice for withdrawals.

2:2.5.6 Pensioners' Guaranteed Income Bonds

These bonds provide a fixed rate of interest for a fixed period. They are only available to those aged 60 and over. Interest is paid monthly without deduction of income tax, making the investment particularly attractive to non-taxpayers.

The minimum investment is £500 and the maximum is £1 million. Withdrawals, in whole or part, can be made at the end of the fixed period without penalty. If the bonds are encashed at any other time, 60 days' notice has to be given and no interest will be paid during the notice period. Alternatively, encashments can be made immediately, but subject to a 90-day interest penalty. The interest rate needs to be assessed in the light of likely changes in rates generally.

At September 2000, two issues of Pensioners' Guaranteed Income Bonds were available

Series 15 five-year bonds: interest 5.75% per annum

Series 6 two-year bonds: interest 6.0% per annum

2.2.5.7 Fixed Rate Savings Bonds

These bonds, introduced in 1999 to replace FIRST Option Bonds, are issued for fixed periods at fixed rates of interest. Interest is paid after deduction of income tax at the savings rate and may be credited monthly, annually or at maturity or paid out monthly. The investment periods and annual interest rates at September 2000 were

	£500– £19,999	£20,000– £49,999	£50,000– £1 million
6 months (issue 4)	5.8%	6.0%	6.2%
1 year (issue 3)	5.85%	6.1%	6.35%
18 months (issue 3)	5.9%	6.15%	6.4%

Initially, three-year bonds were also available, but these were withdrawn in June 2000.

The minimum investment is £500 and the maximum (for all bonds held) is £1 million. Applications may be made by post, by telephone (with payment by debit card) or in person at a post office. The bonds can be encashed fully or partially before maturity, but there is a penalty of 90 days' interest. The bonds are suitable for investors who like the security of fixed interest rates and government backing, but more attractive rates may be available from banks and building societies.

2:2.5.8   Capital Bonds (Series V)

At September 2000, these bonds offer a return which averages 5.65% per annum compound if held for the full five-year period. The interest rises from 4.9% per annum in the first year to 6.56% per annum in the fifth and is paid out at maturity. Although the interest is earned gross and added to the bonds, it is subject to tax (see below). If the bonds are encashed within five years, the return is lower and depends on the length of time the bonds are held. The minimum investment is £100 and the maximum is £250,000. There is no provision for the bonds to earn interest after the maturity date. The bondholder is liable to income tax on the interest added each year even though it is not actually paid to him. The real net return to a taxpayer at maturity is difficult to determine, due to the payment of tax in advance of receiving the proceeds and the uncertainty of future income tax rates. Capital bonds are most attractive to individuals not liable to income tax who require guaranteed capital growth over a five-year period.

2:2.5.9   Children's Bonus Bonds (Issue S)

These bonds can be purchased for children under the age of 16 by anyone aged over 16. The guaranteed rate of return is at present (September 2000) 5.25% per annum for the first five years that the investment is held. This consists of a basic rate of interest of 3.5% per annum plus a bonus at maturity of 10.36% of the purchase cost. The return is free from tax and no liability arises on parents who gift bonds to their children. The bonds will only provide a return until the holder's 21st birthday and are automatically encashed then. The minimum investment is £25, whilst the maximum for each issue is currently £1,000. Bonds are repayable on one month's notice, but the rate of return will only be 3.5% per annum if they are held for less than five years. No interest is paid on bonds held for less than 12 months.

2:2.5.10   Premium Bonds

A Premium Bond is effectively a lottery ticket which can be encashed for its face value (£1 per bond) at any time. Instead of being paid to bondholders, the interest is used to provide prizes for a limited number of investors. Monthly prize draws take place with the maximum prize being £1 million. At September 2000 the prize fund represents approximately 4.25% per annum of the total value of eligible bonds and all prizes (currently nearly 690,000 each month worth over £48 million) are received free of tax. Bonds are not eligible for inclusion in the prize draw until they have been held for one clear calendar month. The minimum initial holding of Premium Bonds is £100 per individual and the maximum holding £20,000.

Premium Bonds cannot strictly be classified as investments as the only return provided depends on the luck of the draw. The odds against winning any prize are 20,000 to 1. However, it is only the interest which is at stake, as the return of the capital is guaranteed. Consequently, this will be satisfactory for persons who are prepared to forgo the interest on their Premium Bonds in order to obtain the chance of receiving a large, tax-free windfall without risk to the value of their capital, other than by inflation. Public interest in Premium Bonds has increased since the introduction of the National Lottery, whose odds (for larger prizes) are considerably longer.

2.2.5.11   National Savings Individual Savings Accounts

National Savings offers a cash mini-ISA (see **Chapter 5**) and a TESSA-only ISA (see **2:2.4** above), both of which meet the CAT standards. The minimum deposit for both is £10. At September 2000, the rate on these accounts was 6.25% per annum, and interest is credited annually.

2:2.6   'Instant access' insurance bonds

Insurance bonds offering immediate withdrawals have been developed from guaranteed income bonds (see **2:2.7** below). They offer variable rates of interest which are attractive in relation to those on bank or building society deposits; at September 2000, they ranged from 4.15% per annum, net of basic rate tax on £5,000, to 4.65% p.a. on £50,000 or more (equivalent to 5.18% and 5.81% p.a. gross for a basic rate taxpayer and 5.67% and 6.35% per annum gross for a higher rate taxpayer). Higher rate taxpayers benefit from the fact that, although the insurance company has paid corporation tax on its income at 20% (or, possibly, effectively less), the tax credit attaching to the net interest is deemed to be at 22%, leaving only tax at 18% payable.

2:2.7　Guaranteed income and guaranteed growth bonds

The purpose of guaranteed bonds is to provide a fixed rate of income or growth over a preselected term (usually one to five years) in addition to the return of the original capital sum at the end of that period. There are four main types of guaranteed bonds, all issued by life assurance companies. Each has a different structure and accordingly is taxed in a different way, as follows

(a) a combination of temporary and deferred annuities;

(b) a single premium endowment policy (this is the most common);

(c) a series of single premium endowment policies;

(d) a series of single premium endowment policies plus term assurance.

The following are the principal considerations relating to guaranteed income and guaranteed growth bonds

(a) The rate of income or growth quoted is net of basic rate tax, but is subject to higher rate tax at the time of payment of the income or at maturity. On income bonds, there may also be a potential higher rate tax charge on the return of capital (where deferred annuities are included as part of the income bonds, a charge to lower rate tax will also arise).

(b) Income payments are generally made annually, although sometimes half-yearly, quarterly or monthly.

(c) If the individual should die during the term of the bond, the amount of the investment is returned (accrued income to the date of death will be paid).

(d) Surrender values, where allowed, are not normally guaranteed and will generally depend on financial conditions at the time. An investor who wishes to dispose of his bond before its maturity may, as an alternative to surrendering it, be able to sell it to a dealer in traded endowment policies (see **section 10:5**).

(e) The returns are fixed. Therefore, before an investor becomes locked in at a fixed rate of interest, he should take the view that interest rates are unlikely to rise. However, if he considers that higher rates are likely, it may be appropriate for him to invest in a variable interest investment, such as a building society account, on a temporary basis and then reinvest in guaranteed bonds at a later date if he proves to be correct.

(f) Since guaranteed bonds are frequently offered by less established insurance companies, potential investors should ensure as far as possible that the financial position of the company concerned is soundly based.

(g) If a person normally qualifies for age allowance, it should be remembered that their position could be affected by the taxation treatment of the guaranteed bonds.

(h) The rates of interest provided under guaranteed income and guaranteed growth bonds tend to lag behind general market interest rates. Therefore, potential investors should be prepared to act quickly when market rates have fallen, but before this is reflected in the rates offered by the guaranteed bonds.

At September 2000, returns of approximately 5.0% per annum net of basic rate tax can be obtained for periods of both one and five years, on amounts of £10,000 or more.

For amounts of £50,000 or more invested for at least three months, two insurance companies will arrange a guaranteed bond to mature on a date specified by the investor, for which it will quote a 'bespoke' rate. This is particularly useful for investors who have a known liability (e.g. a tax payment) on a specific date.

2:2.8   High income insurance bonds

From time to time, insurance companies offer bonds which will pay an 'income' of 8–10% per annum (monthly, quarterly or annually) for a period of three to six years. Such offers are available for a limited period of four to six weeks.

The counterbalance to these exceptionally high rates is the risk to the capital invested. Repayment of the initial capital in full is dependent on the performance of one or more equity indices – typically, the FTSE-100 in the UK, the Standard & Poor's 500 in the US and/or the Dow Jones Eurostoxx 50 index in Europe. If all the indices are higher at the end of the investment period or have not fallen by more than a specified amount (often the closing index readings are averaged over six or twelve months), all the capital is repaid; if not, only the initial capital less the 'income' payments is returned. These contracts are based on derivative contracts constructed by leading investment banks. Investors need to appreciate the equity risk which underlies these superficially attractive arrangements.

2:2.9   Gilt-edged securities

Gilt-edged securities (gilts) are issued by the British government in the form of loans in order to finance its expenditure. Since the loans are government backed, their repayment on the relevant maturity dates is assured, although in the interim prices will fluctuate according to market forces. The following are some of the more important characteristics of the gilt-edged market for the private investor (the tax treatment of income and capital gains is discussed in **Chapter 12**)

(a) Due to the very wide choice of gilt-edged securities offered, it is usually possible to select a particular issue to fit the investor's circumstances. The various types available are as follows

    (i)   short-dated (with maturity dates within five years);

    (ii)   medium-dated (with maturity dates after five years but within fifteen years);

    (iii) long-dated (with maturity dates after fifteen years);

    (iv)   undated (with no maturity dates);

    (v)   convertible (gilts with an option for the holder to switch into a longer-dated gilt at a series of fixed dates, typically six months apart, during the life of the convertible stock);

    (vi)   index-linked (where both capital growth and income are based on changes in the RPI. See **(f)** below).

    Dated gilts (other than index-linked gilts) can be further divided into low-, medium- and high-coupon stocks. Coupons range from 2% to $13^{1}/2\%$. Normally, high-coupon stocks will be more suitable for pension funds, charities and individuals not liable to tax, while low coupon issues will be more appropriate for individuals paying tax at the higher rate due to the greater potential for tax-free capital growth. At September 2000, most fixed interest gilts were standing at prices above their repayment values, because of the fall in interest rates in recent years. Prospective investors must, therefore, take the certainty of a capital loss at redemption into account before buying stock.

(b) At maturity, £100 nominal of stock will be redeemed for £100 except in the case of index-linked stocks.

(c) The volatility of the price of a gilt will mainly depend on the nominal rate of the coupon and the length of the period until the redemption date. Low-coupon and long-dated stocks will generally be more volatile than high-coupon and short-dated stocks.

(d) The shape of the yield curve, which plots the current redemption yields of different gilts against their periods to maturity, will normally indicate general expectations for movements in interest rates and the outlook for inflation. Short-dated gilts are more affected by interest rates while longer issues also reflect views on inflation. The redemption yields on very short-dated gilts reflect current interest rates, whereas those on long-dated gilts are slightly lower, reflecting the expectation of lower interest rates and inflation as European economies converge.

(e) Price anomalies can arise in the gilt-edged market, and, by being alert, it is possible for an investor to obtain benefit from them. These anomalies usually occur due to there being a shortage or excess of a particular stock at a particular time. They are, however, usually so small that, after taking dealing expenses into account, the benefit of switching is, for a private investor, minimal.

(f) Index-linked gilts, whereby both the capital and interest exactly reflect the change in the RPI, were first issued in March 1981 and subsequently became available to private investors in March 1982. As a result, an individual was able for the first time to obtain a guaranteed real rate of return on his investments. (The change in the RPI is measured over the period from eight months before the issue date of a gilt to eight months before its redemption date.)

However, in order for this return to be guaranteed, the gilt must be held until redemption, since its price in the interim will be mainly determined by the following factors

(i)   the supply and demand in the market;

(ii)   the current level and outlook for interest rates;

(iii)   the yields offered by conventional gilts;

(iv)   the rate of inflation which has occurred for the period from eight months before the issue date to the present time;

(v)   the outlook for inflation from the present time until eight months before the redemption date.

Currently (September 2000), investors can obtain a real rate of return to redemption (capital plus income) of around 1.8% to 3.8% per annum before tax, assuming inflation at 3% per annum.

Index-linked gilts are a worthwhile investment for those investors wishing to obtain a guaranteed real return from part of their capital. This particularly applies to individuals paying tax at the higher rate. Where a gilt is unlikely to be held until its redemption date, it should be remembered that, as in the case of conventional gilts, the stocks with the earlier maturity dates will carry less risk.

(g) Where gilt-edged securities are purchased directly from the Bank of England rather than through a stockbroker, dealing costs are lower, especially for smaller bargains. This route does, however, have the following disadvantages

    (i)   a maximum investment is permitted in any one stock of only £25,000 per day (this does not apply to sales); and

    (ii)   it is not possible to specify either the date of the transaction or the price at which a stock should be purchased or sold.

(h) Interest payments are made without deduction of tax. The investor may, however, request that income tax at the savings rate is deducted before payment of the net amount. All gilt interest is free of tax to non-UK residents.

2:2.10   Eurobonds

Eurobonds are bonds, usually issued in a foreign currency, which are traded internationally. Interest is normally paid gross on an annual basis. Although marketability is usually good in high-quality bonds (Triple A bonds), an investment of less than £20,000 is not practical. Due to the complexity of settlement and the variety of bonds available, professional advice is generally necessary when making an investment.

2:2.11   Local authority loans

Local authorities raise loans in order to assist in financing their expenditure. Although the security provided is generally of a high order, these loans do not have the same backing as gilt-edged securities, or the same marketability. As a result, the yields from local authority loans are usually greater than those available from comparable gilts.

There are two main types of local authority loan

(a) Fixed-term unquoted corporation bonds. These bonds are issued and repaid at par for a fixed period (up to seven years) and at a fixed interest rate. Consequently, the return provided will be in the form of interest only and this will be based on general market rates at the time the loans are raised. Since fixed-term unquoted corporation loans are not marketable, an individual is unable to obtain the repayment of his investment until maturity (or death if earlier).

(b) Quoted corporation loans. These loans have many of the features of gilt-edged securities, including a wide range of coupons and maturity dates.

However, the market is often small and consequently it is not always possible to buy in reasonable amounts.

The tax treatment of an individual investing in local authority bonds is discussed in **Chapter 12**.

2:2.12   Company debentures and unsecured loan stocks

These loans, which are normally raised by companies to provide, for example, working capital, are often traded on the Stock Exchange. In the case of company debentures, the loans are secured on particular company assets, or a floating charge is made on the assets generally. However, no specific security is provided for unsecured loan stocks.

Company debentures and unsecured loan stocks can be issued in convertible or non-convertible form. When issued in convertible form, stockholders are provided with the option to convert their investments into the ordinary shares of the company at fixed dates on stated terms. The market value of these 'convertibles' would then reflect the value of the company's ordinary shares in addition to the general level of interest rates and the status of the company concerned. A major disadvantage of some company debentures and loan stocks is that there is often a narrow market, with the result that deals cannot always be transacted. Even where they can be arranged, it is not unusual for there to be a wide margin between the bid and offer prices.

Mainly due to the greater risks involved and their inferior marketability, higher yields are available from non-convertible company debentures and loan stocks than from comparable gilt-edged securities. However, from the point of view of security, gilts would still generally be more suitable for most investors.

The tax treatment of an individual investing in company debentures and unsecured loan stocks is discussed in **Chapter 12**.

2:2.13   Permanent interest bearing shares (PIBs)

PIBs form part of the permanent capital of a building society. They have no repayment date and rank after the society's liabilities on its borrowed capital and balances due to depositors. They are more in the nature of an irredeemable loan than 'ordinary' shares.

PIBs are listed on the Stock Exchange and must be purchased through a stockbroker in units of £1,000 (£10,000 for some issues). Their prices are broadly subject to the same factors as affect gilt-edged securities, but, to reflect the lower degree of security, the interest coupons and yields of PIBs are higher (yields were around 8.0% p.a. at September 2000). Interest is paid half-yearly, net of savings rate tax.

When building societies are converted into banks, PIBs become perpetual subordinated bonds.

2:2.14   Preference shares

Preference shares rank after debentures and unsecured loan stocks in order of security. In the event of the company being wound up, the holders of preference shares would not receive payment until after the loans had first been repaid. Therefore, higher yields would normally be expected from preference shares due to the greater risk involved.

However, there are additional factors which may affect yields on preference shares including, for example, the dividends paid being treated as franked income in a company's hands, whereas interest from debentures and unsecured loan stocks is treated as unfranked income. Since this makes preference shares more attractive to companies, reduced yields are generally offered. Other factors would be the particular terms offered by the preference shares, such as whether they are cumulative or non-cumulative (cumulative means that, if a dividend is missed, it accumulates for later payment), participating rights, voting rights and redemption dates, which could result in lower yields being available.

Like debentures and loan stocks, the higher yields usually offered by preference shares would not generally provide sufficient compensation for most private investors for the greater security and marketability of gilt-edged securities. Furthermore, capital gains arising from preference shares are subject to capital gains tax (this is not the case with gilt-edged securities).

It is now also possible to purchase convertible preference shares, which are treated as wider range investments for trust investment purposes. These are convertible into the company's ordinary shares at fixed dates on stated terms in a similar way to convertible debentures and unsecured loan stocks.

2:2.15   Zero dividend preference shares of investment trusts

Investment trusts invest in portfolios of listed (and sometimes unlisted) investments. As they are companies, investment trusts are able to raise capital not only through ordinary shares, but also through other types of share as well as loans and debentures.

Zero dividend preference shares ('zeros') pay no income (hence their name). However, they have three additional features

(a) they have first claim on the assets when the trust is wound up;

(b) the date and value of their repayment are fixed in advance; and

(c) their entitlement to part of the trust's assets grows each month.

So the capital growth of zero coupon preference shares is assured, subject only to adequate growth in the trust's underlying investments. They are therefore attractive to investors who do not require income but are looking for secure capital appreciation.

The repayment value is set at a level which compensates for the lack of income.

Example 1

   Issue price 52.5p on 31 October 1993
   Redemption price 100p on 31 October 1999
   Appreciation 90.47% over 6 years – 11.33% per annum

The annualised rate of appreciation is called the 'gross redemption yield'. The average yield across the sector at September 2000 was 9.3% per annum and tends to reflect prevailing interest rates. Potential investors will compare the yields on different trusts' shares and will also have regard for the amount of 'cover' – the extent to which the current value of the trusts' assets exceeds the amount required to repay the zeros in full. This is also expressed as the 'hurdle rate' – the amount by which the assets must grow in order to meet the repayment value. When the value of the assets exceeds this value, the hurdle rate is negative.

Zero dividend preference shares are listed on the Stock Exchange and their price may go down as well as up. Their appreciation towards their redemption value is unlikely to follow a straight line. A sale or redemption of zero dividend preference shares may give rise to a chargeable disposal for capital gains tax. If the holding is significant, a liability to tax may be avoided by spreading sales over more than one tax year, using the annual exemption.

2:2.16 Purchased life annuities

Although there are several different types of purchased life annuities (including immediate annuities which commence immediately and deferred annuities which commence at a future date), the following are common features

(a) In return for a lump sum payment, annuity instalments will be received at regular intervals by the investor either for the remainder of his life or for a preselected term. The annuity can be arranged on a joint life and last survivor basis so that, if required, a guaranteed income can be provided for the annuitant and his wife during their lifetimes. The annuity can also be arranged to increase each year on a preselected fixed basis or in line with a preselected index (see **(b)** below).

(b) The annuity payments may be fixed or variable on one of the following bases

    (i)   without-profits level annuity, where the gross payment is determined at the outset and will not change;

    (ii)   without-profits increasing annuity, where the gross payment increases by a fixed percentage each year (usually between 3% and 10%);

    (iii)   without-profits index-linked annuity, where the gross payment is fixed for the first year and thereafter varies in line with an index (usually the RPI);

    (iv)   with-profits annuities, where part of the gross payment is guaranteed, and annual bonuses are declared which increase it and, once declared, become part of the guaranteed payment;

    (v)   unit-linked annuities, where the gross payment is linked to the investment performance of a selected fund.

The gross annuity is the sum of the capital and income elements before deduction of tax (see **(c)** below);

(c) The annuity paid consists of a capital element and an income element. The capital element represents a partial return of the original investment and accordingly is tax free. The income element is subject to taxation in the normal way. (Where an annuity is subject to guaranteed escalations, the capital content rises pro rata with the gross payments. This is unlike the other forms of annuity described above where the capital content remains the same as at the outset so that any increase in the annuity is subject to income tax.)

(d) The returns provided by annuities will be mainly determined by the following factors

    (i)   the type of annuity;

    (ii)   the general level of interest rates;

    (iii)   the age and sex of the individual (or individuals in the case of a joint life and last survivor annuity – with this type of annuity, it is the age and sex of the younger person which will have considerably more importance);

(iv) the guarantee period (if any) for which the annuity is to be paid;

(v) whether or not the contract is 'capital protected' (see below);

(vi) the basis of the annuity (see **(b)** above);

(vii) the frequency of payment; and

(viii) the rates offered by individual insurance companies at the particular time. For tax reasons or a company's desire to be competitive (or not) in this market, there are often significant differences between them. It is therefore essential for several quotations to be obtained. A few companies will pay higher rates to those who smoke or are in poor health.

(e) Since annuity rates are constantly changing, individuals should take immediate action if they wish to purchase an annuity at a time of falling interest rates. Annuities should not be purchased when interest rates are towards the bottom of their cycle. The main disadvantage of purchased life annuities is that there is no access to the capital sum paid. In addition, in the event of an individual's death soon after arranging the annuity, there would be no return to his estate unless the annuity was effected with a guaranteed minimum period of payment or on a capital protected basis. Under a capital protected annuity, the insurance company guarantees in the event of death to return any excess of the purchase consideration over the total of the gross instalments paid. Also, unless the annuity is arranged on an increasing or an indexed basis, there is no hedge against the effects of inflation.

A purchased life annuity will be mainly suitable in the circumstances outlined below

(a) For individuals normally with a minimum age of, say, 75 who wish to increase their net spendable income, but who will not require the return of their capital. This situation could arise when the annuity is included as part of a package. An example of this would be in a home income plan where an annuity is combined with a loan to provide additional income for an elderly home owner (see **Chapter 13**).

(b) For funding purposes at any age, for example, a nine-year temporary annuity to provide the premiums for a qualifying life policy (the first premium being paid directly out of capital);

(c) For inheritance tax purposes, when an annuity may be effected to reduce an individual's estate, whilst at the same time securing a high income for life. This action may also make it possible for him to give away other assets during his lifetime, which would otherwise have been retained to produce income or to fund the premiums to a whole of life policy written on trust to fund his potential inheritance tax liability (see **12:5** below).

2:3   Variable investments

Unlike fixed investments where either the capital and/or the income remains fixed once the investment has been made, in the case of variable investments both the capital and income can vary. Therefore, they should only be considered for the third part of the capital, namely higher risk/higher reward investments (this was considered earlier, see **2:1** above).

Shown below are the main characteristics and some timing indicators with regard to variable investments. Also discussed are some particular types of investment (unit trusts, OEICs, investment bonds, investment trusts, venture capital trusts, investments under the Enterprise Investment Scheme, personal equity plans and Individual Savings Accounts are dealt with in later chapters).

2:3.1   Main characteristics

Although there are many different types of variable investments, they are all governed by the following common rules

(a) since an individual can obtain a guaranteed real return over the rate of inflation by investing in index-linked gilts, he should normally only invest in variable investments if he considers it likely that they will provide a higher return;

(b) due to their particular nature, an individual should only invest in variable investments the proportion of his capital which he is prepared to put at risk with the objective of obtaining an above average return;

(c) variable investments should be made on a medium- to long-term basis, with the actual period depending on the particular type of investment and the investor's circumstances.

2:3.2   Timing indicators

Timing is of the utmost importance with many investments, especially where those of a higher risk/higher reward nature are concerned. It is often more likely that an investor will make a profit from a poor investment in a rising market than he will from a quality investment in a falling market.

Although timing is often the most difficult aspect of investment – there is no automatic way of knowing when is the right time to buy or to sell – the indicators shown below, which particularly relate to equity investments, frequently apply

(a) It is often best to take a contrary view to the general consensus, especially where a longer-term approach can be taken.

(b) An opportune time to make an investment is often when both the relevant market and the investment under consideration have shown major falls. Although it may be worthwhile to wait until the market has steadied, if investment is delayed too long until the outlook has clearly improved, the market is likely to have taken this improvement into account and risen.

(c) When bad news is out and widely known, this is frequently a favourable time to invest. When eventually the news does improve, the stock market is likely to rise.

(d) After a period of general gloom, the institutions, who generally have a large positive cash flow, will normally have a substantial amount of money waiting for investment. When they do invest (and no advance notice is given of this) the weight of money will often cause the stock market to show a sharp rise over a very short period.

(e) A suitable time to sell an investment is often when both the investment concerned and the underlying market have shown considerable rises but have since started to decline.

(f) An indication that a stock market rise may be coming to an end is when there are a large number of rights issues from companies and new unit trust launches.

(g) The trend of the movement in interest rates can indicate the direction of the stock market. If the trend appears to be upwards, this is likely to have a depressing effect on the market, whereas if the trend is downwards, the reverse would generally apply. A rise in interest rates may, however, be welcomed by the stock market as a move to forestall rising inflation.

(h) The stockmarket anticipates events 12 to 18 months ahead. Investors need to do the same.

2:3.3   Ordinary stocks and shares (equities)

The shares of quoted companies provide a popular method of participating in the growth of individual companies and of the economy in general. In addition, most shares provide an income by way of quarterly, half-yearly or annual dividends. While the number of shareholders has grown in the last

20 years as the result of the privatisation of national and regional utilities and the conversion of building societies and mutual insurance companies into public companies, investors must always be aware that share prices are subject to a wide range of factors which may cause them to fall. Equity shareholders must accept the volatility associated with the potential for growth and take an appropriately long-term view.

As a part-owner of a company, the investor in ordinary shares is entitled to vote at general meetings and needs to deal with corporate events, which may include

(a) a bonus issue of shares (also called a scrip or capitalisation issue). This involves the capitalisation of the company's retained profits or other reserves through the allotment of additional shares pro rata to all ordinary shareholders;

(b) a rights issue. This is an offer to all shareholders of the opportunity to subscribe for new shares at a price below the current market price. It is a way for the company to raise new long-term capital; or

(c) a takeover offer, either made by the company or received by it.

In all these cases, the investor is likely to receive a quantity of correspondence from the company, particularly when there is more than one company seeking to take over the company whose shares he holds.

Unless an individual has the time, the knowledge and the inclination to manage his own investments, he will usually benefit if his investments are handled instead by a stockbroker or investment manager specialising in private portfolio management. However, if the investor does satisfy these requirements, he may sometimes produce superior results to a stockbroker or other discretionary portfolio management service due to the personal attention he is able to provide. It should also be remembered that, in addition to any financial benefit (and the saving in charges), an individual may also obtain considerable satisfaction from choosing his own investments. Where an individual does decide to manage his own investments, these should be spread sufficiently in order to avoid undue concentration of risk. It is mainly for this reason that direct investment in stocks and shares is more appropriate for larger investors.

With the introduction of taper relief for capital gains tax from 6 April 1998 (see **Chapter 12**), individual holdings of stocks and shares may be at a tax disadvantage to collective equity investments, such as unit trusts. This is because every time a share is sold and a replacement purchased, there is potentially a charge to capital gains tax and the taper relief clock will be restarted for the new holding. Unit trusts, OEICs and investment trusts are, however, exempt from capital gains tax on gains realised within the fund; the investor is only liable to tax if he sells his interest in the fund.

2:3.4   Offshore funds

Although offshore funds are usually more suitable for expatriate investors due to their special tax position, they are also generally available to UK residents, to whom they can be attractive in appropriate circumstances (see page 36).

Offshore funds operate in a similar way to unit trusts with many of the same characteristics, such as full-time professional management, a wide investment spread and the price of their shares being directly related to the value of the underlying assets. However, as offshore funds are not registered in the UK, the following special considerations apply.

(a) To be marketed in the UK, an offshore fund must be either

    (i)   recognised by the Financial Services Authority. This means that the managers have obtained specific approval of the fund and its proposed method of operation; or

    (ii)   regulated in the territory where it is based under legislation which in the opinion of the Department of Trade and Industry provides protection to investors at least equivalent to that in the UK.

In the 'Offshore and Overseas' section of the Financial Times Managed Funds Service, recognised and regulated funds are listed under separate headings for each territory, so that the status of a fund can easily be seen.

The territories which have been designated as providing adequate investor protection are Bermuda, Guernsey, Jersey and the Isle of Man.

(b) The taxation position of UK investors in respect of offshore funds is as follows

    (i)   the offshore fund itself is generally exempt from taxation apart from perhaps a small amount of corporation tax and in some cases withholding tax on dividends and interest;

    (ii)   UK residents are liable to income tax, rather than capital gains tax, on any realised gains, unless a particular fund has obtained 'distributor' status;

    (iii) the main condition for distributor status is that at least 85% of the net income arising in the fund must be distributed and not accumulated (since distributor status is not granted by the Inland Revenue until after the end of each accounting period, this cannot be guaranteed at the time the investment is made);

    (iv) where a fund does not obtain distributor status it is called an 'accumulator' or 'roll-up' fund. Its income is accumulated within the fund and no tax liability will arise until the investment (or part of it) is sold, when the whole of the gain (capital gain plus undistributed income) will be taxed as income in the year of disposal. This can be very advantageous where the investment is sold in a tax year when the individual's income is low, for example, after retirement or during a period of employment overseas;

(v)   the income distributed to investors is payable gross. Investors will then be personally subject to income tax thereon if they are UK residents. Consequently, this produces a cash flow advantage until the tax due is paid. In the case of a non-taxpayer, the need to make a repayment claim may be avoided.

(c) Offshore funds are permitted to invest in a wider range of assets than UK authorised unit trusts. Accordingly, if an individual wishes to invest, say, in currency or commodity funds, only offshore funds would be available.

(d) Several offshore funds (generally known as 'umbrella' funds) are available which effectively allow an investor to switch between a wide range of currency, equity and fixed-interest sub-funds. The basis for umbrella funds is that they are investment companies with a range of separate classes of shares but having a single embracing structure – hence the term 'umbrella'. Investors can buy shares in one or more of these classes of shares, or sub-funds, and can then switch (or convert) from one class to another. Usually, a limited number of switches is permitted each year without charge.

One of the main reasons for forming umbrella funds was to postpone the payment of capital gains tax, as conversions within the fund were not deemed to constitute a sale and purchase. However, such conversions are now regarded as disposals and are therefore chargeable to income tax or capital gains tax as described in paragraph **(b)** above. Consequently, umbrella funds now appear to offer little attraction apart from ease of administration, the low costs of switching between different asset classes and the ability to receive interest or dividends gross.

The following matters should be borne in mind

(i)   A larger commitment may need to be made to one particular management group than would usually be the case on normal investment grounds. Only a small minority of groups have been able to produce a good past performance record across the whole range of their funds.

(ii)   The timing of the switches between the sub-funds is vital. Therefore, unless this is likely to be done regularly to advantage, a well managed general fund is likely to produce superior results.

(iii) If the Inland Revenue considers that there has been an unacceptably high level of investment change within the fund, it may not grant distributor status. This is particularly relevant when actively managed sub-funds are included, such as managed currency funds or bond funds.

(e) Unlike UK unit trusts, few offshore funds at the present time are authorised to advertise for direct subscription in the UK, except during the initial offer of shares through a filed prospectus.

Mainly due to the greater protection provided, onshore funds are usually more suitable for UK investors than offshore funds, except in the following circumstances

(a) where the investor is a non-taxpayer (this applies particularly to a high yielding fund such as a sterling deposit fund or a fixed-interest income fund);

(b) where the type of investment fund required is not available onshore, for example currency funds;

(c) where there is no intention for the fund selected to seek distributor status and the investor plans to sell his investment in a tax year when his or her income is low.

2:3.5   Currency funds

Currency funds are a particular type of offshore fund and consequently the considerations discussed above will also apply to them. They may form part of an umbrella fund. The two main types of currency funds which are considered below are

● deposit funds denominated in a single currency; and

● managed currency funds.

2:3.5.1   Deposit funds

For an investment in a currency other than sterling, it will be necessary for a view to be taken of the likely movement of that currency relative to sterling. The result of the investment will then depend on the amount of the currency gain (or loss) and the interest received on the chosen fund.

2:3.5.2   Managed currency funds

The main considerations with regard to managed currency funds are as follows

(a) as in the case of all managed investments, the expertise of the investment managers is of paramount importance;

(b) movements in currencies are often more difficult to predict than movements in stock markets;

(c) since the rules of most managed currency funds require the managers to invest in a minimum number of different currencies, the relative strength of sterling will have a major influence on the result of the investment. Accordingly, if it is considered that sterling will be generally weak against most foreign currencies, an investment in a managed currency fund should appreciate. However, if sterling should be relatively strong against other currencies, the reverse is likely to apply;

(d) in choosing a specific fund, it is important to compare 'like with like' as far as possible.

A direct equity investment or one made via a fund in an overseas stock market will be affected by both stock market and currency movements (unless, in the case of a fund, the managers have taken action to reduce exposure to movements in the particular currency). Accordingly, if the investment being considered is to be made on a long-term basis, a carefully chosen equity fund investing overseas may be a more suitable alternative to the currency fund alone, unless the investor does not wish to take a position in the stock market concerned.

2.3.6   Foreign currency bank accounts

A bank account in a foreign currency can be opened at a UK bank (subject to the normal rules) as either a current or a deposit account. Accounts may also be opened with banks overseas or with foreign banks in the UK or, if the funds are required for investment in overseas securities, with a stockbroker or investment manager.

Investors will normally open such accounts for reasons of convenience (for example, to pay personal expenses while abroad) or to meet a particular need, rather than as an investment. Exchange rate movements are notoriously difficult to predict and any gains are likely to be the result of chance rather than foresight. Gains arising on the conversion of withdrawals into sterling are subject to capital gains tax (and losses are allowable), if the account is held by an individual resident or ordinarily resident in the UK, unless

(a) the currency was acquired to meet personal expenses outside the UK; or

(b) the exchange gain is made by a non-UK domiciled individual on an account held overseas. In this case, the gain is taxed only if it is remitted to the UK and no relief is available for losses.

Interest rates will be different from those on sterling accounts and the charges may be higher than in the UK. If the account is in the UK, income tax at the savings rate will be deducted from interest credited (under Schedule D, Case V) on the gross amount arising in the current year.

2:4 Construction of an investment portfolio

The following examples illustrate broad investment portfolios for two individuals aged 30 and 50 respectively, based on their respective circumstances

Example 2

A man aged 30 has a capital sum of £200,000 available for investment. His main personal particulars and requirements are as below

(a) he is married with two young children but does not wish to educate them privately;

(b) he is employed by a company and is a member of their pension scheme. His wife has earnings of £4,500 per annum;

(c) he pays tax at the basic rate and is not liable to higher rate tax;

(d) he is buying a house with the assistance of a low-cost endowment mortgage;

(e) he has already effected the permanent health and life assurance protection policies which he considers necessary;

(f) his principal requirements for the capital are as follows

   (i)   a combination of income and growth;

   (ii)   part of the capital should be easily accessible;

   (iii) £130,000 can be invested on a long-term basis. He is prepared to take some risk with this part of the capital;

   (iv)   some of the capital can be invested in his wife's name.

Since the permanent health and life assurance cover, house purchase and pension requirements have all been dealt with, the entire £200,000 can be used solely for investment purposes. A suitable arrangement could be as follows

First part of capital

	£	£
Deposit account with immediate access without loss of interest (see **Note 1**)		25,000

Second part of capital

	£	£
A short dated, medium coupon British Government Stock	10,000	
A medium dated, index-linked British Government Stock	10,000	
'Instant access' insurance bond	25,000	
		45,000

Third part of capital

Two individual savings accounts of £7,000 invested in UK equity income unit trusts, OEICs or investment trusts in the names of each of the husband and wife	14,000	
A UK equity income unit trust, OEIC or investment trust with the objective of providing an increasing income and potential for capital growth	20,000	
Three UK growth unit trusts, OEICs or investment trusts with the objective of providing capital growth	60,000	
Two international growth unit trusts, OEICs or investment trusts holding UK and overseas equities with the objective of providing capital growth	36,000	
		130,000
		£200,000

Notes

1. For the purpose of this example, it is assumed that there is no existing investment in a deposit account.

2. Part of the capital should be invested in the wife's name, as her annual exemption may be needed for the saving of capital gains tax. Investment income will be taxed at 20%, whoever holds the investment.

Example 3

A man aged 50 inherits £150,000 from his mother and asks for investment advice. His main personal particulars and requirements are

(a) he is married with three children who have all left home and are in paid employment;

(b) he is self-employed and is providing for his retirement mainly through personal pension policies. He would like to retire at age 60. His wife does not have any earnings;

(c) he is already subject to a marginal rate of income tax of 40% before his inheritance is taken into account;

(d) his house is jointly owned with his wife and the mortgage has been repaid;

(e) he has effected appropriate life assurance policies to fund for inheritance tax;

(f) his assets already include a portfolio of equities managed by his stockbroker. His wife has relatively few investments;

(g) his principal requirements for the £150,000 inherited are

    (i)   to have access to one third of the capital at short notice;

    (ii)   to supplement his existing pension benefits;

    (iii)   to achieve capital growth during the next ten years but with risk being kept to a realistic minimum;

    (iv)   to purchase a country cottage;

    (v)   to use a relatively small amount of the inheritance to acquire some antique furniture for his house.

The above requirements could be met by the following arrangement of his capital

First part of capital

	£	£
Deposit account with immediate access without loss of interest (see **Note 1**)		10,000

Second part of capital

	£	£
3rd Issue 2-year Index-Linked National Savings Certificates	10,000	
A medium-dated, index-linked British Government Stock	12,000	
Zero dividend preference shares	18,000	
		40,000

Third part of capital

	£	
Additional personal pension contributions paid under the unused relief provisions (this is discussed in **Chapter 9**)	20,000	
Two individual savings accounts of £7,000 invested in UK equity income unit trusts, OEICs or investment trusts in the names of each of the husband and wife	14,000	
Two international growth unit trusts, OEICs or investment trusts with the objective of providing capital growth	11,000	
Country cottage	50,000	
Antique furniture	5,000	
		100,000
		£150,000

Notes

1. For the purpose of this example, it is assumed that there is no existing investment in a deposit account.

2. Part of the capital should be invested in the wife's name, as this results in the utilisation of her personal allowance and in income being taxed at the lower rate. Also her annual exemption may be needed for the saving of capital gains tax, for example on the sale of the cottage.

3. The deposit account, index-linked stock, zeros and unit trusts, OEICs or investment trusts (totalling £65,000) can all be realised at short notice, if necessary.

3   Unit trusts, OEICs, investment bonds and investment trusts

The purpose of this chapter is to consider the main characteristics and principal differences between unit trusts, open-ended investment companies (OEICs), investment bonds and investment trusts. In order to achieve this, unit trusts and investment bonds are first considered together. OEICs and unit trusts are very similar vehicles, both from the perspective of taxation and the underlying investments they hold. Indeed, unit trusts and OEICs are listed together in many performance tables and most OEICs which are available in the UK have been formed by conversion of unit trusts. For this reason, when comparisons are being made between the different collective investment vehicles it may be assumed that OEICs will have the same characteristics as unit trusts, unless specifically stated.

Nevertheless, there are significant differences between unit trusts and OEICs in terms of structure and administration. These areas are dealt with under the section on OEICs (see **3:3**).

At the end of the chapter, a comparison is made between unit trusts and investment trusts. Throughout the book, unless otherwise stated, unit trusts should be taken to mean UK authorised unit trusts.

3:1   Advantages of unit trusts and investment bonds

Unit trusts and investment bonds both enable individual investors to pool their resources, providing the following advantages when compared to investing directly in stock exchange securities

(a) Full-time professional management is available on a day-to-day basis. However, the investment expertise of fund managers varies considerably and this is likely to be reflected in the results of their portfolios.

(b) As a result of the wide investment spread, the impact of disappointing results from individual investments is reduced. In addition, a spread of management can be obtained by investing in a number of different unit trusts or bonds, thereby further reducing risk. However, the likelihood of making exceptional gains is also reduced.

(c) Due to the large number of different types of unit trusts available, both by country and sector, the exact equity investment requirements of most individuals can usually be met by a careful selection of trusts.

(d) There is a considerable saving in paperwork for the investor, as dealing with scrip issues, rights issues and take-over bids is avoided. In addition, the preparation of tax returns is simplified.

(e) Both unit trusts and investment bonds are tax efficient when properly used. Unit trusts are exempt from capital gains tax on their realised gains, with the result that a fund manager is not inhibited in his investment decisions by tax considerations. Holders of investment bonds are permitted to withdraw 5% of their initial investment each year with the income tax liability deferred until disposal. As far as the unit trust investor is concerned, no capital gains tax liability can arise until the units are sold. This provides an important cash flow advantage in comparison to a direct investment in equities which are actively managed. Furthermore, under the capital gains tax taper relief rules, the taper relief 'clock' will run from the date of purchase of units in a unit trust regardless of any dealings within the trust. This may produce a tax advantage for unit trusts over individually held share portfolios.

(f) Investment bonds provide a convenient method of investing in assets such as property, particularly for relatively small amounts (a few property unit trusts are now also available).

(g) Unit trusts and investment bonds provide an easy and convenient way of investing in overseas equities and fixed-interest securities. This method is often adopted by stockbrokers to obtain the required overseas exposure for their private clients.

(h) Investment bonds generally provide a switching facility between funds at very low cost with no tax being payable by the bondholder on the exercise of this facility.

(i) Since the size of the bargains carried out by unit trusts and investment bonds is usually relatively large, an active investment policy can be undertaken less expensively than by the individual investor himself.

(j) The annual management charge of a unit trust is not subject to VAT and in most cases is deducted in calculating the amount of trust income to be paid out. Effectively, therefore, tax relief is given on the charge. The fees of the manager of a directly invested portfolio, however, are subject to VAT and are not tax deductible.

3:2   Advantages of management by stockbrokers

The main advantages of investing directly in stock exchange securities using the management services of stockbrokers compared to indirect investment through unit trusts and investment bonds are listed below

(a) A more personal service is offered with the investor normally receiving a half-yearly valuation and report on his own portfolio. An annual list of dividends and capital gains tax calculations are also usually provided.

(b) An investor may derive more interest from investing directly in companies and following their fortunes.

(c) For very large investors, an investment management service may be more advantageous because the size of their portfolios enables them to have a sufficiently broad spread of holdings at a lower cost than through a unit trust or investment bond.

Direct stock exchange investment may also be appropriate where an individual has the time and inclination to make his own investment decisions. Many investors gain considerable personal satisfaction from choosing their own investments, with or without the assistance of a stockbroker, and following their progress in the press on a regular basis.

3:3   Basic constitution

Unit trusts, OEICs and investment bonds are all collective investment schemes, where the unit price is dependent upon the net asset value of the underlying investments. This contrasts with investment trusts where the share price is dependent upon the supply of and demand for shares.

3:3.1   Unit trusts

A unit trust is constituted by a trust deed which is an agreement between the trustees and the managers of the fund. The trust deed covers the main aspects of the running of the trust and is subject to approval by the Financial Services Authority (FSA). The essential characteristics of the deed are that it lays down

(a) the rights and responsibilities of all concerned;

(b) provisions enabling new members to join;

(c) the maximum charges that can be made by the managers for administering the fund;

(d) provision for calculating the buying (offer) and selling (bid) prices of units;

(e) the objectives of the trust; and

(f) types of investment permitted.

The role of the trustee, whose appointment is subject to approval by the FSA, is that of a watchdog. A trustee's main duties are to ensure that the terms of the trust deed are strictly observed and to hold the cash and securities belonging to the fund. The responsibility for the choice of investments lies with the managers, although the trustee retains the right of veto.

3:3.2   Open ended investment companies (OEICs)

Open ended investment companies (OEICs) became available in the UK in January 1997. They are, effectively, unit trusts established as companies incorporated under UK and European legislation and so comply with the rules for UCITS. Instead of trustees, they have a board of directors, one of whom will be the 'designated corporate director' who will be the fund manager. They also have a single price for their shares, based, as with unit trusts, on the value of their underlying investments. They are, in this respect, simpler than unit trusts (which have separate prices for purchases and sales), although they may impose separate buying or selling charges to prevent dilution of the fund. OEICs may be constituted as umbrella funds, with different classes of share for different sector or regional funds; they may also issue different types of share.

A number of unit trust groups have converted their funds to OEICs and this trend is likely to continue.

3:3.3   Investment bonds

An investment bond is a non-qualifying single premium life assurance policy. The investments of the bond fund form part of the main assets of the life assurance company and the bondholder has no prior charge on the fund. Consequently, if the life assurance company should find itself in financial trouble, the bondholder could suffer loss on his investment despite the protection offered by the Policyholders' Protection Act 1975 (this Act provides that a policyholder would generally receive 90% of the benefits under his policy). It is mainly for this reason that great care should be taken before business is placed with new or small life companies. In the case of unit trusts, there is not the same risk in dealing with newly established or small trusts due to the security provided by the trust deed and the fact that only the unitholders have a claim on the fund. With most life companies, the investments are in a separate bond fund which operates similarly to a unit trust. The performance is a function of the underlying value of the investments in the fund, irrespective of the performance of the life company's other investments. Many bond funds themselves invest in unit trusts as well as directly in equities and other assets.

3:4   Underlying investments

3:4.1   Unit trusts

Unit trusts are authorised by the FSA to invest only in quoted securities (subject to 10% of the fund being allowed in unquoted securities).

The main types of unit trusts may be classified under the following broad headings; these are the classifications used by performance measurement organisations

(a) UK

    (i)   All Companies;

    (ii)   Smaller Companies;

    (iii) Equity Income;

    (iv) Equity and Bond Income;

    (v)   Equity and Bond;

    (vi) Gilts;

    (vii) Corporate Bonds;

    (viii) Other Bonds;

(b) International/global

    (i)   Growth;

    (ii)   Equity Income;

    (iii) Equity and Bond;

    (iv) Bonds;

    (v)   Emerging Markets;

(c) Japan

    (i)   General;

    (ii)   Smaller Companies;

(d) Far East

   (i)   including Japan;

   (ii)   excluding Japan;

(e) North America

   (i)   General;

   (ii)   Smaller Companies;

(f) Europe

   (i)   excluding UK;

   (ii)   including UK;

   (iii)   Smaller Companies;

(g) Managed

   (i)   Active;

   (ii)   Balanced;

   (iii)   Cautious;

   (iv)   Income;

(h) Specialist;

(i) Property;

(j) Index Bear;

(k) Money Market;

(l) Guaranteed/Protected.

3:4.2   Investment bonds

Investment bonds are permitted to invest in an even wider range of assets than unit trusts, including investing in unit trusts themselves. The following are the main investment sectors used by performance measurement organisations

(a) Balanced Managed;

(b) Stockmarket Managed;

(c) Cautious Managed;

(d) Defensive Managed;

(e) Guaranteed Funds;

(f) Distribution Bonds;

(g) UK Equity Income;

(h) UK All Companies;

(i) UK Smaller Companies;

(j) International Fixed Interest;

(k) International;

(l) Europe;

(m) Australasia;

(n) Emerging Markets;

(o) Far East, including Japan;

(p) Far East, excluding Japan;

(q) North America;

(r) Japan;

(s) UK Gilt and Fixed Interest;

(t) Index Linked Gilts;

(u) Money Market;

(v) Currency;

(w) Commodity and Natural Resources;

(x) Property;

(y) Friendly Society – Tax Exempt.

3:4.3 Switching

A switching facility, which is available with most bonds, enables the bondholder to switch from one fund to another within the same policy at very low cost (typically, one free switch in a policy year, with subsequent switches being subject to a minimum charge of £10 and a maximum charge of £25). Since the switch is not considered to be a disposal by the bondholder, no tax is payable on the exercise of this facility.

Despite the apparent attraction of the switching facility, timing and choice of funds are all important. Unless market movements are anticipated correctly, it is possible that switching will not add to the value of the bond.

In the case of unit trusts, switching funds within the same management group can usually be done on preferential terms by reducing (discounting) the initial charge on the units purchased, although the sale is a disposal by the investor for capital gains tax. This also applies to OEICs, even though they are under an umbrella structure. The exception to this is the fund of funds which invests in other unit trusts within the same management group. In these circumstances, a switch between the underlying unit trusts by the fund manager would not be treated as a disposal for capital gains tax purposes by the investor, as he holds units in the 'top' fund.

3:5   Undertakings for Collective Investment in Transferable Securities (UCITS)

Since October 1989, unit trust groups throughout the European Union (EU) have been able to market their schemes in any other EU country. A European agreement on collective investments, UCITS, removed the barriers between individual countries by requiring minimum standards, with the effect that all the schemes became comparable. Under the Financial Services Act 1986, other countries can become 'designated territories' if their financial regulations are at least as stringent as those in the UK. Consequently, collective investment schemes in these territories can be marketed in the UK in a similar manner to unit trusts, provided that they receive recognition from the FSA.

UK unit trusts can now be sold elsewhere in the EU and European funds can be marketed in the UK. However, each unit trust will operate under the regulations of its own country although it must abide by the marketing regulations of the country in which it is sold. A UK fund bought in Germany, while authorised by the FSA, will be marketed under German regulations. A French unit trust bought in Britain does not offer investors the same protection as an authorised UK fund.

3:6   Life assurance cover

3:6.1   Unit trusts

Since a unit trust is not a life policy, there is no life cover attached. Consequently, the realisation value on the death of the unitholder is the bid value of the units. However, units do not necessarily have to be encashed by the executors, but can instead be passed to beneficiaries or held within a trust created by a will.

3:6.2   Investment bonds

As mentioned above, a bond is a non-qualifying single premium life assurance policy and, consequently, on death (or the death of the last survivor if applicable), the contract terminates and a lump sum is provided which is normally a percentage of the bid value of the units at the date of death (often 101%).

A small number of companies base the life cover on the age of the individual at the time they invest in the bond and on the amount of the original investment. On death, the amount receivable will be the greater of the life cover or the bid value of the units in the bond fund.

3:7   Personal requirements and investment objectives

Before anybody invests in a unit trust or investment bond, they should first consider their personal requirements and investment objectives. These would include the following salient points

(a) Whether they require capital growth, income, or a combination of the two, from the investment. Having decided on this, it is important to ensure that the purpose of the fund selected meets this objective.

(b) The degree of risk they are prepared to accept, remembering there is often a close correlation between risk and reward.

(c) The period of time for which it is intended to hold the investment. If the investment is being made on a long-term basis, a general or managed fund providing the investment managers with the greatest flexibility is often the most suitable.

(d) If they wish to invest in a specialised fund or geographical area, such as a fund investing in technology shares or Hong Kong, investment fashions can change and therefore it is important to be alert to dispose of the investment at short notice when market conditions are right.

(e) Whether they require the fund to be fully or substantially invested at all times, or whether it is desirable for the investment managers to take a view by going partially liquid if they think it appropriate. Most managers believe it is their responsibility to remain fully invested and for investors to decide on their own level of liquidity.

(f) Whether they require exposure to a particular currency when making overseas investments.

(g) The particular purpose for which the investment is being made; for example, an equity income unit trust can be very useful in a settlement where the interests of the life tenant and remaindermen have to be met by providing a balance of income and capital growth.

An investment bond is often ideal for a trust where income is to be accumulated until, for example, infant beneficiaries reach majority. However, it is unsuitable where income is required for a life tenant, as any withdrawals are regarded as capital repayments from which generally he is not permitted to benefit. However, it is essential that the trust contains a power to purchase investment bonds as they are not otherwise trustee investments.

3:8   Past performance

The performance record is often the most important factor on which the selection of a fund is based. It is, however, not a guide to the future; other factors (risk, management changes, investment policy) need also to be considered.

In assessing the past performance record of a unit trust or investment bond, it is most important that the results should not be considered in isolation if a realistic investment picture is to be obtained. Past performance figures are commonly shown on a cumulative basis, for example, the growth of £100 over periods from one month to ten years. This makes it difficult to judge the consistency of the results, as good returns in one or two periods can mask poor returns in others. It is preferable to analyse the results of separate time periods, either three months or one year.

The following matters should also be borne in mind

(a) the results should be considered over a reasonable period, at least two years, five if possible;

(b) the trend of the past results should be considered as this could indicate changes which have taken place within the fund;

(c) the results of the fund under consideration should be compared with those of similar funds and also, where possible, with appropriate indices;

(d) it is preferable for the fund to have produced a consistently good performance, rather than a mixture of outstanding and mediocre results;

(e) any changes in the management group or individual fund managers during the period under review should be carefully considered. It should be borne in mind that where a change in management has taken place, the new investment manager may not have the same expertise as the person who was responsible for the past results.

It should also be remembered that a new manager may wish to change the structure of the investment portfolio in accordance with his own ideas and this could initially have an adverse effect on the performance. However, this could be less of a disadvantage than it initially appears, since the new manager will normally follow the overall investment policy of the group concerned and, accordingly, any changes are likely to be limited.

3:9   Assessing management expertise

Although it is not possible to know which investment managers will produce the best results in the future, a considered opinion can be formed as to which managers offer above average expertise. However, to do this, a certain amount of research must take place. The following are indicators of management expertise which should help in the selection of a particular fund

(a) the fund having a good past performance record;

(b) the management group and individual manager having a proven record in the particular sector or geographical area in which the fund will invest;

(c) the management group generally having a good all round performance record.

Additionally, the investor should, where possible, attempt to form an independent opinion of the capabilities of the prospective group or fund manager, for example, by reading any group literature (particularly that relating to the funds he has in mind) and by reading the financial press. The investor should also ask the opinion of a professional financial adviser. He or she may wish to telephone the managers to ask questions; marketing departments are always willing to provide additional information on, for example

(a) the general philosophy of the group for the selection of investments and the degree of authority allowed to the individual fund managers;

(b) the general philosophy of the group as far as currencies are concerned when making overseas investments (this applies particularly to the exposure to any movements in currencies relative to sterling);

(c) the practical way the group operates and how fund managers obtain their information, for example through stockbrokers, company visits or internal research;

(d) the length of time for which the individual fund managers have managed a particular fund, together with their other responsibilities and previous experience;

(e) whether the fund manager has other responsibilities which may leave them with insufficient time to give proper attention to the fund and whether they are only nominally responsible for the fund, with the day-to-day management delegated to another person.

They will also provide a copy of the most recent manager's report and of the current allocation of the fund.

In practice, it is unlikely that an investor would have sufficient time to be able to obtain all this information. Nevertheless, with the judicious use of publications such as Money Management or Planned Savings, sufficient knowledge to make a reasonable assessment of a particular investment can still be gained.

3:10   Unit trusts – general guidelines

The following general guidelines apply in the selection of a unit trust.

3:10.1   General trusts v. specialised trusts

The principal advantage of a general trust is that the fund manager has more scope in his choice of investments with fewer restrictions applying to the type of investments which can be made. General trusts are usually less volatile because of their wider investment spread. In particular, 'portfolio' trusts, whose asset allocation reflects that adopted by the manager for individual private clients, offer a simple way for investors to acquire a broadly spread balanced portfolio through a single holding. With the introduction of taper relief for capital gains tax, this approach to investment will be more tax efficient than a directly invested portfolio.

The main advantage of a specialised trust is that it enables investors to back their own views if they favour a particular sector. In addition, a fund manager can concentrate expertise on the sector concerned. However, if that sector performs poorly, it is difficult for the fund manager to avoid a loss. Unit trust portfolios generally remain fully invested; the managers regard it as the investor's responsibility, not theirs, to increase liquidity if a market fall is anticipated.

Consequently, investors must be prepared to buy and sell unit holdings actively as their views of the investment prospects of different sectors change, although the capital gains tax position and the dealing charges involved should be borne in mind.

3:10.2   Large funds v. small funds

As a general rule, large funds are more likely to perform closely to the average of their sector, while small funds are either excellent or poor. However, although there is no clear evidence to show that the overall performance of small funds is superior to large funds, small funds often have an advantage due to their greater investment flexibility. This applies especially to trusts where the marketability of the underlying investments is restricted, for example unit trusts investing in small companies.

A steadily expanding fund has a definite advantage regardless of its size, as the fund managers are able to build up liquidity if required without the need to sell underlying investments. They can also change the 'slant' of the fund by applying new money differently from the existing investments and thereby avoid selling expenses in order to achieve this.

3:10.3   New trusts

The main advantage for an investor of purchasing units in a completely new trust is that the fund manager and the investment house will be especially keen for the trust to perform well. In addition, the only investments in the trust are those selected by the fund manager in the light of current conditions, rather than having been inherited from a previous manager or bought in a different investment climate. The principal disadvantage of subscribing to a new trust is that it is frequently launched after the sector in which the trust will invest has had a substantial rise. Consequently, it may be over valued and due for a fall. It should also be established whether the new manager has a track record of producing above average returns whilst managing a similar fund.

3:10.4   Index tracking trusts

Some management groups run index tracking unit trusts. These are run in a manner designed to follow the movements of a share index, typically the FTSE 100 Index or FTSE Actuaries All Share Index. They do this by holding either all the constituent shares in the index, in the same weightings, or a representative number of them whose price movements are likely to reflect this index as a whole. Index tracking funds are likely to underperform their chosen indices slightly because they bear expenses and there is the likelihood of tracking error. Nevertheless, over the longer term some of them have demonstrated a consistency which puts them well up the performance tables.

Recent international mergers have, however, created a few very large companies which dominate the FTSE 100 index in particular. This, and the increased volatility of share prices, has increased the risk profile of index-tracking funds.

3:11   With-profits bonds

The substantial market falls that occurred in the late 1980s prompted a number of investors to lose confidence in equity investment. This caused them to seek a means of achieving long-term capital growth, without short-term fluctuations.

Investment bonds investing in insurance companies' with-profits funds provided a solution. The key features of these bonds are as follows

(a) the with-profits fund invests in a mixture of equities, fixed interest securities and property;

(b) the returns from the fund are in the form of annual bonuses and possibly a terminal bonus at encashment or on the death of the life assured;

(c) once allocated, the annual bonuses cannot be removed, but the rate of bonus is not guaranteed from year to year, depending as it does on the returns earned on the fund's investments. The irrevocable declaration of bonuses is subject to point **(f)** below;

(d) an income withdrawal facility is normally available, although higher rate taxpayers may suffer a tax liability if the withdrawal exceeds 5% of the initial investment;

(e) most bonds have no fixed maturity date so all or part of them can be surrendered at any time. In the early years, surrender penalties may apply;

(f) if at the time of surrender, investment returns have not been sufficient to support the bonuses credited, the company will apply a 'market value adjustment factor' which further reduces the surrender proceeds;

(g) on death, as with conventional investment bonds, a lump sum is provided, which is a percentage of the bid value of the units at the date of death (often 101%). To this amount a terminal bonus is often added.

Whilst a with-profits bond offers the investor a lower-risk alternative to conventional equity investment, the following disadvantages should be borne in mind

(a) investors for whom equity investment is appropriate should not be concerned about short-term volatility. Most with-profits bonds should be held for a minimum five-year term and over that period, equity investment (either directly or through unitised funds) should produce better returns. With-profits bonds should principally be taken out by those whose resources are not sufficient to sustain the investment risk attaching to equities;

(b) the insurance companies' right to apply the market value adjustment factor means that investors are not protected, if they wish to encash during adverse market conditions;

(c) as many with-profits bonds are available as limited offers, the choice of insurance companies may be limited at the time when funds are available.

3:12   Distribution bonds

As an alternative to with-profits bonds, many companies are now offering distribution bonds. These bonds invest in funds that have a 'safety first' approach to equity investment. This approach manifests itself in the asset allocation, which has a much lower exposure to equities than a managed fund, with a correspondingly higher exposure to gilts, overseas bonds, cash and property.

A further feature of distribution funds is that they have higher yields than managed funds, making them particularly appropriate for investors who require income. Yields currently vary between 2% and 8% per annum. Investors do not need to take all of the income generated by the fund. Any excess can normally be left to build up further. Particular care must be exercised when selecting a distribution fund as the equity exposure can vary. This will affect both the income generated by the fund and the investment risk.

3:13   Taxation

3:13.1   Investment bonds – final encashment

The taxation position on final encashment of an investment bond is as follows

(a) Final encashment is considered to arise on complete surrender, death (or death of the last survivor of a jointly owned policy), or assignment for money or money's worth.

(b) The gain on the bond is calculated by taking the proceeds on final encashment plus all previous withdrawals and deducting the original cost of the bond and any chargeable amounts already established (known as chargeable excesses – see **section 3:13.3**).

(c) The gain is taxable as if it were an addition to the investor's income, but credited with basic rate income tax having already been paid. Thus only a higher rate taxpayer or a basic rate taxpayer close to the higher rate threshold would be personally liable to pay tax on the gain. The credit given cannot be reclaimed.

(d) If the investor's total taxable income is close to the threshold for higher rate tax (£28,400 plus allowances in 2000/01), the tax payable is calculated by 'top-slicing'. This method was introduced at a time when there were more bands of higher rate income tax than at present, to prevent a large chargeable excess in one year being taxed unduly heavily. The gain on the bond at **(b)** above is divided by the number of complete policy years that the bond has been held, to arrive at the top slice of the gain. This slice is added to the investor's other taxable income for the tax year of encashment and the tax payable with and without the slice is then calculated. The difference less basic rate tax on the slice is multiplied by the complete number of years that the bond has been held to arrive at the tax liability.

(e) If a loss should arise on final encashment, this will only be allowed to the extent of the amount of the chargeable excesses which have already arisen on partial surrenders in policy years commencing after 13 March 1975. This loss will then be permitted as a deduction in calculating the bondholder's higher rate tax liability in the year of final encashment. It should be noted that each policy is considered in isolation. Therefore, it is not permitted to use the loss on one policy to offset the gain on another.

The following example illustrates the calculation of tax on the encashment of a bond

Example 4

A married man aged 50 bought a single premium bond for £10,000 on 1 June 1990 and encashes it on 31 August 2000 for £13,000 having used the 5% per annum withdrawal facility throughout. During 2000/01 his earned income was £32,500.

Under the top-slicing process, the gain of £8,000 (£3,000 on encashment plus previous withdrawals of £5,000) is divided by 10 (the number of complete years the bond has been in force) to arrive at the top slice of the gain, namely £800

	Tax position without top slice of the gain	*Tax position including top slice of the gain*
	£	£
Income	32,500	32,500
Top slice of gain	–	800
	32,500	33,300
Less: personal allowance	4,385	4,385
	£28,115	£28,915

Tax payable thereon	£1,520 @ 10%	152	£1,520 @ 10%	152
	£26,595 @ 22%	5,851	£26,880 @ 22%	5,914
			£515 @ 40%	206
		£6,003		£6,272

	£
Total tax payable including tax on slice	6,272
Total tax payable without tax on slice	6,003
Tax payable including basic rate tax on slice	269
Less: basic rate tax on slice – £800 at 22%	176
Higher rate tax on slice	£93
Total tax on gain – £93 x 10	£930

3:13.2   Planning hints

The maximum higher rate tax liability on a gain made on an investment bond is currently 18% (40% less 22%) – even though the income of the life assurance fund has been taxed at the lower (or savings) rate of 20%. Nevertheless, it is still worthwhile to keep any liability to a practical minimum. The following are some planning hints to enable an investor to do this

(a) Encash the bond in a tax year when the bondholder's marginal tax rate is low. This could be due to retirement, a period of employment overseas or unemployment.

(b) Rearrange the bondholder's affairs to make their income low in the tax year of encashment, perhaps by reinvestment of assets in low or non-income producing securities.

(c) Hold the bond until death, as the bondholder's income in that year is likely to be less than normal since it would be based on that received from the preceding 6 April to the date of death.

(d) Take out a series of smaller bonds, as already mentioned. The bondholder will then be in a position to encash separate bonds completely over a number of years and thereby reduce the amount of the top slice to be added to his other income each year. This is likely to have the effect of the gain being taxed at lower rates, if at all.

(e) Take out bonds on a joint life and last survivor basis. Where a bond is taken out by a husband and wife on a joint life and last survivor basis and the bond is not encashed until the second death, the tax charge will be postponed until that time.

If the husband is the first to die, it is likely that the widow's income would be lower following his death. This would then present a suitable opportunity for her to encash the bond if she required the capital sum.

(f) Arrange for a bond to be taken out by the spouse paying tax at the lower rate. Alternatively, a bond should be assigned from one spouse to another if that results in a tax saving on encashment. This assignment must not be for money or money's worth and must be absolute with no control being retained by the transferring spouse.

(g) At some time before encashment, make an additional investment into an existing bond. This is treated for top-slicing purposes as if made at the date of the original investment. Consequently, any gain arising on final encashment on both the original and subsequent investments will be top sliced over the whole period of the original investment, with the result that the overall tax liability can be considerably reduced. This does not, however, reduce the tax liability on the original investment.

Particular care should be taken by a person who would normally qualify for age allowance, since chargeable excesses or gains on a bond are counted as income for the purpose of determining whether the age allowance should be reduced. Top-slicing relief has no effect in these circumstances. However, the 5% per annum withdrawals can be taken without affecting the age allowance.

3:13.3   Investment bonds – partial withdrawals

The taxation position of partial withdrawals from an investment bond is as follows

(a) Any tax liability is based on the realisation proceeds and not the actual profit thereon. This can produce very harsh results where withdrawals are substantial (see planning hint (a), section **3:13.4**).

(b) Annual withdrawals of 5% per annum of the original investment can be made with no immediate liability to tax but these will be taken into account on final encashment.

(c) The 5% allowances operate on a cumulative basis so, for example, if withdrawals are not taken in the first four years, a tax deferred withdrawal of 25% of the original investment can be taken in the fifth year.

(d) Tax deferred withdrawals are limited to 100% of the original investment (20 years at 5%).

(e) When a withdrawal is made in excess of the above allowances, a chargeable event is deemed to occur. If the bondholder is subject to higher rate tax, the excess may then be liable to income tax at the difference between the higher and basic rate. All withdrawals in a policy year are added together for the purposes of the calculation.

(f) The tax payable is calculated with reference to top-slicing relief which is explained in section **3:13.1(d)**. However, the period over which the gain is top sliced for partial encashments is limited to the number of years which have expired since the most recent chargeable event, or the start of the contract if there has not been a previous chargeable event. However, the year of the partial encashment counts as a further year for top-slicing. For example, a partial encashment after two-and-a-half years, with no previous chargeable gains, would be top sliced over three years.

This is illustrated in the following example

Example 5

An investment bond is purchased for £10,000 with partial withdrawals having been made as follows

during year 1 –	£ 500
during year 4 –	£1,400
during year 5 –	£2,500
during year 7 –	£2,000

End of year	*Cumulative allowance (5% p.a.)*	*Withdrawals in year*	*Total*	*Chargeable excess*
	£	£	£	£
1	500	500	500	Nil
2	1,000	Nil	500	Nil
3	1,500	Nil	500	Nil
4	2,000	1,400	1,900	Nil
5	2,500	2,500	4,400	1,900
6	500	Nil	Nil	Nil
7	1,000	2,000	2,000	1,000

Note

For the purposes of top-slicing relief, the chargeable excess of £1,900 in year 5 is divided by 5 and the chargeable excess of £1,000 in year 7 is divided by 2.

(g) Chargeable excesses are calculated on a policy year (not a tax year) basis, for example

(i)   bond purchased for £10,000 on 1 January 1996;

(ii) partial withdrawal of £2,500 on 10 January 2000 (bringing cumulative withdrawals to £4,400 after five complete policy years);

(iii) tax based on policy year ending 31 December 2000, in fiscal year 2000/01;

(iv) cumulative allowances to 31 December 2000 are £2,500, resulting in chargeable excess of £1,900;

(v)   tax due on chargeable excess payable in January 2002.

3:13.4 Planning hints

The following courses are suggested

(a) Take out a series of smaller bonds in lieu of one larger bond to provide greater flexibility (this is often achieved by dividing a bond into a number of identical cluster policies or segments). In this way, the bondholder can totally encash a smaller bond if required, rather than resort to a partial encashment of a larger bond with the possible penal tax consequences.

(b) Postpone taking withdrawals when markets are low to avoid the encashment of an undue number of units in the bond fund. This also applies to any automatic withdrawal facility where the bondholder does not need to rely on the withdrawals for income; it is best to defer the first payment for at least six months to allow the price time to recover part of the bid/offer spread.

3:14 Position on death

3:14.1 Unit trusts

At present, there is no capital gains tax payable on gains at death. Consequently, if a unit trust is held until death, capital gains tax will be avoided.

3:14.2 Investment bonds

As already mentioned, death is one of the 'chargeable events', when the bid value of the units of the bond is used in calculating the amount of the gain. If the life cover exceeds the bid value of the units, the excess will not be taken into account in calculating the tax charge. This charge will be an allowable deduction from the estate in calculating the inheritance tax liability.

3:15 Trusts and settlements

A bond can, in certain cases, be advantageous for some trusts and settlements in that it is a non-income producing asset and there is no tax liability on the settlor, trustee or beneficiary until it is encashed. However, before an investment is made in a bond, it is necessary to ensure that the trustees have the power to invest in non-income producing assets and also the power to invest in life assurance policies. A bond can be particularly suitable in the following circumstances

- in accumulation and maintenance settlements for the benefit of children;

- as gifts to children either absolutely or contingent upon their attainment of a certain age.

As previously mentioned, an equity income unit trust can be very useful in a trust situation where the requirement is to provide a balance of income for the life tenant and capital growth for the remaindermen. Bonds are not suitable for this purpose because they produce no income. All withdrawals are regarded as coming out of capital.

3:16   Personalised bond funds

Some insurance companies permit individuals with a large investment portfolio to have their own private bond fund for these investments. This enables investors to retain some influence over the management of their investments while receiving the same tax treatment as that applying to investment bonds. The introduction in the Finance Act 1998 of an additional tax charge on personalised bonds issued by offshore life assurance companies in respect of any policy year ending after 5 April 2000 will mean that these bonds will become unattractive to all but a minority of investors.

This tax charge is based on a deemed 'gain' equal to 15% of the premiums paid each year, and the total of deemed 'gains' from previous years. A deemed gain will also arise on termination of the policy – in addition to the normal tax charge. The additional charge will not be imposed in respect of any policy year ending before 6 April 2000. A policy year ends on the day before each anniversary of the creation of the policy.

3:17   Share exchange schemes

If an individual already owns stocks and shares, it will often be possible to exchange these investments for unit trusts or investment bonds on favourable terms such as the following

- Where the individual has stocks and shares with a minimum value of typically £1,000 and these investments are accepted into the portfolios of the unit trust or insurance company, the offer or middle prices are normally allowed on the stocks and shares exchanged, with no deduction being made for selling expenses.

- Where the stocks and shares have a ready market but the unit trust or insurance company does not wish to take them into its portfolios, they will usually be sold on the individual's behalf, often with a waiver of the selling expenses. Accordingly, the gross proceeds are applied to the purchase of the unit trust holding or investment bond.

In all other cases, the individual would be required to dispose of his own investments and bear the charges. Where a person exchanges an investment in this way, it will be treated as a disposal for capital gains tax purposes. Although the terms offered by some share exchange schemes are more advantageous than others, it should be remembered that it is the future performance of the unit trust or investment bond selected that will generally be of far greater importance.

3:18   Unit trusts or investment bonds?

Before a decision is taken as to which of these is the more suitable investment medium, it will be necessary to consider the following

(a) Whether the particular fund being considered is available in the form of both a unit trust and an investment bond. In many cases, the fund is only one or the other.

(b) The current and future tax position of the individual. This is of particular importance in the case of investment bonds where the marginal rate of tax payable by the individual in the year of final encashment will be a major factor in determining the amount of any tax liability. Although the maximum personal tax liability is restricted to 18% in 2000/01, this is likely to change if there is an alteration in income tax rates in subsequent years.

(c) The age of the individual. A bond is not normally so suitable for a younger person (say, under age 50) since it is more difficult to postpone final encashment until the time when the investor's income is low, such as following retirement. A bond may also not be suitable for a very elderly person, since death may cause tax to become payable.

(d) The investor's potential capital gains tax position. If the investment objective is capital growth, a unit trust will usually be more suitable if the investor rarely makes use of the annual capital gains tax exemption. Realised gains made within an investment bond are currently subject to capital gains tax at 20% and this cannot be recovered by the bondholder.

(e) Whether a regular 'income' is required. Investment bonds normally provide greater flexibility in this respect, although a number of unit trust managers have started to offer regular income facilities (which may involve selling some units to make the payments up to the required level).

(f) Whether the investment is to be used for a particular purpose, such as in an accumulation and maintenance settlement, or as a gift to children.

(g) Whether the individual is likely to make use of the fund switching facility available within most investment bonds, which, unlike a unit trust switch, does not crystallize a capital gain.

3:19   Investment trusts and unit trusts compared

Investment trusts, although companies quoted on the stock market, have many features similar to unit trusts, including full-time professional management, a wide investment spread and the same tax treatment for investors. However, investment trusts have several characteristics which distinguish them from unit trusts

(a) Investment trust shares may be bought and sold through a stockbroker, but many management groups now offer a cheap dealing service for private investors. By using their own stockbrokers and dealing in large quantities, they are able to offer very low commission rates. The disadvantage is that smaller transactions may only take place weekly, so that the share price may well have changed since the investor made the decision to buy or sell.

Unit trusts are open-ended funds which create or redeem units according to demand. Units are always bought from and sold to their managers. An initial charge of 5% to 6% is usually made when units are sold to an investor.

(b) The share capital of an investment trust is fixed. Consequently, its shares are not redeemed when a large number of investors wish to sell, for example in plummeting markets. With a unit trust, the number of units in issue can be increased or reduced, and if a lot of unitholders sell, the fund manager has to realise investments to provide the cash with which to pay them. A fund which is gradually expanding is normally easier to manage from an investment viewpoint than a fund which is static or contracting.

(c) The share price of an investment trust fluctuates in accordance with the supply and demand for its shares, which can usually be purchased at a discount to the value of its underlying assets. The price at which a unit trust is bought and sold is based directly on the value of its underlying assets (subject to the provisions regarding the calculation of the bid/offer spread). Fluctuations in an investment trust's discount (or premium) will enhance or damage its share price performance.

(d) An investment trust may be converted into a unit trust, or subjected to a takeover (the buyer's object being to acquire an investment portfolio cheaply). In both cases, the investment trust shareholder is likely to make a windfall profit as the discount is eliminated. Unit trusts can only be merged at their net asset value.

(e) The mood of the UK stock market normally has a greater effect on the share price of an investment trust than on the price of a unit trust (the price of an investment trust can be affected even when its underlying assets are wholly invested outside the UK). Accordingly, investment trust prices will often show greater movements than their underlying assets, even before taking into account the effect of any gearing (see (g) below). This could, therefore, have an adverse result for shareholders wishing to dispose of their shares in a falling market when the discount on assets often widens, with the reverse applying in a rising market when the discount frequently narrows.

(f) An investment trust has the freedom to invest entirely in unquoted securities, while no more than 10% of a unit trust portfolio may be invested in this way.

(g) An investment trust is able to effect 'gearing' by issuing prior capital in the form of preference shares, debentures or loan stocks and by utilising short-term borrowing facilities. The effect of gearing on an investment trust is that an increase or decrease in the value of its total assets will have an exaggerated effect on the change in the value of the net assets per ordinary share. This arises because the holders of prior capital are entitled to a fixed return of capital if the investment trust is wound up, with the value of the remaining assets being divided between the ordinary shareholders. Gearing also has a similar effect on income. A unit trust is only permitted to borrow within very strict limits and therefore gearing can only be introduced to a minor extent.

(h) A particular type of investment trust which could be suitable to investors seeking specifically either income or capital growth is a split capital trust. These trusts, which were first introduced in the mid-1960s, have a fixed winding-up date and can have several different classes of share capital, with clearly defined rights

   (i)   *Zero dividend preference shares* (zeros) have a fixed entitlement on winding up, in priority to other classes of share. As their name implies, they pay no dividends; their return is entirely in the form of a predetermined rate of capital appreciation. They are therefore suitable for higher rate income taxpayers who can use their annual capital gains tax exemption to minimise the impact of tax on their gains;

(ii) *Stepped preference shares* are also prior capital. They offer a fixed and increasing (hence 'stepped') rate of income and a fixed capital entitlement at the end of the trust's life. They are therefore suitable for cautious investors who require predictable returns.

(iii) *Income shares* are entitled to the whole of the trust's income (after prior charges). Since, as a class, they represent only part of the capital but receive all its income, they are 'geared' and are able to pay dividends at a much higher rate than conventional ordinary shares. Their capital entitlement varies: a 'traditional' income share will be repaid at its par value or its original subscription price when the trust is wound up, whereas the repayment price of an 'annuity' income share may be 1p or less. 'Traditional' shares are usually issued with capital shares; 'annuity' shares with zeros and capital shares.

(iv) *Ordinary income shares* are sometimes (more accurately) called highly geared income shares; the latter term highlights the risks of buying them. They are issued in conjunction with zeros and are entitled to the whole of the trust's income and, on winding up, all the assets remaining after the zeros have been repaid. Their price is therefore very sensitive to changes in the value of the underlying portfolio. All types of income share are useful for those seeking a high income, although this will often be at the expense of capital appreciation.

(v) *Capital shares* have no rights to income, but on winding up are entitled to the whole of the assets remaining after all other classes of capital have been repaid. They therefore suit investors who can accept above average risk in pursuit of high capital gains.

There are two other types of investment trust security, both of which entitle their holders to acquire ordinary or income shares

(i) *Convertible loan stock*, which may be exchanged into shares at the holder's option on fixed dates and in a predetermined proportion.

(ii) *Warrants*, which are no more than a right to subscribe for new shares in the trust at a predetermined price. They are frequently offered 'free' to those who subscribe for shares when a trust is launched. They can, however, be traded independently of the shares – but are for speculators only.

A unit trust is only able to offer one type of unit, since all investors have a *pro rata* share of the fund. Investors do, however, sometimes have a choice between income units and accumulation units. Holders of income units are paid the income to which they are entitled or have it applied to secure additional units, whereas holders of accumulation units have the income accumulated within the fund to enhance the value of their existing units. The reinvested income is nevertheless treated as taxable income of the unitholder.

(i) An investment trust may retain some of its income and use the revenue resources created to supplement its dividend payments when its portfolio income drops. Unit trusts have to pay out all of their income.

(j) An investment trust is effectively prohibited from advertising its shares in the way a unit trust can advertise its units.

(k) The annual management charges of the older and larger investment trusts tend to be lower than those of unit trusts.

3:19.1   Conclusion

Although the choice between an investment trust and a unit trust or OEIC will depend on individual circumstances, the factors which are likely to be of particular importance in determining which will prove to be a better investment are

(a) the expertise of the investment managers;

(b) the investment scope of the fund (the desired combination of investments may only be available in one form or the other);

(c) the size of the discount on assets at which an investment trust may be bought.

3:20   Unit trust and investment trust regular savings plans

Unit trust and investment trust regular savings plans are investment schemes whereby a fixed amount is invested on a regular basis (usually monthly). These plans are particularly useful to an individual who wishes to spread his investment over a period, rather than commit a lump sum at a particular time. However, although a decision on timing is largely removed, it should be remembered that the investor will only benefit from rising values to the extent that he has already invested in the savings plan.

One of the benefits of regular savings plans is that of 'pound cost averaging', whereby more units are automatically acquired from the regular investment when prices are low than when they are high. Consequently, the average cost per unit purchased over a period is lower than the average of the market prices during that period. Although pound cost averaging is likely to produce greater benefits with a volatile fund than with a more stable fund, it is even more important if a volatile fund is selected that the investor should have the flexibility to be able to postpone encashment until the market is considered high.

The same care should be taken in choosing a regular savings plan as with a lump sum investment. If large regular investments are to be made, it is normally worthwhile to divide the contributions into a number of different plans.

One particular problem which can arise with regular savings plans is the calculation of capital gains tax. Since each contribution to a plan counts as a separate investment, a large number of capital gains tax calculations may be necessary to calculate the indexation allowance when the plans are encashed. However, for disposals made after 5 April 1988, it is possible for an investor to apply for a simplified method to operate, whereby fixed monthly savings are aggregated each year and treated as a single sum invested in the seventh month of the trust's accounting year. Additional payments can also be included, provided they do not exceed twice the regular monthly contribution. Otherwise, lump sums will be treated separately.

This problem does not arise for contributions since 6 April 1998, as taper relief operates by reference to the number of complete years after that date an asset has been held at the date of its disposal. Each 'batch' of monthly contributions in a 12-month period will, therefore, qualify for the same rate of relief. Contributions paid before 5 April 1998 constitute a single asset, and those paid before 17 March 1998 benefit from an extra year's taper relief. Contributions paid within three years before the disposal do not qualify for any taper relief.

3:21   Guaranteed equity bonds

Guaranteed equity bonds are technically insurance bonds issued for a fixed period which offer a combination of

(a) a minimum guaranteed return, which may be

     (i)   the return of the initial investment, either as a capital payment or (in the case of high income bonds) as a combination of income during the period and capital at maturity; or

(ii)   the return of a multiple (say 1.25 times) of the initial investment; and

(b) an additional return based on the performance of a share index, which may either be in line with the movement of the index or an enhanced multiple (say 120%) of it.

They are thus, at first glance, attractive to investors who wish to obtain an equity-based return but without the risk of losing money.

The guarantees do, however, have a price. Among the disadvantages are

(a) The investor may not receive a return in line with that from the index. Often only a percentage (say 95%) of the initial investment moves with the index and there is sometimes a limit on the extent of the gains.

(b) To avoid the effect of a sudden drop in the index near the end of the fixed period, the final index figure is averaged, say over the last six months.

(c) The investor receives no income.

(d) Capital is tied up for the fixed period. Encashment is either not permitted or is subject to a severe penalty.

(e) Higher rate taxpayers will have an additional liability on the maturity of the bond.

(f) If only the initial capital is returned, it will have been eroded by inflation.

3:22   Protected unit trusts

With recent excellent stock market returns, there has been an increased interest in products which offer a degree of protection against a market fall. The protection comes in a variety of forms: one is a promise that the bid price of the fund will not fall by more than, say, 2% over a three-month period. The upside return is usually linked to the FTSE-100 Index.

The investment managers generally provide the guarantees by investing the majority of the fund in cash and then using the remaining small proportion of the fund to buy an exposure to the FTSE-100 Index through call options. There are, however, a variety of other techniques.

The potential investor in this type of fund needs to be aware of the following disadvantages, which counterbalance the greater security in the event of a stock market fall

(a) the degree of protection is often related to the bid (selling) price. Since the units are acquired at the offer price, the investor will suffer the full bid/offer spread in spite of having the impact of the market fall limited;

(b) some of the funds pay no income; and

(c) the need to commit some of the fund to assets providing the protection may result in growth lower than on the underlying portfolio.

4 Personal equity plans and individual savings accounts

In order to promote individual share ownership and to give investors a personal interest and a direct stake in UK companies, personal equity plans (PEPs) were introduced with effect from 1 January 1987. Substantial improvements to PEPs were made in subsequent Finance Acts, and from 1 January 1992, investors could take out a 'single company' PEP, in addition to a general PEP, in each tax year. The last subscriptions to PEPs were paid on 5 April 1999; they were succeeded by Individual Savings Accounts (ISAs), but plans in existence on that date continue.

4:1   Main features of PEPs

The main features of PEPs are as follows

(a) Any UK resident aged 18 or over was able to invest up to £6,000 per annum in a general PEP and £3,000 in a single company PEP. Subscriptions had to be paid by cheque; shares could be transferred into a PEP only in the following circumstances, and subject to time limits

    (i)   shares newly issued in a public offer;

    (ii)   shares allotted under a savings-related share option scheme or an approved profit-sharing scheme into a single company PEP; and

    (iii) shares issued to members on the demutualisation of a building society or life assurance company.

In the first two cases, the cost or value of the shares counted towards the annual subscription limit. In the third case, the shares were treated as having a 'nil' value, and so did not count towards the limit.

(b) Authorised PEP managers included members of the stock exchange, licensed security dealers, banks, building societies and unit and investment trust managers. Some companies offered plans invested only in their own shares (corporate PEPs); these could have been either general or single company plans.

(c) No tax is payable either on capital gains or income, whether paid out or reinvested, in respect of investments held within a PEP or on withdrawals of capital. However, interest arising from cash holdings is subject to lower rate tax in the same way as bank or building society deposits if the amount paid to the investor exceeds £180 in any tax year.

(d) Investments which may be held in a PEP are

    (i)   ordinary shares of UK companies which have a full stock exchange listing;

    (ii)   quoted equities of companies incorporated in other EU Member States;

    (iii) UK authorised unit trusts and investment trusts which are at least 50% invested in equities (both quoted and unquoted) in the UK or EU Member States;

    (iv) UK authorised unit trusts and investment trusts which are less than 50% invested in the UK or EU, but subject to a maximum initial investment of £1,500 per tax year and, subsequently, 25% of the value of the plan if the holding is changed;

    (v)   corporate bonds denominated in sterling, issued by non-financial UK companies and having a minimum term of five years to maturity;

    (vi) preference shares of UK and EU non-financial companies; and

    (vii) cash.

Single company PEPs may only hold

    (i)   ordinary shares of UK companies which have a full stock exchange listing; and

    (ii)   unquoted shares transferred under **(a)(ii)** above.

(e) There is no need for an investor to report details of his plans to the Inland Revenue as the plan manager is responsible for reclaiming the tax on income and for all the paperwork.

(f) A series of PEPs can be planned to form a unified portfolio, although each year's plan has to be accounted for separately. A PEP can be transferred from one plan manager to another at any stage.

(g) Planholders must be sent regular statements, at least annually, showing details of all plan investments and cash held, the value of the investments, the prices at which purchases and sales have been made and details of all dividends and interest.

(h) There is no limit to the plan manager's charges, but they must be clearly disclosed. Charges can include an initial fee, annual charges for both first and subsequent years, dealing costs, charges on the number of assets held, withdrawal from the plan (including switching to another plan manager), receiving the annual report and accounts and attendance at annual general meetings of companies whose shares are held, and other sundry expenses mainly covering portfolio valuations additional to the first in a year.

4:2 Main features of individual savings accounts

Like PEPs, ISAs are governed by their own regulations. The main features are as follows

(a) Any UK resident aged 18 or over is able to invest up to £5,000 in each tax year (£7,000 in 1999/2000 and 2000/01). Accounts may not be opened in joint names but, in the case of married couples, both husband and wife may have independent accounts. Subscriptions may be paid by cheque or electronically and applications can have effect for successive years. The only shares which may be transferred into an ISA are those allotted under a savings-related share option scheme or an approved profit sharing scheme. The transfer must take place within 90 days of their transfer to the investor.

(b) An ISA may consist of up to three components

(i) a cash component, with a subscription limit of £1,000 each year (£3,000 in 1999/2000 and 2000/01);

(ii) an insurance component, with a subscription limit of £1,000 each year; and

(iii) a stocks and shares component, with a subscription limit of £5,000 (£7,000 in 1999/2000 and 2000/01), less amounts paid to the other components in that year.

An account which contains all three components or consists only of a stocks and shares component is known as a 'maxi-ISA'. An investor may open only one maxi-ISA each year. Each component may, however, exist separately and an investor may use the products of different providers for each one in each year. In this event, each product is classed as a 'mini-ISA'.

(c) Additionally, an investor may hold a 'TESSA-only' ISA, that is, one which has had paid into it the capital element of a matured TESSA (i.e. a maximum of £9,000). The transfer from the TESSA must take place within six months of the maturity date. Alternatively, the investor may transfer the capital element of his matured TESSA to the cash component of a maxi-ISA or to a mini-ISA consisting of a cash component; in both cases, the amount transferred does not count towards the subscription limit.

(d) ISAs will continue to be available at least until 5 April 2009, although the government intends to review them in 2006.

(e) Accounts must be offered by an ISA manager approved by the Inland Revenue. Managers must be

    (i)   authorised under the Financial Services Act 1986;

    (ii)   a European institution permitted to operate in the UK;

    (iii)   a bank, building society or permitted European institution (for a cash component only); or

    (iv)   an insurance company or friendly society (for the life assurance component only).

(f) No tax is payable either on capital gains or income, whether paid out or reinvested, in respect of investments within an ISA, or on withdrawals of capital, with one exception. Interest on cash held within the stocks and shares or insurance component of a maxi-ISA is paid, subject to the deduction of income tax at 20%, but the interest is otherwise tax exempt and does not have to be reported on the investor's tax return. Tax credits on dividends will be recoverable by the account manager for the benefit of investors in the stocks and shares and insurance components only for the first five years (i.e. until 5 April 2004). Tax deducted from interest will be repayable throughout.

(g) There is no minimum period of ownership required to retain the tax reliefs. Capital and income can be withdrawn at any time, but the account provider may impose charges on withdrawals or on transfers to other managers.

(h) No tax relief is given on subscriptions to an ISA.

(i) Investments which may be held in a stocks and shares component are

    (i)   shares issued by a company wherever incorporated and officially listed on a recognised stock exchange;

    (ii)   securities issued by a company (not an investment trust) wherever incorporated, whose shares or securities are listed on a recognised stock exchange. The securities must not be repayable within five years;

    (iii)   shares in or securities of an investment trust, provided its rental income is less than 50% of its total investment income;

(iv)   units in an authorised unit trust or an authorised UK OEIC, including umbrella funds and funds of funds;

(v)   a UCITS (see **Chapter 3**) situated in and authorised by an EC state and recognised under the Financial Services Act 1986;

(vi)   shares acquired under a savings related share option scheme or approved profit sharing scheme; and

(vii)   cash (subject to the limitation at **(f)** above).

(j)   Investments which may be held in the insurance component are

(i)   single premium life assurance policies on the life of the investor, which cannot be assigned (annuities, pension contracts and personal portfolio bonds are specifically excluded); and

(ii)   cash (subject to the limitation at **(f)** above).

(k)   Investments which may be held in a cash component are

(i)   cash deposited in a bank, building society or permitted European institution;

(ii)   units in a money market fund; and

(iii)   deposits or accounts with National Savings.

These accounts must not be linked to another account in an arrangement giving particularly favourable terms.

(l)   There is no need for an investor to report details of his accounts to the Inland Revenue as the account manager is responsible for reclaiming the tax on income and for all the paperwork.

(m)   ISAs may be transferred to a different manager at any time after the year of subscription.

(n)   If requested by investors, the account manager must arrange for them to receive the annual report and accounts of all companies in which they hold shares. Similarly, investors can request to attend shareholders' meetings, exercise voting rights and obtain other shareholder information. A charge can be (and usually is) made by the manager for these facilities.

(o)   Investors must be sent regular statements, at least annually, showing details of all investments and cash held, the value of the investments, the prices at which purchases and sales have been made and details of all dividends and interest.

(p) There is no limit to the account manager's charges, but the government has set benchmarks for ISAs which meet strict criteria for low charges, easy access and fair terms (the 'CAT standards'). Charges must be clearly disclosed and may include one or more of an initial fee, annual charges for both first and subsequent years, dealing costs, charges on the number of assets held, withdrawal from the plan (including switching to another plan manager), receiving the annual report and accounts and attendance at annual general meetings of companies whose shares are held, and other sundry expenses mainly covering portfolio valuations additional to the first in a year.

4:3 Principal advantages and disadvantages

The following are the principal advantages and disadvantages of PEPs and ISAs compared to other main savings media.

4:3.1 Advantages

(a) No tax is payable, either on capital gains or on dividend income, in respect of investments held within a PEP or an ISA (this can be particularly advantageous where the main purpose of the investments is to produce a high income).

(b) Non-taxpayers can avoid the need to reclaim tax by investing in ISAs. Until 5 April 2004, they can also benefit from the recovery of the 10% dividend tax credit, which is not repayable if the holding is owned directly.

(c) There is no additional charge for buying a unit trust through a PEP or ISA; indeed some managers charge less for these plans than for direct investments.

(d) PEPs and ISAs can be discontinued at any time without loss of the tax benefits.

(e) All returns to the Inland Revenue are dealt with by the plan manager. An individual need not disclose the investments or income on his tax return.

4:3.2 Disadvantages

(a) Any specific PEP or ISA administration charge could outweigh the amount of tax relief on dividends, now that the rate of tax credit has fallen to 10%. When the repayment of tax credits to PEPs and ISAs ends on 5 April 2004, the balance between costs and benefits will need to be reviewed even more carefully. Plans which do not levy a separate charge are, therefore, to be preferred.

(b) The maximum investment in ISAs is restricted to £5,000 per tax year per person (£7,000 in 1999/2000 and 2000/01).

4:4   Other considerations

Other considerations which should be borne in mind are as follows

(a) The quality of investment management, whether in a discretionary plan or a collective fund, is of paramount importance. This is likely to have a greater bearing on the final investment return than the level of charges.

(b) PEPs and ISAs should normally be regarded as medium- to long-term investments, in the same way as the underlying securities. Any additional initial charges are diluted over a period and the tax benefits increase as the capital and income grow.

(c) The ISA regulations allow investors to invest their own funds and subscriptions may also be paid as a gift.

(d) ISA managers must allow a 14-day 'cooling-off' period, within which an investor must be allowed to change his mind and withdraw his application. If he does so, he will not receive a refund of his full subscription if the value of his investment has fallen.

4:5   Conclusion

The tax reliefs provided are relatively small in view of the fact that

(a) dividend tax credits are now at only 10%, and, if attached to taxable dividends, satisfy a basic rate taxpayer's liability on that income;

(b) the majority of investors do not pay capital gains tax, as their gains are normally within their annual exemption; and

(c) long-term capital gains are subject to taper relief, which for a higher rate taxpayer reduces the effective tax rate to 24% after ten years.

Accordingly, PEPs and ISAs are most advantageous for higher rate taxpayers who regularly make use of their annual capital gains tax exemption. However, for those investors who wish to start unit trust or investment trust portfolios, an investment within an ISA will be more advantageous because of the tax-exempt environment. For this reason, ISAs are useful vehicles for funding the repayment of mortgages, long-term saving for education fees and as a supplement to approved pension arrangements when saving for retirement.

It should be noted that the favourable tax and charging structure and the lack of penalties on ceasing payments make monthly ISA savings plans a considerably more attractive proposition than ten-year life assurance savings plans, for even the smallest investor.

5   Land and property investments

As an asset class, land and property investments provide a useful complement to stockmarket investments in a portfolio. This has the benefit of reducing the overall risk, as the prices of different types of property move in different (and usually, longer) cycles to those of shares and fixed interest securities.

Property (particularly commercial property) has the following characteristics, some of which it shares with equities and gilts

(a) it is a 'real' asset, being tangible and, over many periods, a useful hedge against inflation;

(b) it has the potential to appreciate in value, reflecting an expanding economy and/or the benefit of refurbishment or other improvements;

(c) price movements are less volatile than those of equities – and, in the last ten years, gilts as well; and

(d) it provides a stable and growing income, with yields on commercial property (in June 2000) above those of both equities and gilts. Rent increases are reflected in higher capital values. The security of rental income does, however, depend on the quality of the tenant.

There are, however, a number of disadvantages of which potential investors should be aware

(a) although the property market is well established and efficient, it can be illiquid. It may take some time to arrange a purchase or sale at the right price;

(b) there are significant acquisition costs in the form of legal fees and associated costs and stamp duty;

(c) there are essential running costs, such as insurance and maintenance; and

(d) there will be no income from a let property if a tenant cannot be found or the occupant defaults.

5:1   Main residence

Most investors will already have an investment in property through the ownership of their own home. Given the substantial value which this may represent, it may not be appropriate for them to make any further investment in property.

An individual should, however, regard his main residence primarily as a home for himself and his family and not as an investment or as a financial planning tool. In most cases it will produce no income and, if sold, the proceeds are likely to be needed to purchase another home.

Home ownership has been encouraged by

(a) the granting of income tax relief on interest on the first £30,000 of loans for house purchase (although this was ended on 5 April 2000 except for home income plans purchased by the elderly before that date – see **13:8.1** below); and

(b) the exemption of the sale proceeds from capital gains tax. The rules for this include a deemed extension of the period of residence for periods of absence for

 (i) any reason totalling up to three years;

 (ii) employment elsewhere in the UK totalling up to four years; or

 (iii) employment abroad with no limit.

The exemption normally applies to the house and grounds of up to half a hectare, but a larger area is allowed if it is appropriate to the size and character of the house.

Further income tax relief for owner-occupiers covers income from letting a furnished room in their main residence. This 'rent-a-room' relief was introduced as an incentive to those with spare rooms to let them out. Gross rents from such lettings (including the provision of certain services, for example, meals) are exempt from tax if they do not exceed an annual amount of £4,250. If the gross rents do exceed this, taxpayers can elect to pay tax on the excess over £4,250 (without relief for expenses) or to compute the taxable amount in the normal way (i.e. rent less expenses).

5:2 Second homes

Some families buy a second home (e.g. a cottage in the country or at the seaside) for use at weekends and for holidays. Having been acquired for their personal use and enjoyment, the property will not, in many cases, be let and so will produce no income. There may be a return in the form of a capital gain when the property is sold, but in the meantime the owner will have to bear the cost of insurance, maintenance, etc. If the second home is only used occasionally, security will also be a concern.

Where an individual owns two homes, he may, within two years of the purchase of the second, elect (by giving notice to the Inland Revenue) for one of them to be regarded as his principal private residence for capital gains tax purposes. This need not be the property which is occupied for most of the time and the election can be varied subsequently. Any gain on the home which is not so designated will, on disposal, be subject to capital gains tax and so should be the one which is likely to show the smaller gain. If the owner will, in time, use the property as his home in retirement, then it should be borne in mind that any gain on death is exempt. If it is possible that a loss may arise on the sale of either property, the election should be made for that property not to be the principle private residence, so that the loss is allowable.

There is no tax relief on interest on a loan for the purchase of a second home.

5:3 Let residential property

Any type of residential accommodation which is suitable for occupation, from flats for students to luxury apartments and country mansions, can be purchased for letting to occupational tenants. Because of their own experience in the residential property market, many investors favour this type of asset and, as interest rates fell, the late 1990s saw the emergence of a number of 'buy to let' schemes for new properties promoted by developers. For a time, the level of rents which could be achieved provided a significant margin over the cost of finance, but, as the result of over supply and rising interest rates, investors needed to exercise greater care to ensure that their investment would be profitable.

The key to successful letting is to find a satisfactory tenant who will not only pay the rent promptly but also look after the property. Some investors rely on an agent to find a tenant, prepare a proper tenancy agreement, collect the rent and deal with all other aspects of management. The agent's fees for this will be deducted from the rent collected. Others prefer to take care of the property management themselves.

For income tax, the management expenses, an allowance for wear and tear of furniture and any mortgage interest paid may be deducted from the rental income to arrive at the net income subject to tax. If more than one let property is owned, the income and expenses for all of them, both furnished and unfurnished, are combined. In general, any gain on sale is subject to capital gains tax; if the property has been occupied by the owner, however, the gain is time apportioned to exclude the period of owner-occupation. There is, however, an additional exemption, being the lower of an absolute limit of

£40,000 and the amount of the gain exempted by virtue of the principal private residence provisions.

5:3.1 Furnished holiday accommodation

A special set of tax rules applies to property which qualifies as furnished holiday accommodation. Briefly, the rental income is deemed to be trading income and so is classified as earned income. It can, therefore, form the basis for contributions to a personal pension plan and losses can be offset under the usual rules for trading losses. For capital gains tax

(a) the property is treated as business property for taper relief (see **12:2** below);

(b) relief for the replacement of business assets (roll-over relief) is available if the whole of the proceeds of the sale are reinvested in further assets to be used for a trade. The purchase of the property may also serve to defer a chargeable gain on a business asset previously sold; and

(c) retirement relief is available until 5 April 2003 (see **12:2** below).

The legislation provides a detailed definition of what qualifies as a holiday letting. It is worth noting that the property does not have to be located in a holiday resort. The principal requirement is that it must be available to be let for at least 140 days in a 12-month period, and must actually be let for at least 70 days in that period, of which no more than 31 consecutive days are to the same person.

5:4   Residential property overseas

Many of the principles discussed in previous sections of this chapter also apply to residential property overseas – with the added problems of distance, local laws and taxes and fluctuating exchange rates. In investment terms the principal financial return is likely to be from capital appreciation, although property may also be let at least for part of the time. Expert local advice on both the property market and aspects of property ownership in the overseas location must be taken before purchasing.

UK-resident and domiciled individuals are taxable on rental income, less expenses and mortgage interest, from letting property overseas. Only a proportion of the expenses will be deductible if the property is partly occupied by the owner and travel expenses will not be allowable at all if there is an element of private purpose to a visit. Foreign tax can normally be offset against the UK liability. If the owner is either not domiciled in the UK or a British subject not ordinarily resident in the UK, he or she will be assessable to income tax only on net rental income remitted to the UK.

On the sale of the overseas property, any gain will be subject to capital gains tax if the owner is UK-resident or ordinarily resident and domiciled. If he is not UK-domiciled, however, the gain is only taxable if the proceeds are remitted to the UK. Any foreign tax paid on the capital gain can be offset against the UK liability.

5:5   Time-sharing and multi-ownership

Time-sharing schemes have become popular as a more convenient and cheaper method of financing a holiday home, particularly when outside the UK. Under such a scheme, a person acquires a right to occupy holiday accommodation for an agreed period each year, either indefinitely or for a set number of years, depending on the particular legal requirements in the country concerned. It is achieved by payment of a capital sum at the start of the scheme followed by an annual management or service charge. Properties can be purchased in the UK, many countries within Europe and the United States. To improve flexibility for the time-sharer, weeks can be exchanged from one property to another so that the individual is not tied to a particular holiday destination. Properties may also be sub-let if required. Schemes are organised in a number of formats, including clubs, corporate schemes, licences or leases. The latter two are more common in the United States than in Europe.

The taxation of income (depending on whether the property is in the UK or overseas) and capital gains is as described in previous sections. If, however, there are less than 50 years outstanding on a lease at the date of sale, only a proportion of the cost can be deducted, depending on the period still outstanding.

Most time-share investors purchase for their personal use and thus the opportunity for creating income is limited. The annual maintenance charge is likely to rise with inflation and as the properties get older. The quality of management is all important. The investment may not be easy to realise and should be regarded as a medium to long-term asset.

5:6   Commercial property

Commercial property represents by far the largest sector in the property market. It includes

(a) retail – high street shops, out of town centres and retail warehouses;

(b) offices;

(c) commercial – hotels, public houses, nursing homes, etc; and

(d) industrial – factories and warehouses.

The principal investors in commercial property are the listed property companies, life assurance companies and pension funds. Private investors may also buy property directly, and as all four types of commercial property can be found in all parts of the country, there is an enormous variety of buildings and locations to choose from.

Income and capital gains from a commercial property are taxed in the same way as let residential property and interest on a loan taken to finance a purchase can be deducted in calculating the owner's taxable income.

For the average private investor, however, exposure to commercial property is best obtained through some form of collective investment. The following are available

(a) *Property company shares.* Although not strictly a collective investment, the shares of a listed property company are easy to buy and sell. The prices of such shares, however, tend to move more in line with share prices generally than with property values and can for long periods stand at a discount to the value of the company's property portfolio.

(b) *Insurance bonds.* Most insurance companies include a property fund in their range of unit-linked funds. The portfolio will usually be widely spread between the main sub-sectors. The funds vary considerably in size and performance, but details about the underlying holdings and their returns are not readily available, making selection difficult.

(c) *Investment trusts.* There are only two authorised investment trusts investing in property. They hold a mixture of directly owned properties and property company shares. Their share prices normally trade at a discount to the net value of their portfolios.

(d) *Authorised unit trusts.* The discount problem does not arise in the case of unit trusts, the value of whose units is based on the value of their assets. The three authorised unit trusts investing in property are however permitted to hold no more than 70% of their funds in directly owned property, with the other 30% in readily realisable assets such as listed property company shares and cash deposits.

(e) *Unauthorised unit trusts and OEICs.* This group includes enterprise zone property trusts (see **5:7**) and specialist funds investing in, for example, residential property and freehold ground rents. They have more freedom in their choice of investments than authorised unit trusts and may in some cases be able to borrow to enlarge their portfolios. Dealings in their units or shares is likely to take place once a month, rather than on a daily basis.

The tax treatment of each of these types of investment is covered in **Chapter 3**. No tax relief is given on interest on a loan taken for the purpose of buying collective funds (except enterprise zone property trusts) or property company shares.

5:7   Enterprise zone property

Enterprise zones are areas designated by the Government under the Local Government, Planning and Land Act 1980. Typically, they are located where the local economy was heavily dependent on a major industry which had fallen into decline (e.g. ship-building, steel-making, mining and, in London, the docks). The area is, therefore, in need of regeneration and the various benefits of designation as an enterprise zone are intended to attract developers, new industries and both institutional and private investors to finance it.

The principal benefit of investing in an enterprise zone is the 100% industrial buildings capital allowances given on the cost of a qualifying industrial or commercial building. The allowances are not given on the cost of the land element, which may be up to 20% of the total cost. The capital allowances can, if the investor wishes, be taken in the year the investment is made and offset against the rental income from the property and his other income to reduce his overall income tax liability. If he prefers, part of the allowances may be taken in the first year and the balance subsequently.

This type of investment was very popular in the healthy property market of the 1980s, when over 20 zones were designated. The general decline in the market in the 1990s, the expiry of many of the earlier zones (designation lasts for only ten years) and the significant problems encountered by some of the enterprise zone trusts have made it less attractive. Only a few zones remain and there is little property available for retail investors. Partly as a result of this, rental yields have fallen to around 6% per annum.

An investor would need at least £100,000 to buy a reasonable building (although smaller units were available in the 1980s). As the owner, he would be responsible for finding a tenant and managing and maintaining the building. For most investors, however, the more practical ways of acquiring an interest are through a syndicate or a trust. In both cases, a manager finds a suitable property, markets the fund to potential investors and uses their subscriptions to buy the property. Syndicates and trusts are, therefore, available for only a limited period of up to six weeks. The manager then finds a tenant (sometimes a property is pre-let before the fund is launched), collects the rents, pays the expenses, and distributes the net rents to investors. Both structures are transparent for income tax, so, instead of the fund being taxed, each member is taxable on his proportionate share of the net rental income and has the benefit of his share of the total capital allowances.

Enterprise zone syndicates and trusts differ in two main respects

(a) Syndicates consist of a relatively small number of wealthy individuals, who are required to subscribe at least £50,000 (sometimes £100,000). The minimum subscription for a trust, however, is normally £5,000 and there are, therefore, likely to be many more investors.

(b) The financing of a syndicate includes a bank loan, which is arranged by the manager. This and the tax relief result in the actual cash outlay by a syndicate member being a relatively small percentage of his total subscription. Trusts do not borrow, although the manager usually arranges for a bank to provide a loan facility for investors who wish to make use of it.

Because in both cases the interest can be deducted from the rental income for tax purposes, this is an attractive option, which 'gears' the capital and income returns. If, however, the tenant defaults or one is not found, the investor is left to pay the interest out of his other income.

Potential investors in enterprise zone syndicates and trusts need to be aware of the following potential problems and risks

(a) the price at which an enterprise zone property is acquired from a developer is typically higher than its open market value. This is a way of allowing the developer to share the benefit of the capital allowances given to investors;

(b) the tax relief given through the capital allowances becomes repayable (through a balancing charge) if

 (i) the property is sold or a capital payment is received within seven years of acquisition;

 (ii) the property is sold between seven and 25 years from acquisition. If, however, a lesser interest is disposed of (e.g. a long lease is created out of a freehold), the allowances are not reclaimed, because the owner retains his original interest; or

 (iii) the investor disposes of his shares in a syndicate or trust.

After 25 years the allowances cannot be clawed back.

(c) the investment is potentially very long term. Though trust and syndicate managers will normally seek to sell the property at some stage between seven and 15 years after purchase, this cannot be guaranteed and will depend on conditions in the property market in general and in the enterprise zone in particular. The purchasers will not have the benefit of the initial capital allowances;

(d) at least 75% of the members must agree to the sale or a major alteration to the fund. No one member has control and the members are therefore very reliant on the integrity and efficiency of the manager.

(e) a sound tenant – backed if necessary by a bank or parent company guarantees or rental deposits – is essential. If the rent ceases, not only do the members have no income, they may also be called upon to pay the expenses, in addition to any loan interest. Again, the investors have to rely on the manager to carry out appropriate due diligence.

Any gain on the sale of an enterprise zone property (or shares in an enterprise zone trust) will be subject to capital gains tax, with indexation and taper reliefs applying as appropriate. On the disposal of a property by an enterprise zone trust, and the subsequent distribution of the proceeds to the shareholders, capital gains tax is charged both on the trust and (on the net proceeds paid out) on the individual shareholders.

5:8 Farmland

Investment in farmland can be made in two ways

(a) By purchasing the land outright and commencing a farming business either personally or in partnership. Although the day-to-day running of the business can be delegated to a manager or to a contract farmer, a degree of personal involvement will be necessary. Returns from agriculture have historically been low and changes brought about by EU regulations and the low prices of some produce have pushed many farming businesses into losses. Any profits are taxable as earned income and there are provisions for profits of consecutive years to be averaged if there are severe fluctuations. Trading losses can be set against other income of the same or the previous year, but this relief may be restricted if losses are made for more than five consecutive years. On a sale, business asset taper relief, retirement relief and roll-over relief may apply when calculating the capital gains tax liability.

(b) By purchasing tenanted farmland. This is a pure investment, like any other in let property, the income deriving from the rent charged to the tenant. This is unearned income, from which relevant expenses and loan interest may be deducted for tax purposes. Any gain on sale will not benefit from the reliefs mentioned in **(a)** above.

5:9 Woodlands

Investment in woodlands was popular with high earning individuals before April 1988 because of the income tax relief given (at the investor's marginal rate) on planting expenditure. Since then, the rate of establishment of new woodlands has dropped and most investment is now made in young and semi-mature plantations by those seeking the capital gains tax and inheritance tax benefits. Some also buy for the pleasure of owning a piece of the British countryside, especially if the property has other amenities such as a holiday home, fishing or stalking. There is also some investment in new woodlands on agricultural land for which special grants are available.

Since conifers take 40 years to mature and deciduous trees over 100 years, woodlands are a long-term investment. Properties are, however, available with crops at differing ages and it is possible to buy a property to suit particular needs for capital growth or income (from the proceeds of felling part of the timber each year).

The principal value of a property is in the growing timber; the land value is relatively low. Most woodlands are purchased through specialist estate agents or forestry management companies. Ownership may be

(a) As an individual. The owner then has complete control of and responsibility for the property. He is likely to engage a manager or management company to ensure that the timber crop is properly looked after.

(b) As a member of a forestry syndicate. Each syndicate member contributes a proportion of the initial cost of purchasing a property and then participates pro rata in the expenses, income and eventual sale proceeds. A manager deals with all the administration and the care of the trees.

(c) As a unitholder in a forestry trust. From time to time, forestry managers set up unit trusts to raise capital to purchase woodland properties. These are open for subscriptions for only a limited period and normally for a specific capital growth or income objective. There is often a fixed winding-up date.

Following the reform of the taxation of woodlands in the Finance Act 1988, income from the sale of timber and fellings from woodlands run on a commercial basis is exempt from income tax and there is no relief for expenses. Grants are available, subject to conditions, to offset the costs of planting and maintenance.

The proceeds of timber sales are also exempt from capital gains tax, which is, however, chargeable on any appreciation in value of the land element when the property is sold. The capital cost of the woodland (i.e. the land and any capital works, for example, roads) qualifies as a business asset for the purpose of roll-over relief following the sale of a previous business asset.

If woodlands are the subject of a gift or are owned at death, and have been owned for at least two years, business property relief (currently at 100%) will apply, so that no inheritance tax is charged. If tax is payable, an election can be made to defer payment on the timber (but not on the land element) until it is sold. Inheritance tax is then charged on the sale proceeds, not on the value at death.

6   Higher risk and alternative investments

6:1   Introduction

The investments discussed in this chapter are principally those which offer the opportunity of above average returns in exchange for a higher risk of loss. In some cases the potential returns are enhanced (or the potential loss reduced) by the presence of tax reliefs. It is these reliefs which attract many investors to the Enterprise Investment Scheme and venture capital trusts, but each proposition must be evaluated primarily on its investment merits and not pursued for the tax reliefs alone.

Investments in Enterprise Zone property and woodlands (see **Chapter 5**) should also be regarded as high risk.

6:2   Reinvestment relief

Although capital gains tax reinvestment relief is not an investment, it should be borne in mind when considering overall investment strategy. Originally introduced in 1993, it was enhanced in 1994 and merged with the EIS relief with effect from 6 April 1998, so that, to qualify for both reliefs, shares must satisfy the same tests (see **6:3** below). Investments in EIS shares up to £150,000 now qualify for both the initial income tax relief and for CGT reinvestment relief, with investments over this limit attracting reinvestment relief only. There is no upper monetary limit for reinvestment relief.

The relief applies where, on realising a chargeable gain on any asset, the investor buys new ordinary shares in a trading company carrying on a qualifying trade or in a venture capital trust. It allows the payment of tax on the realised gains to be deferred, up to the amount of the reinvestment. Reinvestment must be made within one year before the date the gain is realised or

(a) within one year after, if reinvestment is into a venture capital trust; or

(b) within three years after, if reinvestment is into a trading company.

It should be noted that these time limits are not related to tax years.

Companies whose shares qualify for reinvestment relief have to satisfy a number of conditions. In particular they must carry on a qualifying trade for at least three years from the date of investment.

There are five routes to reinvestment relief

(a) *Shares in private companies.* Investors may have the opportunity to buy new shares in small private or family-owned companies. This route will appeal to 'business angels', who are able to bring their expertise to assist the business and who may, following their investment, become a director. 'Passive' investors also qualify. Potential investors are responsible for carrying out 'due diligence' on the company and for agreeing an appropriate value for the shares to be issued.

(b) *Shares in public EIS companies.* Many EIS companies invite subscriptions by issuing a public prospectus. The costs of preparing the prospectus make this a relatively expensive course if less than about £1.5 million is to be raised, but it does attract a large number of investors. The information in the prospectus about the company's management and business will enable the prospective investor to form a judgement about its potential for success.

(c) *Personal companies.* Some sponsors of EIS companies also offer the facility to form a 'personal' company for investors seeking reinvestment relief for £400,000 or more. They will provide a qualifying business (usually one conducted by one of their existing EIS companies, and with the same management team), and issue all the shares to the investor. Because his shareholding exceeds the 30% limit for EIS, the investor does not obtain the initial 20% income tax relief, but this does not affect his reinvestment relief. Once the company has carried on its qualifying trade for three years, it is free to conduct any type of business in future (it could, for example, merely hold an investment portfolio). So long as the investor holds his shares the payment of tax on his realised capital gains is deferred, and as he is the sole shareholder he has complete control over the company and its activities.

(d) *AIM shares.* Shares traded on the Alternative Investment Market or the unofficial OFEX market are, for the purposes of reinvestment relief and inheritance tax, regarded as unquoted. Investments into new shares on these markets therefore qualify for reinvestment relief, provided that the company meets all the requirements.

(e) *Venture capital trusts.* These are discussed in more detail at **6:5** below.

6:3　Business Expansion Scheme

The Business Expansion Scheme (BES) was introduced in 1983 to encourage private investment in companies seeking equity finance to start or expand their business. In 1988, the list of qualifying trades was extended to include companies investing in property to be let on 'assured tenancies', a new type of tenancy arrangement which was designed to encourage the provision of housing for residential letting. The attraction of investing in relatively risk-free properties severely limited the amount of BES money going into genuine trading companies. Sponsors then developed the 'arranged exit' scheme, under which an institution (commonly a bank, building society or university college) undertook to purchase the BES companies' properties at a price which would provide a fixed return to investors. The major risk of this type of investment was thus removed. This persuaded the government to abolish the BES with effect from 31 December 1993 and most investors will by now have disposed of their shares. The principal tax reliefs were

(a) income tax relief at the investors' marginal rate on the cost of qualifying ordinary shares (maximum £40,000);

(b) provided the income tax relief was intact after five years, exemption from capital gains tax on disposal; and

(c) if the shares had been held for two years and the company was an unquoted trading company, business property relief (currently at 100%) for inheritance tax. This will still apply to any remaining BES shares.

6:4　Enterprise Investment Scheme

The Finance Act 1994 introduced the Enterprise Investment Scheme (EIS) as a successor to the Business Expansion Scheme for which the CBI and other business organisations had pressed since the announcement of the ending of BES on 31 December 1993. Like the original intention of BES, the objective is to help small companies to raise equity finance and, in a departure from the BES approach, to encourage investors who wish to become involved in their management. It applies to shares in qualifying unquoted companies issued after 1 January 1994. The EIS was amended in the Finance Act 1998, to make it the basis for capital gains tax reinvestment relief from 6 April 1998. The EIS has certain similarities to BES

(a) The company must carry on a qualifying trade. Among businesses specifically excluded are leasing, financial and legal services, property investment and those which require a significant property element (e.g. farming, forestry, nursing homes and hotels).

(b) There is income tax relief on the cost of investment, but this is only given at the lower rate of tax (20%) as a reduction in the investor's income tax liability.

(c) There is an annual limit on the investment qualifying for income tax relief. The maximum amount eligible for relief in each tax year is £150,000 per individual. This gives a husband and wife overall capacity of £300,000 per tax year.

(d) Part of the tax relief on investments made before 6 October in any tax year can be carried back to the previous year. The carry-back is limited to £25,000 or one-half of the amount subscribed, whichever is less.

(e) The shares must be held for five years to keep the income tax relief.

(f) If the EIS shares are sold after five years and the income tax relief is intact, any gain on the sale is exempt from capital gains tax.

There are some differences between the EIS and BES, namely

(a) A qualifying company has to have gross assets of less than £15 million before it raises new capital and no more than £16 million afterwards. From 1 January 1994 to 5 April 1998, there was a limit of £1 million on the amount a company could raise, but this has been removed.

(b) An investment in EIS shares can be used to defer the tax on a capital gain realised after 28 November 1994. The shares must be bought within 12 months before the gain arose or three years afterwards. For a higher rate taxpayer, this effectively takes the relief available to 60% – 40% capital gains tax and 20% income tax. The deferred tax becomes payable when the shares are sold, unless a new qualifying investment is made.

(c) From 6 April 1998, an investment in a qualifying company in excess of the annual income tax relief limit of £150,000 can qualify for capital gains tax reinvestment relief (see **6:2** above).

(d) Where an investor acquires EIS shares after 5 April 1998, sells them in less than five years at a gain on or after 6 April 1999 and reinvests in other EIS shares, he is entitled to claim taper relief on the disposal of the second shareholding by reference to the holding period for both EIS investments. This is intended to encourage 'serial entrepreneurs'.

(e) If EIS shares are sold at a loss (after taking the initial income tax relief into account), relief for the loss may be claimed against either income tax or capital gains tax.

(f) Any investors previously unconnected with the company may become paid directors. To retain the income tax relief, their appointment must take place *after* their shares have been issued.

(g) Companies involved in letting residential property are not permitted under the EIS rules.

(h) The EIS income tax relief will not be granted if, before or at the time the shares are issued, arrangements are made for the disposal of the shares or of the company's assets or trade or to guarantee the shareholders' investment. This is intended to end 'arranged exit' schemes.

The following risks inherent in EIS investment make it an opportunity needing careful consideration

(a) Investment in young, unquoted companies carries a particularly high risk because of the difficulties of establishing new businesses.

(b) If the company fails to establish itself successfully, the whole investment could be lost.

(c) There is usually no market for EIS shares (although they can be dealt in on the unofficial OFEX market), so they are difficult to dispose of.

(d) The investor can be called upon to make a further investment.

(e) The initial tax relief can be withdrawn through no fault of the investor (e.g. if the company breaches one of the many EIS conditions).

The many failures in the early years of BES demonstrated that the risk of investing in an unquoted trading company was high. Many potential investors will probably consider that income tax relief at 20% is not, on its own, a large enough incentive to justify those risks. The EIS may, however, be attractive to those who wish to invest in a business in which they will take an executive role (sometimes called 'business angels') or to obtain reinvestment relief. Potential investors should proceed with extreme caution.

6:5   Venture capital trusts

Venture capital trusts (VCTs) were introduced in the Finance Act 1995 as a further incentive to private investors to finance unquoted companies. Their design was the result of consultations between the Inland Revenue, the Stock Exchange and the venture capital industry. Venture capital trusts are companies and have the same constitution as conventional investment trusts. They are subject to particular constraints and offer a number of tax benefits. To qualify as a venture capital trust the following conditions apply

(a) The company must be listed on the Stock Exchange and approved by the Inland Revenue as a VCT.

(b) Within three years of first issuing shares, it must invest 70% of its assets in qualifying unquoted companies. Of this 70%, 30% (i.e. 21% of the total assets) must consist of ordinary shares; the remainder may be preference shares and loan stock. The other 30% of the assets may be 'non-qualifying' investments such as listed securities (both equity and fixed interest) and cash deposits. Most VCTs aim to invest 80% of their assets in qualifying shares and securities.

(c) From 2 July 1997, at least 10% of the VCT's total investment in a company must be in ordinary shares, and guaranteed loans and securities cannot form part of the 70% of assets invested in qualifying companies.

(d) The VCT must invest in unquoted companies which have gross assets of not more than £15 million before its investment or £16 million afterwards. These companies must only have qualifying subsidiaries, must not be controlled by another company and must carry on a qualifying trade (dealing in land or securities and providing financial services are excluded, as are businesses which require a significant property element (e.g. farming, forestry, nursing homes and hotels)).

(e) There is a limit of £1 million on investments in one company in any financial year.

(f) The VCT must not hold more than 15% of its investments in any one company or group.

(g) It is required to distribute not less than 85% of its income.

The tax benefits for investors in venture capital trusts are

(a) Income tax relief of 20% is given on the cost of new ordinary shares, up to a maximum of £100,000 in each tax year. To retain this relief, the shares must be held for five years.

(b) Capital gains tax reinvestment relief is given on the cost of new ordinary shares. Gains realised after 5 April 1995 can be deferred by investment in a venture capital trust and reinvestment must take place within 12 months before or 12 months after the date the gain was realised.

(c) A capital gain realised on the sale of the ordinary shares of a VCT is exempt from capital gains tax, provided the shares were purchased on issue and have been held for five years. Conversely a loss on such shares is not an allowable loss.

(d) Dividends are exempt from income tax.

(e) Capital gains realised by a venture capital trust on its investments are exempt from corporation tax. Unlike ordinary investment trusts, venture capital trusts are permitted to distribute their capital gains to their shareholders.

The benefits at **(d)** and **(e)** are also available to investors who buy VCT shares in the market.

The success of a venture capital trust will depend upon the skill of its managers, who have to be experienced in raising finance for private companies. An assessment of their past record will be an important part of the process of selecting a VCT investment.

6:6   Options and futures

An option is a contract which gives its owner the right – but not the obligation – to buy or sell a quantity of a particular asset. Originally designed for the benefit of commodity producers wishing to protect themselves from price fluctuations, option contracts are now also dealt in by investors (and speculators) as assets in their own right. Their particular value to investors, however, is their use to protect a portfolio, or particular securities, against loss or to reduce the overall risk of a portfolio. Contracts are available not only for commodities (e.g. metals and soft commodities like wheat, coffee, etc) but also for specific securities and for intangible assets like share indices, interest rates and currencies.

The purchaser pays a premium to acquire an option to buy or sell at a specified price (the strike price) on or before a specified date. If he buys a 'call' option (one for a purchase) and the 'spot' price of the asset (i.e. the current market price, for dealings 'on the spot') rises, he will exercise the option; if the price falls, the investor can buy the asset more cheaply and he will allow the option to lapse. His only loss is the cost of the premium. Conversely, he may buy a 'put' option (the right to sell), which he will exercise if the 'spot' price falls.

Futures contracts are also available for a wide range of assets. They differ from options in that the investor is obliged to buy or sell at the specified price on the specified date. Futures contracts for physical commodities are therefore likely to expire in the hands of professional traders or businesses dealing in those commodities.

Options and futures contracts for commodities can be dealt in through a commodity broker. As well as arranging transactions in individual contracts, brokers run discretionary accounts for clients.

Options on shares and securities on the FTSE-100 Index can be bought and sold through a bank, stockbroker or investment manager. They do not have to be held to maturity but can be traded at any time during their life. Because the price of an option is only a small percentage of the price of the underlying shares, large percentage gains can be obtained from fairly small changes in the share price. Similarly, large percentage losses can be incurred, but the maximum loss is limited to the cost of the option. Because a futures contract *has* to be fulfilled, however, the risk of substantial loss is far higher.

6:7   Spread (or index) betting

Financial bookmakers offer the opportunity to bet on the potential movement (both up and down) of a wide range of commodities, indices, financial instruments and exchange rates. For each 'asset' the investor is quoted the current buying and selling prices (the 'spread'); he then places a bet on the price movement and wins a fixed amount for each point the price moves in his chosen direction. The wager can be closed at any time to realise a profit (or cut a loss). A deposit of between 4% and 15% of the value of the bet is paid at the outset, depending on the type of commodity or index chosen. Price changes on the total bet can, therefore, be significant in relation to the outlay and both gains and losses can be considerable. In isolation, therefore, this activity is highly speculative.

One attraction of spread betting is that all returns are exempt from income tax and capital gains tax and no stamp duty or VAT is payable. The only levy is betting duty, which is paid by the bookmaker.

6:8   Gold, silver or platinum

Gold has long been regarded as the universal currency, particularly recognised as a store of value in times of crisis. During periods of high interest rates and high inflation, however, its appeal as an investment diminishes, as it provides no income. As with all commodities, the returns are dependent on price movements.

Gold can be purchased as bullion, coins or jewellery. Coins can be bought through banks or stockbrokers, and the most common are Krugerrands and

British sovereigns. Other countries have also minted gold coins. Older coins may have a numismatic value and so can trade at a considerable premium over their gold content.

Platinum is also available in modern coins and bars of various weights. Investments in all three metals can be bought through commodity dealers. VAT is chargeable if the asset is bought in the UK, so it is usual to arrange for the purchase, storage and sale to take place in the Channel Islands and other offshore centres.

6:9   Collectors' items

The essential return from the assets in this section is likely to be the enjoyment of seeking, acquiring and owning them. Substantial capital gains are unlikely, but not impossible; in many cases there will be maintenance and insurance costs.

Examples of assets for which there is a collectors' market are

(a) antiques and works of art;

(b) stamps;

(c) rare books and old maps;

(d) old coins and bank notes;

(e) medals;

(f) old toys;

(g) postcards and playing cards;

(h) old bond and share certificates; and

(i) veteran and vintage cars.

All of these can be bought and sold through specialist dealers and at auction and, although the investor may have some knowledge himself, it would be advisable in some cases to seek independent advice.

Although not strictly a 'collectors' item' there is one other asset which in some (but relatively few) cases can prove profitable – racehorses. Most owners, however, participate because of their enjoyment of the sport, recognising that the expenses are likely to outweigh the prize money and betting winnings.

Investment may be in horses in training or in stallions. Typically, a horse in training is owned by a syndicate of up to 12 people. The members have to be approved by the Jockey Club. Most syndicates appoint a professional syndicate manager to be responsible for the day-to-day administration.

An alternative form of investment is through an ownership club, which requires less outlay than a syndicate. This too must be approved by the Jockey Club and has considerably more members than a syndicate. The subscription normally covers the cost of the horse and training, etc, for a two-year period, at the end of which the horse is sold and any surplus funds distributed among the members.

Some horses in training are owned by companies, whose shares can be purchased by investors.

Stallions are normally owned by a syndicate of 40 members run by a committee. There are no restrictions as for horses in training.

7   Membership of Lloyd's

Lloyd's is a corporation, founded over 300 years ago, whose members underwrite UK and international insurance risks. Insurance is underwritten through syndicates, which traditionally specialised in particular classes of business, such as marine, aviation and motor, although the relatively new composite syndicates tend to write a mixture of all classes of business.

Historically, only individuals have been able to become involved with the Lloyd's insurance market with the potentially huge disadvantage of unlimited liability. For the three years 1993, 1994 and 1995, liability was restricted to 80% of total premium income being written, averaged over the three-year period. This was because of the innovative High Level Stop Loss Scheme, which was compulsory for all Names (Lloyd's members) at an annual cost of 1/3% of premium income, but was abolished for 1996. Individual Names once again took on unlimited liability, but may consider arrangements that commenced during 1996, to enable conversion to membership with limited liability. Since 1 January 1994 corporate members were allowed to join and individuals have also been able to invest in quoted corporate members, with investment trust status, as an alternative to full membership of Lloyd's.

7:1   Financial requirements

The overall capacity of the Lloyd's market is around £10 billion and the vast majority of this is now supported by corporate members. Individual members with unlimited liability have dropped in number to less than 3,000, from the peak of over 30,000 during the late 1980s. The concept of the 'Means Statement' and allowing part of the assets outside Lloyd's to support underwriting premium income has been abolished for the 2001 year of account, but the minimum funds at Lloyd's entry requirement for new members is £300,000 for 2001 and £350,000 for 2002.

For existing Names, the minimum capital requirement is being reduced for 2001 to 40% of the overall premium limit of the member. Thus, the minimum of £300,000 will support a premium limit of £750,000.

There is also a risk-based capital ratio, relevant to the risk analysis of the syndicates with which the member is involved, and if this exceeds the 40% minimum Funds at Lloyd's requirement, additional funds will need to be introduced to Lloyd's.

Some individuals find it convenient to provide part of their Funds at Lloyd's by way of a letter of credit secured on other assets. Lloyd's have now relaxed the rules concerning the use of the principal private residence as security, but only on the proviso that the members' agent is satisfied that this is a matter of convenience and not out of necessity.

Costs of membership can be substantial for the individual Name but, with the volatility of the market, the rewards can also be high. There is an entrance fee of £3,000 plus VAT and associated legal costs. Annually, there will be agents' fees, profit commissions, subscriptions to Lloyd's, Central Fund contributions, bank guarantee charges (if the funds at Lloyd's are provided in this way), stop-loss premiums, estate protection premiums, accountancy charges and other expenses of joining Names' associations. All these are allowable deductions for tax purposes.

Lloyd's business is carried on by professional underwriters who exercise their particular skills in taking on risks for an appropriate premium. They work for managing agencies and the capacity for their operation is determined by the number of members, whether individual or corporate, whose support is recommended to syndicates by members' agencies and Lloyd's advisers.

Syndicates prepare accounts for each calendar year at the end of a three-year period in order to allow time for claims to be made, or for there to be sufficient knowledge of likely claims to enable the outstanding risks to be reinsured into the account of the following year. Thus, a name who is involved with a syndicate for the 2001 year of account will have to wait until the spring of 2004 to be told whether that syndicate has made a profit or a loss.

An average Name for 2001 may be writing £750,000 premium income and it is likely that this Name would be involved with a considerable number of different syndicates, all of which will be seeking to generate a profit for their Names. Funds at Lloyd's of at least £300,000 must be lodged by this average Name, although any investment income or capital appreciation from these funds will continue to belong to the individual and be treated as part of the trading result for tax purposes.

An individual member of Lloyd's who commences underwriting activities on 1 January 2001 must have all the financial requirements in place in the autumn of 2000 and, as a pay-out will not be received until the summer of 2004, must be prepared to bear considerable costs in the meantime, which could conceivably amount to £35,000. Membership on this basis should normally only be considered for a long-term period of, say, ten years.

7:2   Advantages of membership

The main attractions of individual membership are as follows

(a) The Names' assets work twice for them; once earning dividends, interest and capital appreciation, but also as collateral for the underwriting business.

(b) The Name is deemed to be carrying on a trade from which the profits are earned income or, conversely, any losses can be set against other income for tax purposes.

(c) After membership for two years, the total Lloyd's connected assets qualify for 100% inheritance tax relief as business property, as long as the Funds at Lloyd's are not out of proportion to the level of business being written.

(d) There is a tax-efficient Special Reserve fund into which Names may transfer up to 50% of annual profits, until this fund reaches a value of 50% of premium income. All amounts transferred are tax deductible and the fund itself grows in a tax-free environment. Taxable withdrawals must be made from the fund to pay losses or calls from the underwriting business. However, transfers to this fund must only be considered as tax-efficient deferrals of income tax because ultimately, on cessation of membership, the full market value of the assets in the fund will be brought into charge to income tax for the final year. As part of the overall Lloyd's interest on death, these assets would attract business property relief.

(e) Pension planning can be considered for all individual Names on profits, once the relevant losses of recent years have been set against profits, as appropriate.

(f) Syndicate participations must be acquired at a cost in the annual auctions and, over a period of time, value will be achieved from good syndicate capacity allocations. On disposal, any proceeds are taxable under the capital gains tax regime and retirement relief may also be due for those over 50 years of age who make a material disposal of business assets, until this relief is finally phased out by 5 April 2003. Otherwise, as business assets, the gains can be rolled over or accepted, with the benefit of taper relief.

7:3   Disadvantages of membership

The main disadvantages are threefold

(a) the risk of unlimited liability;

(b) the lack of control over the business being carried on; and

(c) the further deterioration in gearing that has followed the introduction of risk-weighting each syndicate, which could in some cases increase the Funds at Lloyd's ratio to more than 50%.

7:4 Corporate capital

From 1 January 1994, incorporated members of Lloyd's, with a minimum paid-up capital of £1.5 million, were introduced to the Lloyd's market. They pay much higher entrance fees and have to deposit 50% of their premium income as Funds at Lloyd's. Many of these corporate vehicles operate with investment trust status and are quoted so that individuals now have the option of investing in shares of corporate members. For the first time, therefore, individuals can invest in Lloyd's without the high liability risk that previously applied. The main disadvantage is that their investment is not direct into the Lloyd's market so that their return will be diluted by corporate management charges and profit retentions. There has also been a recent growth of unquoted corporate vehicles dedicated to a particular syndicate or managing agency. These provide capacity for specific syndicates and can detract from the capacity available to individual Names.

7:5 Conversion opportunities

Existing Names have been able to consider converting to limited liability membership in recent years, whether via Scottish Limited Partnerships or individual and collective NameCos. Lloyd's Publications Office provides a Conversion Guide for those who may be interested, as do several Members' Agents.

7:6 Summary

The horrendous losses of the late 1980s and early 1990s have now been reinsured separately into Equitas, set up by Lloyd's specifically for this purpose. The Reconstruction and Renewal settlement enabled the market to survive and assisted those Names who were badly hit, as well as many others, to extricate themselves from the market. The ongoing structure appears to be better organised, most certainly better regulated now that the FSA are involved and, with the due diligence necessary to satisfy corporate members, only the best syndicates and agencies remain. This all points to a reasonable expectation of profit for the future, within a much more financially secure environment. It is some years since new unlimited liability individuals joined the market but, with most of the tax breaks still intact, this is a venture that should still be of interest. Several members' agents have set up corporate arrangements, either for converting Names or new entrants, whereby a degree of control can still be exercised within a personal or family NameCo, and Lloyd's will provide contact details for anyone who is interested in either converting their membership or joining the market. The recent years of 1998, 1999 and 2000 are projected to show losses so that, if the trend towards hardening rates and the cyclical nature of the business is anything to go by, the next few years should have potential for trading profits.

8 Pension arrangements for directors and executives

This chapter has been primarily written from the viewpoint of individual arrangements for directors and executives effected on a 'money purchase' basis (the final benefits being based on the amount in the pension fund at retirement) and not on a 'final salary' basis (where the pension benefits are funded as a proportion of final remuneration). It is not intended to cover medium or large group schemes (although much of the chapter may still be relevant to them), nor the State pension scheme. Personal pensions are discussed in **Chapter 9**.

8:1　Maximum benefits

The maximum benefits which may be provided under exempt approved pension schemes within the Inland Revenue limits, in respect of individuals who joined the scheme before 17 March 1987, are as follows

(a) Member's retirement pension of two thirds of final remuneration provided that ten years' pensionable service has been completed by the normal retirement date.

(b) A lump sum on retirement of $1^1/2$ times final remuneration, provided that 20 years' pensionable service has been completed by the normal retirement date. However, if a lump sum is taken, the maximum member's retirement pension is reduced. Based on the maximum lump sum of $1^1/2$ times final remuneration being provided, the normal maximum pension would be approximately 54% of final remuneration.

(c) Widow's/widower's post-retirement pension of two thirds of the maximum pension that could have been approved for the member before any reduction for lump sum benefits.

(d) Widow's/widower's death-in-service pension of two thirds of the maximum pension that could have been approved for the member had he retired on incapacity grounds at the date of his death. This pension can take into account the whole of the potential service up to normal retirement age.

(e) Dependants' post-retirement and death-in-service pensions. These, together with the widow's/widower's pension, must not exceed the amount of the member's maximum approvable pension.

(f) A lump sum death-in-service benefit of £5,000 or four times final remuneration, whichever is the greater. In addition, there can be a return of the member's contributions, with or without interest.

(g) Escalation of post-retirement and death-in-service pensions in line with the greater of the rise in the cost of living as measured by the RPI or 3% per annum.

The maximum permitted benefits described above assume that there are no 'retained benefits' in pension arrangements relating to previous employments – if these exist, the limits are generally restricted so that total benefits do not exceed the two-thirds pension and 1 1/2 times lump sum limits.

The above benefits are illustrated by the bar chart below

Example 6

A man aged 65 at normal retirement date has final remuneration of £18,000 and 20 years' pensionable service. Maximum permitted benefits are as follows

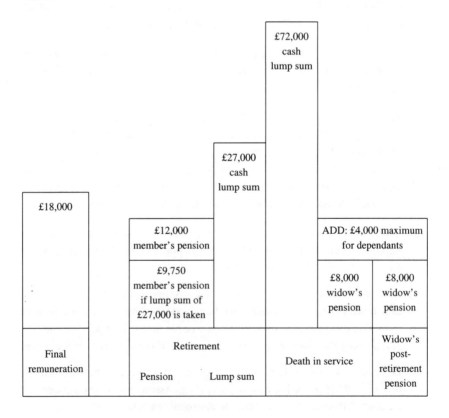

Notes

1. The amount of £12,000 for the member's pension assumes that a cash lump sum is not taken in commutation. However, if a lump sum of £27,000 is taken, the maximum member's pension would be reduced to £9,750.

2. The widow's/widower's pension plus dependants' pensions must not exceed the maximum pension that could have been approved for the member.

3. In addition to the benefits shown in the chart, the post-retirement and death-in-service pensions can be increased in proportion to the increase in the RPI or 3% per annum, if greater.

From 17 March 1987, the following changes, in general, applied to all new schemes and arrangements set up prior to 14 March 1989 and to new members of existing schemes joining before 1 June 1989

(a) The 'accelerated accrual' rate for pension benefits is replaced by a new scale permitting a pension of two thirds of final remuneration after 20 years' service (previously it was possible to qualify for a maximum of two thirds of final remuneration after ten years' service). For shorter periods, a 'straight line' maximum accrual rate of 2/60ths of final remuneration for each year of service will be allowed.

(b) The accelerated accrual rate for the tax-free lump sum, with a maximum of $1^1/2$ times final remuneration after 20 years' service, can be used only if pension benefits accrue on the new accelerated scale. Otherwise 3/80ths of final remuneration for each year of service (with a maximum of 40) will broadly apply, subject to certain relaxation.

(c) Final remuneration for the purpose of calculating the tax-free lump sum on retirement is now restricted to £100,000 and so the maximum amount payable may not exceed £150,000.

Where a member joins his or her company late and so is unable to have 20 years' pensionable service, their maximum approvable retirement pension, expressed as a fraction of final remuneration, is as shown below

	Fraction of final remuneration	
Years of service to	*Before*	*On or after*
normal retirement age	*17 March 1987*	*17 March 1987*
		(see Note 1 below)
1	1/60th	2/60ths
2	2/60ths	4/60ths
3	3/60ths	6/60ths
4	4/60ths	8/60ths
5	5/60ths	10/60ths
6	8/60ths	12/60ths

7	16/60ths	14/60ths
8	24/60ths	16/60ths
9	32/60ths	18/60ths
10	40/60ths	20/60ths
11	40/60ths	22/60ths
12	40/60ths	24/60ths
13	40/60ths	26/60ths
14	40/60ths	28/60ths
15	40/60ths	30/60ths
16	40/60ths	32/60ths
17	40/60ths	34/60ths
18	40/60ths	36/60ths
19	40/60ths	38/60ths
20	40/60ths	40/60ths

Notes

1. From 17 March 1987, the fractions of final remuneration shown in the right-hand column have in general applied to all schemes and arrangements set up since that date and to new members of existing schemes. The fractions in the previous column are applicable in other cases.

2. Fractions of a year may be interpolated into the scale.

3. Where an accrual rate in excess of 1/60th for each year is applied, benefits provided from previous occupations (retained benefits) must generally be taken into account to ensure that the total pension does not exceed two thirds of final remuneration.

For late entrants who are unable to achieve 20 years' pensionable service, the maximum approvable lump sum on retirement, expressed as a fraction of final remuneration, is as shown below

Years of service to normal retirement age	*Fraction of final remuneration*
1-8	3/80ths for each year
9	30/80ths
10	36/80ths
11	42/80ths
12	48/80ths
13	54/80ths
14	63/80ths
15	72/80ths
16	81/80ths
17	90/80ths
18	99/80ths
19	108/80ths
20 or more	120/80ths

Notes

1. For all schemes and arrangements set up between 17 March 1987 and 13 March 1989 (and members who joined existing schemes between 17 March 1987 and 31 May 1989), lump sums based on the accelerated accrual rate (years 9 to 20 or more on the above scale) will be available only to those individuals whose pension is also based on the accelerated accrual rate of 2/60ths. Where the accrual rate lies between 1/60th and 2/60ths, the lump sum may be accordingly enhanced, in proportion from 3/80ths for each year. In any event, the maximum amount which can be taken as a tax-free lump sum with regard to these schemes is £150,000.

2. Fractions of a year may be interpolated into the scale.

3. Where the accelerated accrual rate is applied, benefits provided from previous occupations must generally be taken into account to ensure that the total lump sum does not exceed $1^1/2$ times final remuneration.

Further changes were introduced in the Finance Act 1989, affecting all new schemes set up on or after 14 March 1989 and those joining existing schemes from 1 June 1989

(a) The benefits to be provided, both pensions and cash sums, will be based on 'capped earnings' only. This limit (originally £60,000) may be revalued each year in line with the RPI and currently stands at £91,800 (for the tax year 2000/01).

(b) Employees with at least 20 years' service may retire on a pension of two thirds of final remuneration at any time from age 50 onwards. For shorter periods, 2/60ths of final remuneration for each year of service will be allowed. Any shortfall in funding may be provided by augmentation.

(c) The maximum tax-free lump sum payable on retirement will be calculated as either 3/80ths of final remuneration for each year of service (subject to a maximum of 40) or 2.25 times the annual pension (before reduction for the lump sum), whichever is the greater. The maximum amount permissible is currently £137,700 ($1^1/2$ times remuneration of £91,800).

Employers will be able to provide more generous benefits than the tax rules allow by establishing an unapproved top-up scheme, but the usual tax advantages will not apply. This second scheme can be on a funded or unfunded basis, although contributions to a funded scheme would be taxed as income of the employee. Benefits from an unfunded scheme would be taxed only when they are paid.

Employees not affected by these changes may nevertheless elect that their benefits be subject to the new maxima shown above, but this would include accepting the remuneration restriction in (a) above.

As a consequence of the changes which have occurred since 17 March 1987, many older and highly paid employees could be reluctant to change jobs since their pension and/or lump sum expectation may be reduced.

8:2   Final remuneration

The most usual definition of final remuneration is the remuneration for any one of the five years preceding the normal retirement date. However, where fluctuating emoluments arise, such as commission or bonuses, they would usually be taken as the average of three or more consecutive years ending on the last day of the basic pay year. Directors' fees may rank either as basic pay or as fluctuating emoluments according to the basis on which they are voted.

In the case of a 20% director (a director who, either on his or her own or with associates, is able to control 20% or more of the ordinary share capital of the company), benefits cannot be based on one year's earnings. Instead, final remuneration would normally be defined as the yearly average of the total emoluments for any three or more consecutive years ending not earlier than ten years before the normal retirement date.

For either definition, remuneration may be increased in proportion to the increase in the cost of living for the period from the end of the year on which the remuneration is based up to normal retirement date. This increase is known as 'dynamisation'. Dynamised final remuneration may not be used to permit greater lump sum retirement benefits in isolation.

Benefits in kind may be taken into account when they are assessed to income tax as emoluments under Schedule E and will normally be regarded as fluctuating emoluments. If benefits are not assessable, they may not be included as part of final remuneration except with the agreement of the Inland Revenue. Profit-related pay is an exception.

With effect from 17 March 1987, the following changes have in general applied to all new schemes and arrangements and to new members of existing schemes

- the definition of final remuneration excludes income and gains from share option schemes (this applies to all share options granted after 17 March 1987);

- employees earning more than £100,000 and any employee who has at any time within ten years prior to retirement been a 20% director have final remuneration defined as if they were 20% directors (see above).

For members of schemes set up on or after 14 March 1989 and those joining existing schemes from 1 June 1989, final remuneration cannot exceed the 'earnings cap'.

8:3   Normal retirement date

Normal retirement date may be at any age between 60 and 75. There is no scope to delay the commencement of benefits beyond age 75 except for those members who joined a scheme prior to 1 June 1989.

Following various judgments of the European Court of Justice, all occupational pension schemes were required to equalise the normal retirement age for males and females with effect from 17 May 1990.

An individual may continue to work after the normal retirement date. Members subject to the Finance Act 1989 provisions must normally start to receive benefits at the time of actual retirement (or age 75, if earlier). This is not the case if an individual joined, before 1 June 1989, a scheme set up before 14 March 1989. Such an individual may elect to receive at normal retirement date, or at any later date, before he or she retires, the pension and/or lump sum benefit due, rather than defer all benefits until actual retirement.

Retirement earlier than the normal retirement date is allowed on grounds of incapacity, whatever the age, or if the individual is at least aged 50. In the case of certain occupations, the Inland Revenue will approve earlier normal retirement ages than is the norm, for example, footballers at 35. However, each case has to be considered according to its own individual circumstances.

If the normal retirement date requires changing, this may be possible, provided the member has not yet reached normal retirement date, and the new date is within the acceptable range. However, unless there is a period of at least five years from the date of change to the new retirement date, this may require reference to the Inland Revenue.

8:4   Early leavers

If an individual leaves employment before normal retirement date, the preserved benefits within the company pension scheme can be transferred.

When a member leaves service with more than two years' pensionable service (or less service if the scheme rules provide), the benefits accrued to the date of leaving are preserved for the member.

If the benefits have been earned in a final salary scheme, those preserved benefits will be increased each year, at least in line with the lesser of the increase in the Retail Prices Index and 5% between the date of leaving and date of retirement. Different rules apply to the Guaranteed Minimum Pension (GMP) in respect of any contracted-out service and for those who left service before 1 January 1991.

If the benefits have been accrued in a money purchase scheme, they will continue to reflect investment returns, in the same way as if pensionable service had continued but without further contributions.

As an alternative to leaving the preserved benefits in the pension scheme, the member has the option to transfer them to another approved pension arrangement. Many complex issues need to be taken into account when deciding whether or not to transfer, and evaluated in the light of the needs of the individual. The best way to obtain the right transfer advice is to seek specialist independent advice.

8:4.1   Issues to be considered

An adviser must request full details of the preserved pension that the individual is considering transferring as well as the current transfer value. The transfer value is a capital sum offered in lieu of the benefits under the scheme and, if the transfer option is exercised, it must be transferred to an approved arrangement.

A detailed calculation of the value of the benefits being forgone and the anticipated return needed on the transfer monies to match these benefits should be undertaken in each transfer case. The necessary break-even rate of return should be discussed with the individual in light of the investment risk that he is willing to undertake. Obviously, if the break-even rate of return requires a high-risk investment strategy, a transfer will not be suitable for a cautious investor.

Having established whether it is likely that the benefits will be improved by a transfer, a number of further points need to be considered and discussed with the client. The relevant factors which must be considered, in general, are as follows

(a) loss of a guaranteed pension benefit on transfer;

(b) the spouse's and dependants' pensions at retirement;

(c) indexation of pensions in payment and whether these are discretionary or guaranteed;

(d) the guaranteed minimum pension and other benefits from contracting-out;

(e) statutory indexation of deferred benefits and the history of additional guaranteed or discretionary increases provided;

(f) loss of entitlement to ancillary benefits, such as death benefits;

(g) financial security of the pension scheme;

(h) potential loss of moving from an uncapped occupational scheme to a capped pension scheme;

(i) leaving service benefits;

(j) early retirement provisions;

(k) the state of health of the individual;

(l) pension benefits offered by the new employer's scheme;

(m) proximity of the deferred benefits to the Inland Revenue limits;

(n) any 'transfer club' rights;

(o) the surplus position of the scheme and the trustees' intentions on how any surplus is to be applied;

(p) whether pension ages for males and females are equalised under the scheme and the date at which they were equalised; and

(q) the maximum benefit available as a lump sum on retirement.

8:4.2 Transfer options

If, following consideration of these points, the transfer is to go ahead, the following options are available

Transfer to a new employer's scheme

If the new employment is pensionable, the benefits that the new scheme will grant in exchange for the transfer value should be carefully evaluated.

If the scheme is prepared to offer added years these may initially appear poor. However, it should be borne in mind that the benefit payable at retirement will be based on final remuneration. The future value of these benefits should therefore be carefully assessed especially if the individual plans to stay with the new employer for a long time.

Transfer to a buy-out bond (often called a section 32 policy)

A buy-out bond is a money purchase contract. Any GMP (the part of the pension benefits in a contracted-out scheme that corresponds with SERPS for service prior to 6 April 1997) element of a pension transfer must be guaranteed and the final benefits must mirror the rules of the transferring scheme (for example, retirement age and lump sum limits). Therefore, care needs to be taken if the individual's preserved benefit is already close to the Inland Revenue maximum limits within the transferring scheme. If this is the case, there may be little to gain from switching to a buy-out bond.

Under a buy-out bond, the tax-free cash commutation can be revalued in line with RPI for the period of the policy. This can lead to a higher tax-free lump sum than that allowed under a personal pension arrangement where the tax-free cash is limited to a maximum of 25% of the 'non-protected rights' fund.

If the individual is in poor health, consideration should be given to transferring to a buy out bond which may be able to offer a higher lump sum death benefit.

Transfer to a personal pension

As with a buy-out bond, a personal pension arrangement operates on a money purchase basis. However, it differs from a buy-out bond in that no part of the final benefit is guaranteed. The transfer monies relating to the GMP form 'protected rights', which are invested for the period of the policy, the return depending entirely on investment performance. The accumulated 'protected rights' fund at State pension age must be used to purchase pension benefits only with an attaching 50% spouse's pension. The benefits must increase in payment by 3% per annum compound.

Benefits arising from service after 5 April 1997 in contracted-out final-salary schemes must also be held as a 'protected rights' fund and used to purchase benefits with an attaching 50% spouse's pension (if the individual is married at the time of drawing the pension) and increases in line with RPI up to a maximum of 5% per annum ('Limited Price Indexation').

It is possible to split a transfer between a buy-out bond and a personal pension arrangement so that, for instance, the GMP element of the transfer is guaranteed under the buy-out. However, finding a life office willing to take purely the GMP element may be difficult.

Although there is a restriction on the maximum tax-free cash sum which may be taken, there are no limits to the amount of pension benefit which may emerge from a personal pension. Upon transfer, the tax-free cash sum which may be taken under a personal pension arrangement is the lesser of

(a) 25% of the accumulated 'non-protected rights' fund at retirement; or

(b) the tax-free cash sum as certified by the transferring scheme administrator where the transferring member

(i)   was aged 45 or more at the time that the transfer payment was made; or

(ii)   has at any time within ten years preceding the date of leaving been either a 20% director, or in receipt of annual remuneration in excess of £60,000 or, if greater, the earnings cap for the tax year in which the transfer falls;

(iii)   is entitled to benefits included in the transfer payment which arise from an approved scheme under which the normal retirement date is aged 45 or less.

The certified cash sum may only increase each year in line with the increase in RPI for the term of the personal pension. The resulting lump sum may therefore be lower than 25% of the accumulated 'non-protected rights' fund.

The requirement to treat all benefits for service after 5 April 1997 in contracted-out final-salary schemes as protected rights may also mean that the cash sum available from a personal pension is less than that available from the original scheme.

A personal pension can be used to facilitate phased or staggered retirement as detailed in **Chapter 9**.

8:4.3   Short service periods

Where the individual is a member of a pension scheme and has less than two years' service with a company, he or she is not automatically entitled by legislation to benefits purchased by the company, but this may be a benefit under the scheme rules. They may, instead, receive a refund of up to the level of their own contributions, with or without interest, less their share of the costs of reinstatement in SERPS and a deduction for tax of currently 20%.

8:5   Commutation

It is usually advantageous to commute into cash the maximum amount of pension permitted by the Inland Revenue (up to $1^{1}/2$ times final remuneration) and, if appropriate, to use the cash to purchase an annuity. The reason for this is that the whole of the pension is taxable, whereas the capital element of the annuity is tax-free, with only the income element being subject to taxation (at 20% for basic rate taxpayers). Taking the tax-free lump sum also provides liquidity, a facility not offered by an annuity.

Example 7

A single man aged 65 commutes £4,000 of his pension and applies the resultant cash lump sum to purchase a life annuity

	Without commutation	*With commutation*
	£	£
Pension	16,000	12,000
Other investment income	9,000	9,000
Income element of annuity	–	1,291
	25,000	22,291
Tax	4,173	3,551
Net	20,827	18,740
Capital element of annuity	–	2,230
	£20,827	£20,970

Notes

1. One quarter of the amount in the pension fund has been taken as cash to purchase the life annuity.

2. The annuity is non-increasing, payable monthly in arrears and guaranteed for five years.

3. Although the £4,000 of gross pension forgone is replaced by a gross annuity of £3,521, the tax treatment results in an improved net income situation.

4. Tax is calculated using 2000/01 rates and allowances.

In practice, the purchase of the annuity could be delayed if the income is not required, with the object of obtaining the benefit of improved annuity rates available at older ages. However, besides personal circumstances, this decision would also be influenced by the general level of interest rates prevailing at the time together with their future outlook. Prevailing high interest rates, which are expected to fall in the near future often indicate that the annuity should be purchased immediately. Some will wish to consider the delayed annuity purchase option detailed in **Chapter 9**, which was introduced by the Finance Act 1995.

8:6 Simplified schemes

Simplified occupational pension schemes, providing 'no frills' benefits designed to suit the small employer, first became available in 1987. The Inland Revenue will provide on request standard documentation enabling approval for these schemes to be automatically forthcoming. Under this type of scheme, the benefits must be provided on a money purchase basis. In order to achieve the simplified procedure, special restrictions are imposed on the scheme.

8:7 Taxation position

The provision of pensions is favourably regarded by the Government and, in order to encourage their development, the following advantageous taxation treatment currently applies

(a) Investment income and capital gains accumulate within approved pension funds free of all UK tax. However, pension schemes have been unable to recover tax credits attaching to UK dividends since 2 July 1997.

(b) The resulting pension is treated as earned income.

(c) Lump sum benefits arising on death and at retirement are normally received tax-free. The main exception to this is where the trustees of the pension scheme do not have discretion to nominate who should receive the lump sum death-in-service benefit, with the result that the payment is made into the estate of the deceased member.

(d) Annual contributions payable by a company are allowable as an expense for corporation tax purposes. However, the contribution should be paid and cleared through the bank account before the end of the company's accounting year in order to obtain tax relief in that year. The contributions to approved pension schemes are not taxable as a benefit of the member.

In order for a scheme to be approved, the company's contributions must not be insignificant (generally, a minimum of 10% of the total contributions payable).

(e) Special contributions (contributions which are not ordinary annual contributions) made by the company to purchase additional benefits for a member in respect of past service may have to be spread for corporation tax purposes. The aggregate amount allowed in a single year is normally £500,000, but the Inland Revenue must be

119

notified of all special contributions which exceed the employer's total normal scheme contributions or half of the earnings cap (£45,900 in 2000/01).

Where the special contribution exceeds the amount stated above, the period over which the contribution is to be spread is determined by the size of the aggregate special contribution, normally as follows

Special contribution	Period of spread
£500,000 – £1,000,000	2 years
£1,000,001 – £2,000,000	3 years
over £2,000,000	4 years

The tax relief for the contribution will be spread evenly over the period.

Spreading is not normally required where a contribution is actuarily certified as required solely to finance inflationary increases for pensioners; such contributions will be excluded from aggregation.

(f) Contributions by a member of up to 15% of remuneration in any year of assessment are treated as allowable deductions for income tax purposes. Remuneration for this purpose must not exceed £91,800 in 2000/01 (possibly increasing in subsequent years in line with the increases in the RPI) for those affected by the Finance Act 1989 capping provisions.

(g) Where a refund of contributions is taken, a deduction for tax is made, currently at 20%.

(h) Although not strictly a taxation advantage, no national insurance contributions are payable on either pension contributions made by a company or on the resulting pensions.

8:8   Main uses of pension arrangements

Some of the main uses of pension arrangements are outlined below

(a) Retirement planning for directors and executives. Additional benefits over those of the main scheme can be provided as appropriate for the individual.

(b) Mitigation of corporation tax liabilities. Payment of pension contributions is an allowable expense in whole or in part (if a special contribution, it may be necessary for it to be spread) against corporation tax in the accounting year of payment.

(c) Reduction of the value of the shares in a company for both capital gains tax and inheritance tax purposes. By paying pension contributions, the value of a company is generally reduced.

(d) In inheritance tax planning

(i) A good pension arrangement provides a continuing income for the member and his or her spouse, and it is therefore more likely they would be willing to dispose of assets during their lifetimes and thereby benefit from the annual exemptions or even avoid inheritance tax entirely (lifetime transfers which are potentially exempt become completely exempt after seven years, but will be chargeable if death occurs within that time).

(ii) A lump sum death-in-service benefit may be provided free of tax for the benefit of children and dependants, by way of an 'expression of wish letter' to the trustees of the pension scheme. This letter should be regularly reviewed in case it becomes appropriate to change the individuals nominated.

(e) Funding for cash. A member's retirement pension may be commuted into cash up to the Inland Revenue limit of $1^1/2$ times final remuneration. In order to receive the maximum cash (which must not exceed £137,700 (for the tax year 2000/01) for employees joining new schemes set up on or after 14 March 1989 and existing schemes from 1 June 1989 onwards), individuals will need to complete 20 years' pensionable service by retirement. In many cases, 40 years' service will often be necessary.

8:9 Maximising benefits

Due to the considerable advantages offered by company pension schemes, it is a major benefit to directors and executives if their pension arrangements can be maximised. In order to achieve this, the amount treated as final remuneration should be as high as possible and the pension contributions paid should be as large as possible without over-funding. The following are some of the ways in which these requirements can be met

(a) Dynamising past salaries. As previously mentioned, remuneration may be dynamised in proportion to the increase in the cost of living for the period from the end of the year on which the remuneration is based up to retirement date. Therefore, when the rate of inflation has exceeded the actual increases in remuneration, notional final remuneration should be calculated by taking the actual remuneration for an earlier period and applying the increase in the RPI up to retirement date. This would then produce a larger amount on which pension benefits can be based than the final remuneration actually paid.

(b) Arranging for the normal retirement age to be the earliest allowed by the Inland Revenue. As a result of this, larger contributions would be required for the pension fund to build up to produce the required benefits, due to the shorter period available and fewer contributions payable. In addition, a larger fund would be required to provide the pension benefits as they would normally be payable for a longer period.

(c) Funding for post-retirement pensions to escalate by the maximum permitted (the greater of the increase in the cost of living, as measured by the RPI, or 3% per annum).

(d) Maximising all death-in-service benefits.

(e) Employing spouses and making them directors where appropriate. In this way, they can be paid salaries and be provided with pensions in their own right. The Inland Revenue will need to be satisfied that spouses are genuine employees actively working on a regular basis in the business, however.

(f) Paying additional voluntary contributions (AVCs) to provide further benefits within the permitted maxima. However, it is not possible for members who entered into arrangements to pay AVCs on or after 8 April 1987 to receive benefits arising from AVCs in the form of a tax-free lump sum.

The funds within a money purchase company pension scheme are earmarked so that the monies relating to each member can be separately identified. Money purchase arrangements are subject to maximum funding restrictions which are less generous in the early years of an executive's working life. From 1 September 1994, the maximum contributions which the employer could pay to a scheme were substantially reduced. Schemes which commenced before this date were granted a transitional period of five years, after which overall contributions had to be reduced to the new restricted levels. Small self-administered schemes (SSASs), which are discussed later in this chapter, are also subject to these maximum funding restrictions although these were only introduced from 1 June 1996 for SSASs and the transitional periods may run until at least 1 June 2001, except where special or increased contributions are made or undisclosed retained benefits come to light.

Since July 1999, members of money purchase occupational pension schemes have had the option (provided the scheme rules permit it) to transfer their funds into income drawdown instead of purchasing a pension annuity. This puts them on a par with investors in personal pensions (see **9:10.3**), although it will normally be better to transfer to a personal pension, as this permits 'staggered vesting' and removes occupational scheme restrictions on benefits.

8:10   Additional voluntary contributions

As mentioned above, a further method available to directors and executives to increase their pension benefits is for them to make additional voluntary contributions (AVCs), with the maximum permitted being 15% of their remuneration in any year of assessment (this would include any contributions which they have already paid). Remuneration for this purpose must not exceed £91,800 in 2000/01 for those affected by the Finance Act 1989 capping provision.

Scheme members are able to pay 'free-standing' AVCs to a pension provider of their own choice, although employer's schemes are generally to be preferred on grounds of cost, unless the range of funds available is restricted or has an unsatisfactory record. Because of concern that free-standing AVCs had been mis-sold in circumstances where an employer's scheme was more appropriate, the Financial Services Authority has ordered a review of such contracts (similar to the personal pension mis-selling review).

The individual will be able to deduct basic rate tax before paying the AVC to the pension provider, which will then reclaim this amount from the Inland Revenue and apply it on the employee's behalf to the contract. A higher-rate taxpayer should claim relief at the higher rate through his tax coding or assessment. The overall limit on personal contributions will remain at 15%, but with a maximum of £13,770 per annum (for tax year 2000/01), revalued each year in line with the RPI, in the cases of all new schemes set up on or after 14 March 1989 and employees joining existing schemes from 1 June 1989 onwards. Since benefits provided by free-standing AVCs have to be taken in the form of pension, it will not be possible to commute any of the benefits into a tax-free lump sum. This also generally applies to contributions under AVC arrangements entered into by employees on or after 8 April 1987, although employees who were already in such arrangements on 7 April 1987 may commute pension benefits within the Inland Revenue limits.

The Finance Act 1989 simplified existing reporting procedures for free-standing AVCs. For payments up to £2,400 a year, the pension provider carries out a small number of simple checks which do not involve the employer. Further checks before retirement are not normally necessary. If the benefits at retirement exceed the Inland Revenue limits, the AVC monies in respect of the excess benefits will be returned to the employee subject to a tax charge. This is at a rate reflecting the tax relief received on contributions and on the build up of funds. For payments over £2,400 a year, members are now entitled to the information necessary to calculate the 'headroom' for further contributions.

From April 2001, stakeholder pension contracts may be used as an alternative to AVCs and FSAVCs in some circumstances (see **Chapter 9**).

Although no part of the benefits secured by AVC arrangements effected on or after 8 April 1987 can be taken in the form of cash at retirement, the scheme can take into account the total benefits available from the scheme when calculating the maximum tax-free cash sum at retirement. This may give an advantage to AVCs paid within the scheme rather than to a free-standing AVC, unless the scheme also takes into account the benefits from free-standing AVCs alongside any normal AVCs.

The payment of AVCs may be worthwhile in the following cases

(a) Where the benefits offered by the pension scheme are low. Moreover, although commutation from the AVC scheme may no longer be allowed, it might still be possible to increase the overall pension benefits by the payment of AVCs and then take the maximum tax-free lump sum at retirement from the main scheme. However, this would cause a reduction in the pension provided from the main scheme and consequently post-retirement increases may be lost, although the AVC fund can be used for this purpose (see **(f)** below).

(b) Although the company may have introduced improved benefits for directors, they may not have been made retrospective due to the cost involved.

(c) The pension scheme may have been introduced late in the individual's working life with the result that he may receive only low pension benefits at retirement.

(d) A change of job may not allow an individual sufficient time in his new pension scheme to build up the maximum pension.

(e) Earnings for the purposes of the pension scheme may not reflect an individual's total earnings, with commissions or bonuses not having been taken into account.

(f) No provision may have been made in the pension scheme for escalation of post-retirement pensions earned before 6 April 1997.

However, before an individual decides to pay AVCs, the following matters should be borne in mind

(a) the likelihood or otherwise of the company improving pension benefits before the individual retires, making the payment of AVCs unnecessary;

(b) the fund built up from the AVCs used to be locked in until the pension benefits became available at retirement. From July 1999, however, AVC benefits may be taken at any time from age 50 (or any date of earlier incapacity) to age 75. If taken before the main scheme benefits, they must be taken entirely as income, even if contributions started before April 1987;

(c) the position should the individual change jobs before retirement.

Whether it is preferable for pension contributions to be made by the individual in the form of AVCs or in the form of salary sacrifice, whereby the individual's salary is reduced, or rights to a bonus waived, but the company pays an additional pension contribution for their benefit, will depend on the exact circumstances.

With the removal of the upper earnings limit on employers' national insurance contributions from 6 October 1985, salary sacrifice can be an ideal method for a company of reducing the salaries paid to directors and executives and thereby mitigating national insurance costs. Salary sacrifices need to be carefully documented and specialist advice should be sought before action is taken. Under the salary/bonus sacrifice route, any excess funds cannot be returned to the member at retirement and must remain within the scheme for the benefit of other members. It should be noted that life assurance benefits, or even maximum retirement benefits, could be reduced by a salary sacrifice. However, from the individual's viewpoint, the advantage of AVCs is that the limits on pension and death-in-service benefits are based on the gross remuneration and not on the remuneration after the deduction of the contributions. As previously mentioned, remuneration for this purpose must not exceed £91,800 in 2000/01. In the event of the individual's death-in-service, the normal lump sum death benefits may be increased by the return (with or without interest) of his or her own contributions.

It can therefore be seen that there are conflicting factors operating in the choice between AVCs and salary sacrifice. The following example shows AVCs as an investment

Example 8

A single man is aged 45 next birthday with a normal retirement age of 65 and current remuneration of £26,000 per annum. AVCs of £1,000 per annum are to be paid

	Contributions paid	*Contributions not paid*
	£	£
Gross remuneration	26,000	26,000
Less: additional voluntary contributions	1,000	–
	25,000	26,000
Less: personal allowance	4,385	4,385
	£20,615	£21,615
Income tax payable	£ 4,353	£ 4,573
Net income	£20,647	£21,427
Difference in net income	£780 per annum	

Illustrative benefits provided by pension scheme at age 65 in respect of £1,000 per annum payable for 20 years

Illustrative fund	£39,000
Illustrative pension	£3,580 per year

Net return is approximately 8.1% per annum compound based on the net income reduction of £780 per annum.

Notes

1. The illustrated fund shown at £39,000 is based on the rules laid down by the Financial Services Authority and assumes that contributions, after allowing for a deduction for expenses, will be invested to earn 7% per annum.

2. In the event of death before age 65, the full amount of the accumulated fund would be returned.

3. Since employees joining new or established AVC schemes on or after 8 April 1987 cannot commute any of the benefits into a tax-free lump sum, the benefits will have to be taken in the form of pension.

4. Tax is calculated using 2000/01 rates and allowances.

8:11   Insured schemes

The main types of insured schemes are as follows

(a) *With-profits*. Under this method, the pension fund is increased each year by the declaration of bonuses which, once declared, cannot be taken away. In addition, most insurance companies also pay terminal bonuses, the amount of which will be mainly based on the capital appreciation over the term of the policy. Most insurance companies now write these contracts on a unitised basis, where bonuses increase the rate of growth in unit prices. The benefit of a with-profits investment is that investment returns are 'smoothed' over the duration of the policy. While with-profits contracts produce 'smoothed' proceeds at retirement in cash terms, this is not necessarily true of the annuity which can be purchased with the proceeds. Other investments can offer protection against changing annuity rates nearer retirement.

(b) *Non-profit*. This type of scheme can be suitable when it is required that the amount in the pension fund or the pension itself at pension age should be guaranteed. It is not normally recommended except in cases when there is a comparatively short period to retirement. This type of scheme is now exceedingly rare, although old schemes may still be in existence.

(c) *Unit-linked*. The value of the pension fund under this method will fluctuate with the value of the underlying assets on which the price of the units is based. Unit-linked schemes, although capable of producing very good results, usually involve a greater level of volatility in the value of the fund. Some providers offer a 'lifestyle' option which switches investments progressively in the period up to anticipated retirement, to protect against sudden falls in both equity markets and annuity rates at retirement.

(d) *Deposit administration*. This method is often operated in a similar way to a bank deposit account, where interest is added periodically to the amount in the pension fund. Therefore, the value of the fund is guaranteed to show annual growth and cannot depreciate. This type of scheme is also rare but can be broadly replicated by investing in a with-profits or cash fund.

It is now normal practice, in the case of all types of insured schemes, for an open market option to be available without penalty at retirement age. An open market option is where the full value of the member's benefit is made available to purchase a pension from an insurance company other than that with which the pension scheme was effected. The amount normally transferred would be the fund after payment of any retirement lump sum. Therefore, it is usually worthwhile for several quotations to be obtained at retirement from leading life assurance companies in the annuity market and then for the pension benefits to be taken with an appropriate company.

8:12   Small self-administered schemes

Small self-administered schemes are very popular for directors, particularly of owner-managed businesses. The main difference between insured and self-administered pension schemes is that the administration and the management of the investments are undertaken by the trustees, who can be nominated by the company, so that control of the assets of the scheme is not passed to an insurance company.

Although small self-administered schemes have been in existence for a number of years, it was not until February 1979 that the first proper guidance was given, when Memorandum No. 58 was issued by the Inland Revenue. This Memorandum was replaced with effect from 15 July 1991 by the Retirement Benefit Schemes (Restriction on Discretion to Approve Small Self Administered Schemes) Regulations 1991 (SI 1991 No. 1614).

Since 1979, many insurance companies have brought out their own hybrid schemes (part-insured, part self-administered) and loanback schemes, mainly to compete with the pure self-administered schemes.

A 'small' scheme is one with fewer than 12 members and in this interpretation the Inland Revenue will ignore relatively low-paid employees with derisory benefits whose inclusion brings the total membership to 12 or slightly more. Schemes will also not be regarded as 'small' if no members are 'connected' to any other member, to the employer (normally as a director) or to the trustees. An insurance company scheme established under self-administered documentation, but with all its assets fully insured, is not recognised as a small self-administered scheme.

It is necessary for every small self-administered scheme to have a pensioneer trustee (an independent individual or body, widely involved with occupational pension schemes and having dealings with the Inland Revenue, who is prepared to give an undertaking that he will not consent to any improper termination of a scheme of which he is a trustee). A pensioneer trustee is not a watchdog for the Inland Revenue in any other area. The resignation or replacement of the pensioneer trustee must be reported to the Inland Revenue within specified timescales.

In order to obtain Inland Revenue approval for a small self-administered scheme, its purpose must be pension provision and not tax avoidance. A company will only be permitted to have one small self-administered scheme. It should be noted that, in order to comply with the provisions of the Financial Services Act, all members must be trustees.

In the first two years after the scheme is established, the trustees may only invest a maximum of 25% of the scheme's assets in shares of the employer or loans to the employer. Here, the valuation of the scheme's assets cannot include assets arising from the payment of a transfer value or held because beneficiaries have deferred purchasing annuities.

After the initial two-year period, the trustees may invest up to 50% of the total market value of the scheme assets (excluding those from deferring annuity purchase) in the employer. Any loans to the employer must be at a commercial rate of interest. It is not possible for a small self-administered scheme to secure a member's benefits against particular scheme assets. However, an asset can be notionally used to calculate a member's benefit.

There must be an actuarial valuation of the scheme's assets and liabilities at its inception and thereafter at three-year intervals. Contributions cannot be paid to the scheme unless justified by the latest actuarial report.

In general, the trustees may not invest in the following assets

(a) personal chattels, such as works of art;

(b) residential property except in specific circumstances; and

(c) shares in an unlisted company which carry more than 30% of the voting rights in that company or entitle the trustees to more than 30% of any dividends declared by that company.

Special arrangements apply to schemes where the trustees held investments in the above assets prior to 15 July 1991 (the date of implementation of the regulations).

The scheme administrator must report to the Inland Revenue within 90 days the following transactions

(a) acquisition or disposal of land, including buildings and other structures;

(b) lending of money to an employer or associated employer;

(c) acquisition or disposal of shares in the employer or associated employer;

(d) acquisition or disposal of shares in an unlisted company;

(e) borrowing money; and

(f) the purchase, sale or lease from or to an employer or associated employer of any asset other than one as described in **(a)**, **(c)** or **(d)** above.

The Inland Revenue does not require the purchase of an annuity on the retirement of a scheme member until age 75. By exercising this delay in the annuity purchase, the trustees can avoid the expense of securing benefits for the member during periods of poor annuity rates. Trustees must take professional advice on the most opportune time to purchase an annuity and keep deferral under continuous review, however.

8:12.1 Suitability

Small self-administered schemes are more likely to be suitable in the following circumstances

(a) Where the minimum annual contribution is £10,000.

(b) Where all the beneficiaries are not due to retire in the near future (until at least five years from the inception of the scheme).

(c) Where the fund will be used to make specific investments, such as a loan to the company or an investment in property where the company may be the lessee. However, in these cases, the transactions must be arranged at arm's length and on full commercial terms.

8:12.2 Advantages and disadvantages

The main advantages of small self-administered pension schemes compared to insured schemes are as follows

(a) Greater investment freedom, since

    (i)   direct control of the investments of the pension scheme is with the trustees who often include the directors of the company;

    (ii)   the choice of investment is very wide;

    (iii) it is usually possible to change investment managers at low cost.

(b) Greater flexibility as to the amount and timing of contributions. Consequently, there is less risk to future cash flow.

(c) Generally lower costs for larger contributions. Charges which are based on a percentage of the size of the pension fund can be extremely high and should be avoided.

(d) If the fund purchases a property, either owned by the company or which can be leased to the company, the rent is paid to the fund with no liability to tax. When the property is sold, any capital gain is tax-free.

(e) If assets are built up in a fund rather than in a company, it is often possible to transfer substantial sums from one generation to another, free of inheritance tax.

The principal disadvantage is that there is often more administration and, as a result, additional costs may be incurred. Also, responsibility must be assumed for investment. It should be remembered that the size of the pension to be received will mainly depend on the success or otherwise of the scheme's investments.

9   Personal pensions

9:1   Introduction

Personal pensions were introduced in the Finance (No. 2) Act 1987 and came into effect on 1 July 1988, replacing section 226 retirement annuities. They can be effected by either the self-employed (including partners) or those not in an occupational pension scheme either because the employer does not provide one or because the employee has opted not to belong to it. An employee, covered for death-in-service benefits only under an occupational scheme, is allowed to arrange a personal pension. Personal pensions can be provided by life assurance companies (including friendly societies), building societies, banks and unit trust management groups.

Unlike company pension arrangements where contribution limits are determined by final salary and length of service, the benefits under personal pensions are restricted by the maximum contributions which it is permissible to pay. These contributions are based on a percentage of net relevant earnings and the maximum varies according to the age of the person concerned at the beginning of the tax year in which the tax deduction is sought.

Net relevant earnings may be broadly defined as any earnings which are chargeable to tax and to which no approved occupational pension scheme relates or earnings from a business or self-employment, less certain deductions such as expenses, trading losses and capital allowances. A precise definition of relevant earnings (the admissible income before deductions) can be found in section 644 of the Income and Corporation Taxes Act 1988. Personal charges such as mortgage interest are not deducted.

Precise notes on the operation of personal pension schemes can be found in the Inland Revenue booklet IR76.

9:2   Main benefits

The following are the main benefits that can be available under personal pensions

(a) Retirement pension. This will normally commence at a minimum age of 50 with the maximum age at which the pension must be taken being 75. However, for certain professions and occupations, the Inland Revenue has agreed earlier retirement ages (see **Appendix 3**).

As an alternative to a full pension, a tax-free lump sum may be taken together with a reduced pension. The pension and lump sum must be taken simultaneously (unless income drawdown is used – see **9:9.3** below). The maximum cash sum allowed is 25% of the overall fund excluding the value of the 'Protected Rights fund' (see **9:3** below).

In practice, it is generally worthwhile to take the lump sum together with the reduced pension as the lump sum can then be used to purchase an annuity. If this is done, a higher net income is normally obtained than from the full pension, as part of the annuity is tax-free (see Example **7** in **Chapter 8**). In addition, taking the lump sum provides liquid funds, a facility not offered by an annuity.

(b) Dependant's retirement pension (this must not exceed the amount of the individual's pension) payable to a spouse or other person financially dependent on the retired person.

(c) Annual increases in the individual's and dependant's retirement pensions.

(d) Lump sum death-in-service benefit with the maximum allowed being the value of the pension fund at the time of death.

(e) Supplementary death-in-service benefits to provide a cash lump sum or pension for any named individual. These benefits can be provided only by an insurance company or friendly society.

9:3 Contracting out

Employed persons, including those in contracted-in occupational schemes, can use the personal pension as a vehicle to contract out of the State Earnings Related Pension Scheme (SERPS). It is then described as an 'appropriate personal pension scheme'. Such a scheme can be divided into two parts. The first part is the compulsory minimum contribution, which is equal to the national insurance contracting out rebate (see below) and is paid by the Department of Social Security (DSS) direct to the pension provider chosen by the individual. The fund built up by these contributions is called the 'Protected Rights fund', the benefits from which may be taken only from State pension age or later. The second part is for additional contributions which may be made by either an employer and/or the employee (see **9:4** below).

From 1993 until 6 April 1997, the national insurance rebate was 4.8% of 'band earnings', which are earnings between the Class I national insurance lower and upper earnings limits (£3,484 and £27,820 per annum for 2000/01). Since

6 April 1997, the level of national insurance rebate has been age-related. The minimum rebate from age 16 is 3.8% and this increases to 9% at age 47.

The level of rebate was calculated by the Government Actuary trying to estimate the contributions that would be required, over a specified period, for the benefits from a personal pension to match those available under SERPS. The calculations took account of the expenses that would be levied by personal pension providers.

9:4   Contributions

Contribution limits based on age rather than date of birth were introduced with effect from 6 April 1987 and these limits applied to personal pensions when they were introduced on 1 July 1988. Following changes in the Finance Act 1989, the allowable contributions are as follows

Age at beginning of year of assessment	Maximum contributions (% of earnings)
35 or less	17.5
36-45	20
46-50	25
51-55	30
56-60	35
61-75	40

These limits will be overlaid with further contribution allowances from 6 April 2001, as described in **9:7(k)** and **(l)** below.

Where a contract is effected by an employee, it will also be possible for a contribution to be paid by his employer, although the overall limits shown above must not be exceeded. Minimum contributions and age-related rebates paid by the DSS for an arrangement which is used to contract out of SERPS are not included when determining the maximum contributions payable.

The maximum contributions qualifying for tax relief in respect of the provision of death-in-service benefits are limited to 5% of net relevant earnings. The limit reduces to 10% of contributions for new schemes set up after 5 April 2001 or for employees joining employers' schemes that exist at that date. The contributions paid reduce the maximum contributions available to provide the benefits **(a)** to **(d)** in **9:2** above.

The Finance Act 1989 introduced a cap on the earnings that can be included when calculating maximum contributions. The initial level of the cap was set at £60,000 and the intention was that this would rise in line with RPI, although the uplift was missed in 1993/94.

The earnings caps have been as follows

Tax year	Earnings cap £
1989/90	60,000
1990/91	64,800
1991/92	71,400
1992/93	75,000
1993/94	75,000
1994/95	76,800
1995/96	78,600
1996/97	82,200
1997/98	84,000
1998/99	87,600
1999/00	90,600
2000/01	91,800

9:5 Taxation position

As with company pensions, the provision of personal pensions is regarded very favourably by the Inland Revenue, with the taxation position being broadly as follows

(a) Contributions up to the maximum permitted are effectively allowed against the highest income tax rates payable in the tax year in which the contribution is paid. For the self-employed, contributions made on or before 6 April 2001 are paid gross with the tax relief being claimed from the Inland Revenue, either using form PP120 or via the tax return. For those in employment, employee contributions are paid net of basic rate tax. Any claim for higher rate tax relief is made in the same manner as for the self-employed. From 6 April 2001, all contributions made by the self-employed and employed will be paid net of basic rate tax. Employer contributions are paid gross. Contributions must not exceed taxable earned income for the year in which relief is claimed.

(b) By election, a contribution paid in one tax year may be treated for tax purposes as having been paid in the previous tax year. Where there are no relevant earnings in the previous tax year, an election may be made to go back to the last but one tax year. From 6 April 2001, a contribution must be paid by 31 January in the following tax year to be eligible for 'carry back' treatment. The election for this treatment must be made before or at the time the contribution is made. The election to carry back two years is withdrawn from 6 April 2001.

(c) Where contributions paid in a fiscal year are less than the maximum contributions permitted, the difference (known as unused relief) may be carried forward for up to six years. Relief will be given in the year in which the excess contribution is paid, or deemed to have been paid, at the tax rates applicable for that year.

Before unused relief can be utilised, the maximum contribution permitted must first be paid in respect of the tax year in question. Any excess contributions can then be paid in respect of unused relief starting with the earliest years on a first in, first out basis.

This facility to relate premiums to a tax year, other than the year of payment, does not apply to contributions paid by an employer. The 'carry forward' relief will not be available after 5 April 2001, although by using carry back, the unused relief can be preserved until 31 January 2002. The carry forward provisions are replaced by the facility described in **9:7(l)** below.

(d) Investment income and capital gains accumulate within the pension fund free of all UK tax. However, since 2 July 1997, pension schemes have been unable to recover tax credits attaching to UK dividends.

(e) The resulting pension is treated as earned income.

(f) The lump sum benefit on retirement is tax-free.

(g) The lump sum death-in-service benefits are free of income tax. These benefits, apart from any amount payable in respect of the Protected Rights fund, are usually paid at the scheme administrators' discretion (it is normal for the policyholder to nominate to whom he would like the benefits paid) and are therefore free of inheritance tax liability. It is also possible to make all lump sum death-in-service benefits the subject of an individual trust and this will again remove any inheritance tax liability.

9:6　Options available

Personal pensions are very flexible contracts, with the following options often being available

(a) Regular contribution contracts can allow payments to be increased, decreased, temporarily stopped and restarted or entirely omitted. However, depending upon the charging structure of the contract, penalties may arise on reduction or cessation of regular contributions. Contracts may also be set up with 'one-off' single contributions.

(b) Switching facilities are now available within the same pension plan whereby both the existing fund and/or future contributions can be switched from a with-profits basis to a unit-linked basis and vice versa (under these plans, with-profits funds are themselves on a unitised basis).

(c) Until 6 April 2001, waiver of contributions under regular contribution contracts can be arranged by the payment of small additional contributions. These would qualify for tax relief in the same way as the normal pension contributions. Consequently, if the person concerned is unable to work due to a prolonged period of sickness or disability, the contributions falling due are waived, thus enabling benefits to be maintained. Without the waiver of contribution option, benefits could not be maintained due to the lack of net relevant earnings, even if the individual had the necessary money to pay the contributions. This option is particularly important when the tax-free lump sum on retirement is to be used to repay a loan. From 6 April 2001, those wishing to insure the continuity of their contributions will have to take out a separate policy.

(d) In the event of death before retirement, the contributions paid can be returned, either with or without interest. Alternatively, the full value of the pension fund can be returned.

(e) An open market option is generally available whereby the pension fund can be built up with one pension provider but the actual pension taken with a different company if this offers higher annuity rates at retirement.

Although the open market option can be very important, it is the general level of interest rates prevailing at the time the pension is taken that is likely to have an even greater influence on the actual amount to be received.

(f) At retirement, it is usually possible for a person to elect for his pension benefits to be guaranteed for a period of up to ten years or taken on a joint life, second death basis. This can be particularly useful if he is not in the best of health at that time. If the individual has only a short life expectancy, it may be worthwhile for him to delay taking his benefits. In these circumstances, the amount payable on death before retirement will often exceed the guaranteed retirement benefits. Alternatively, an 'impaired life' annuity can be purchased; however, detailed medical evidence will be required.

(g) An option is often available for the pension benefits to be taken in stages rather than the entire benefits commencing at the same time. This phased retirement is normally arranged by the pension plan being divided into multiple policies which can then be dealt with independently.

(h) Instead of taking level pension benefits, it is possible to arrange for them to increase in accordance with one of the following methods

   (i) by a fixed percentage annually;

   (ii) on a with-profits basis (the pension is dependent on bonuses credited);

   (iii) in line with the RPI;

   (iv) in line with the value of the underlying fund in the case of a unit-linked policy (under this method, the amount of the pension can also decrease).

   Where an increasing pension is taken, it will generally commence at a significantly lower amount than the corresponding level pension and consequently it will usually take several years (often more than ten years) before the amount of the level pension is reached. Therefore, unless the person concerned believes he has an above average life expectancy or expects the increasing pension to rise rapidly, a level pension can be more attractive.

(i) Term assurance can be taken out with tax relief effectively allowed at the individual's highest rates of income tax payable. The benefits can be written under trust to pass free of inheritance tax to any dependant.

   If net relevant earnings should cease, some life companies may permit the conversion of the policy into a term assurance policy with no medical evidence required.

(j) Loan facilities are often available prior to the proposed retirement date (the main advantages of loan facilities are discussed later in this chapter).

(k) The benefits under a personal pension may be transferred to most other types of pension arrangement but special conditions apply to the benefits, if any, in the Protected Rights fund. Transfer payments from any pension arrangement may be made to a personal pension, although in certain cases it may be necessary for additional restrictions to be imposed and guarantees may be lost.

9:7 Stakeholder pension schemes

From April 2001, individuals will be able to contribute to a new type of pension arrangement known as a stakeholder pension. This scheme has been introduced with the aim of encouraging a greater number of individuals to save for their retirement.

The 'wrapping' is very much like that of a personal pension plan. The main features of a stakeholder pension are set out below

(a) Defined contribution (money purchase) benefit structure.

(b) Approved tax status.

(c) Benefits may be taken from age 50.

(d) Up to 25% of the fund can be taken as a tax-free lump sum.

(e) An annual limit on charges of 1% of the value of the fund.

(f) Given this limit on charges, investment options may be restricted.

(g) Benefits can be phased in to allow greater flexibility.

(h) Benefit statements will be issued to members on a yearly basis.

(i) Plans may be established under contract or trust.

(j) Life assurance can be purchased using up to 10% of contributions.

(k) Contributions of up to £3,600 a year can be paid regardless of earnings and age. This will enable investors to pay contributions in years when they receive no earned income (e.g. during a career break) and also on behalf of non-earning spouses and children.

(l) Contributions can be paid for up to five years after earnings have ceased, based on the earnings of the last year.

An employer will be required to nominate a stakeholder scheme for eligible employees and deduct from pay any contributions those employees may want to make. Employers are not required to contribute. Such schemes do not have to be made available where

(a) An employer has less than five employees.

(b) An employee has earned below the national insurance lower earnings limit during the last three months.

(c) An employee has been employed for less than three months.

(d) An employee is eligible to join an occupational pension scheme after a waiting period of not more than 12 months.

(e) An employer has agreed to contribute to a personal pension plan for all employees over age 18, with a minimum contribution of 3% of basic salary.

Those employers who are required to provide stakeholder schemes will need to have nominated a provider and have the necessary systems in place ready for 8 October 2001.

9:8　With-profits policies

The main types of insured schemes available for personal pensions are similar to those for company pension arrangements for directors and executives and have already been considered in **Chapter 8**.

The following are the principal types of with-profits policies together with their characteristics

(a) *Funding for cash.* Under this type of contract, a cash fund is built up by the addition of reversionary bonuses to the guaranteed basic sum. A terminal bonus, representing mainly the investment surplus earned over the lifetime of the policy, will also often be added to the pension fund when the policy proceeds are taken. At retirement, if beneficial, the open market option can be exercised. The contract may be arranged on a unitised basis.

(b) *Deferred annuities with guaranteed cash conversion rates.* Unlike the funding for cash contract, this type of arrangement provides a guaranteed basic pension to which pension additions are made in the form of reversionary bonuses and a terminal bonus, if applicable. At retirement, guaranteed conversion factors from pension to cash are applied based on the age and sex of the person concerned. The open market option can then be applied to the converted cash sum. The level of benefits under this contract generally tends to be less volatile than in the case of the funding for cash contract.

(c) *True deferred annuities.* This type of arrangement operates in a similar way to **(b)** above, except that there are no guaranteed conversion rates with the pension being unaffected by the rates of interest at the time of retirement. The pensions receivable under this contract are likely to be more predictable than for the more common with-profits contracts shown under **(a)** and **(b)** above.

9:9　Unit-linked policies

The main considerations relating to unit-linked policies are as follows

(a) The amount of the pension benefits receivable under a unit-linked policy (and also largely under a with-profits policy) will partly depend on the cash fund at retirement, which results from

　(i)　the amounts and dates of the contributions paid;

　(ii)　the performance of the investment fund;

(iii)   the charges levied by the life office.

It will also be influenced by the translation of this fund into pension, which depends on

(i)   the sex of the individual and the age at retirement;

(ii)   the level of annuity rates at the time the pension commences;

(iii)   the form in which the benefits are taken – cash/pension and such factors as guaranteed period, escalation rate and provision of a dependant's pension.

(b) Although unit-linked policies are normally of a higher risk/higher reward nature than with-profits policies, this need not necessarily be the case. For example, by switching, as retirement approaches, into a deposit fund where the pension fund is credited with a rate of interest, the value of the fund cannot fall but must increase with interest additions. A switch to a gilt fund will broadly 'purchase' the annuity at the time the switch is made. This is because movements in the value of the fund should match annuity market movements.

(c) Investment market conditions are reflected more immediately in the value of unit-linked policies, whereas there is a 'smoothing' effect in the case of with-profits policies.

(d) It is normally possible to switch at low cost both the amount already accumulated and future contributions between the available underlying investment funds.

(e) Equity-linked funds are often suitable when it is possible to have flexibility in choosing a retirement date in order for it to coincide with a time when stock market values are considered high. However, if this flexibility is not available, consideration should be given to switching into a deposit fund shortly before retirement at a time when stock market values are considered high.

(f) Charges on unit-linked policies can be incurred in the following ways

(i)   policy fees;

(ii)   bid/offer spread or other initial charge;

(iii)   unit allocations;

(iv)   capital levy, usually on units allocated during the first one or two years;

(v)   periodic fund management charge;

(vi)   early retirement penalties which represent the outstanding balance of the capital levy;

(vii)   transfer penalties;

(viii) fund switch charges.

9:10   Drawing benefits

9:10.1   Phased retirement

For those in corporate arrangements, the drawing of pension benefits is usually a one-off event; however, personal pension policyholders have always had the opportunity to phase encashment, by drawing benefits from their various policies when extra income is required. This is particularly useful for the self-employed who are often able to reduce their workload gradually as retirement approaches. Pension benefits can then be used to top-up income as earnings reduce.

The advantages of phased retirement are

(a) there is flexibility over the amount of income that can be drawn;

(b) there is an opportunity to obtain different types of annuities;

(c) there is an opportunity to defer annuity purchase if annuity rates are low and expected to rise;

(d) the unencashed portfolio remains invested in a tax-free environment; and

(e) the unencashed portfolio remains available for return to the estate or a trust in the event of death.

The disadvantages are

(a) the tax-free cash lump sum becomes phased;

(b) the 'open-market' option must be carried out each time a policy is encashed;

(c) the pension becomes potentially payable from several offices;

(d) annuity rates could reduce over time.

9:10.2 Staggered vesting

As personal pension administration systems are now sophisticated, policies can be divided into a huge number of segments to enable the process of phased retirement to become more flexible. A new concept called 'staggered vesting' has become available and it is not unusual to find policies for this purpose divided into as many as 1,000 segments.

A staggered vesting policy is usually established once contributions have ceased. The accumulated fund is consolidated into a multi-segmented personal pension. Whenever income is needed, a number of segments are encashed, through the cancellation of units, to produce income. The tax-free lump sum element of each policy is used to enhance the income. This means that as little of the fund as possible is used to purchase a conventional annuity. The balance of the fund remains in a tax-free environment until further income is required.

The idea of staggered vesting is that as time passes, annuity rates improve with age and the remaining funds continue to benefit from growth within a tax-free fund. The advantages and disadvantages of staggered vesting are similar to those for phased retirement. However, staggered vesting does have the disadvantage of leaving all invested funds with one life office. This can be overcome by taking out plans with more than one office when consolidating the pension portfolio at the outset, although this does increase the administration burden. Staggered vesting will be the only option in cases where the pension portfolio is not sufficiently well spread to enable the desired phased retirement programme to take place.

9:10.3 Deferral of personal pension annuity purchase – 'income drawdown'

The Finance Act 1995 introduced the option of deferring the purchase of a personal pension annuity whilst drawing benefits. The option has the following features

(a) The option allows the policyholder to delay the purchase of an annuity and instead withdraw an income based on upper and lower limits set by the Government Actuary. Currently these limits are that income must be withdrawn from the fund (after tax-free cash has been taken) at a rate of between 35% and 100% of the amount of single life level annuity that could have been purchased each year.

(b) The level of income taken each year can vary (within the limits prescribed) to meet the varying personal cash-flow needs of the individual. The option could also be a useful tool in planning, as a means of reducing income tax liabilities on a year-by-year basis, in the event that tiered tax rates are re-introduced.

The income drawdown parameters are re-calculated at three-yearly intervals. This ensures that the original purpose of the pension fund (to provide an income throughout retirement) is being maintained, i.e. that the level of income withdrawals is not excessive and may comfortably be supported by the remaining pension fund.

(c) The policyholder must purchase an annuity by his or her 75th birthday. If a policyholder dies before an annuity has been purchased, a greater level of flexibility is now available to the widow(er) or dependants. These options are

    (i)   take the remaining fund as cash. A 35% tax charge is levied on a total withdrawal; or

    (ii)   purchase an annuity; or

    (iii)   continue with the drawdown until the earlier of when the original policyholder would have reached 75 or the 75th birthday of the survivor or dependant. On the death of the survivor, the remaining fund can be passed on as cash, subject to the 35% tax charge and possibly inheritance tax. An annuity can be purchased at any time.

If the beneficiary is neither the spouse nor a financial dependant, payment must be made as a lump sum less the 35% tax charge. There may be circumstances where the full fund value is not available to the beneficiary. This could be where

    (i)   the spouse is older than the policyholder; or

    (ii)   the policyholder is female and her spouse is younger or roughly equal in age; or

    (iii)   the beneficiary is a child.

(d) The option of a tax-free cash lump sum is still available upon retirement at the rate applicable to all personal pensions (25% of the 'non-protected rights' fund). Once the lump sum has been taken, income drawdown must start.

(e) After the tax-free cash lump sum has been taken and income drawdown has begun, no additional contributions can be made to the income drawdown plan. However, the fund itself will still benefit from the tax-free status of pension funds.

(f) One of the reasons behind the introduction of income drawdown was to give personal pension holders an alternative to annuities, which in recent years have provided disappointing income levels. Regrettably, a pensioner then has to live with these disappointing returns for the remainder of his or her life.

(g) For income drawdown to be worthwhile, the rate of return from the plan needs to be at least equal to that which could have been obtained from an annuity. This rate of return needs to be after expenses and the ongoing costs of professional advice and investment management. The 'cross subsidy' effect of mortality within an annuity further increases the investment return required for drawdown to match the return from an annuity. It is likely that for an adequate return to be achieved by the income drawdown plan, it will have to be invested in equities. This requirement automatically restricts the potential users of the option to those with a relatively high investment risk threshold and a substantial fund.

(h) As a broad guideline, the withdrawal facility should not normally be considered for pension funds of less than £250,000 (or arguably more). At this level, a reasonable amount of investment diversification can be obtained and the transaction costs are sensible in the context of the funds at issue. Due to the risks involved in deferring the purchase of an annuity, the option will be more suitable for those who are younger and able to ride out short-term volatility within equity markets. By definition, it will not suit those approaching age 75, the point at which an annuity must be purchased.

(i) The key decision is choosing the right moment to switch to an annuity. The optimum time will be when equity markets are high and annuity conversion rates are good. It will be necessary to look at equity markets and annuity rates from a historic perspective, in order to determine whether the switch is merited.

(j) The basic cost of the option far exceeds the charges incurred in arranging an annuity. Annual investment management charges, along with the professional advice needed on a continuing basis, push up the rate of return needed to better the return from an annuity. If this option is taken, the pensioner needs to be comfortable with continuing to be involved with professional advisers.

Potentially all pensioners benefit from the introduction of income drawdown, in that it provides a further choice as to how benefits are taken. Specific beneficiaries are likely to be

(a) Those wishing to delay the purchase of an annuity, in the expectation of annuity rate rises.

(b) Those who believe the fund remaining invested will produce a return materially in excess of the return available from a portfolio of long-dated gilts (on which annuity rates are based). A tolerance to and an understanding of the risks inherent in equity investment is essential for those using the option for this reason.

(c) Those who are already investing in self-invested personal pensions, as the option is a natural extension of that concept.

(d) Those with much younger spouses wishing to maintain flexibility over the level of the survivor's pension.

(e) Those wishing to dovetail income drawdown with their State benefits. This would entail taking a higher income level at outset and reducing it once State benefits become available.

(f) Those with substantial pension portfolios who wish to maintain an equity market exposure for as long as possible, perhaps having purchased an annuity with part of their fund.

(g) Those for whom the benefits available to the family on death before purchasing an annuity are equally or more important than the level of pension. The death benefits can play a useful role in estate planning.

Inevitably there will be those for whom the cost of and the risks inherent in taking up the option will not match the benefits of additional flexibility. Categories who may not benefit are

(a) those who are cautious, do not require flexibility or consider annuity rates to be at a reasonable level;

(b) those with smaller funds, where the contract costs and the cost of ongoing professional advice are likely to outweigh any benefits or flexibility;

(c) those in retirement annuities and company schemes, when the transfer to a personal pension causes a material reduction in the tax-free cash lump sum;

(d) those not requiring the lump sum or income until near age 75; and

(e) those who do not wish to be involved in monitoring their funds or continuing professional advice.

Pensioners who are contemplating this option should be very clear that, unless they expose themselves to a substantial amount of investment risk, they are unlikely to exceed the return from an annuity. The option should therefore be regarded as a means of providing flexibility, rather than improving the total retirement income.

While the income drawdown plan must be provided by and administered by a life assurance company, it is possible for the investor to appoint his own investment manager. It is recommended that income drawdown plans are established as self-invested personal pensions (see **9:15** below), so that the investor is able to change the investment manager if he becomes dissatisfied with the performance of his fund, without having to change plan provider.

Since July 1999, income drawdown has also been permitted from money purchase occupational pension schemes, although the terms may not be as generous as for personal pensions.

9:11   General principles

Before any firm recommendations can be made, it is necessary to consider the exact circumstances of the person concerned. These include

(a) the age of the person;

(b) the number of years until the pension is to be taken and whether the pension date is flexible;

(c) the degree of risk the person is prepared to take;

(d) the likelihood of the person remaining self-employed or not joining an occupational pension scheme;

(e) the extent to which earnings are likely to fluctuate;

(f) the state of health of the person;

(g) the family circumstances of the person;

(h) the extent of surplus income.

Subject to the particular requirements and circumstances of the person concerned, the following general principles will normally apply

(a) Since contributions paid cannot be carried forward for tax purposes, the ability to vary the amount of the payments can be extremely important.

(b) The more volatile funds available under unit-linked policies are usually more appropriate for younger persons, unless the retirement date is flexible.

(c) With-profits, fixed interest and cash deposit funds are often more suitable for persons within five years of retirement.

(d) In many cases, it is most appropriate to pay single contributions rather than start regular contribution policies. Contributions paid on a single-premium basis often carry far lower charges than annual premium contracts. They also allow an element of flexibility, as a decision can be taken each year as to the company to which additional contributions are to be paid.

(e) It is normally recommended that contributions should be paid to several different companies, in order to obtain a spread of investment management.

(f) Due to the higher charges made by some companies in respect of longer-term annual contribution contracts, policies should often be written to age 50 as the retirement age. Late retirement rarely incurs a penalty. In addition, many life companies offer regular contribution policies costed on a single premium basis.

9:11.1   The cost of delay

It is generally advantageous to start the payment of contributions to a personal pension at the earliest possible age. By so doing, the amount of the pension to be received is usually considerably enhanced.

This is illustrated in the following examples

Example 9

Two men aged 39 next birthday and 40 next birthday with a retirement age of 60 pay pension contributions of £1,000 per annum for 21 and 20 years respectively

	Man aged 39 next birthday paying 21 contributions	*Man aged 40 next birthday paying 20 contributions*
	£	£
Illustration of benefits at age 60		
Cash value of pension fund	40,000	36,800
Tax-free lump sum	10,000	9,220
Annual pension	2,380	2,190
Increase in illustrated pension fund by payment of additional contribution	8.7%	

Notes

1. The figures shown in **Examples 9** and **10** are based on the rules laid down by the Financial Services Authority and assume that contributions, before allowing for a deduction for expenses, grow at 7% per annum. Immediate annuity rates are based on an interest rate of 6% per annum.

2. In the event of death before retirement, the full value of the pension fund would be paid.

3. The pension is non-increasing and payable monthly in advance for a guaranteed period of five years.

Example 10

Two men aged 39 next birthday and 40 next birthday with a retirement age of 60 each pay a single contribution of £2,000

	Man aged 39 next birthday	Man aged 40 next birthday
	£	£
Illustration of benefits at age 60		
Cash value of pension fund	7,130	6,700
Tax-free lump sum	1,780	1,670
Annual pension	424	398
Increase in illustrated pension fund by earlier payment of contribution	6.4%	

9:11.2   Immediate vesting

Where other resources are available at retirement, it is often preferable to take the pension benefits as late as possible due to the favourable taxation treatment of the pension fund and improved annuity rates at older ages. However, it may be that an individual can only afford to pay a contribution if the pension benefits are received immediately. Such an arrangement (known as an immediate vesting personal pension) can be advantageous, particularly for higher rate taxpayers, but is subject to the following requirements

(a) the individual must be aged between 50 (or within a few weeks thereof) and 75;

(b) the individual must have sufficient allowable relief to make the payment;

(c) the amount to be paid must not exceed taxable earned income in the year of payment, even if there are sufficient available reliefs;

(d) preferably, the individual should be in good health so that he is likely to live for a longer period than that for which the pension is guaranteed.

The following example illustrates an immediate vesting personal pension for a man paying tax at the higher rate

Example 11

A man aged 59 years 11 months subject to tax at 40% pays a single contribution of £10,000 and chooses to take the pension benefits at age 60

	£	Net cost £
Gross contribution		10,000
Tax relief at 40%		4,000
		£6,000

Benefits provided

	£	£
Tax-free lump sum payable at age 60 (25% of £10,000)		£2,500
Gross annual pension	563	
Less: tax payable at 40%	225	
		£338

Notes

1. The pension is non-increasing, payable monthly in arrears for life, but in any event guaranteed for five years. Therefore, the man or his estate would receive in the first five years after retirement, based on present tax rates, a total amount after tax of £4,190 (lump-sum of £2,500 plus annual net pension of £338 payable for five years).

2. The net cost of the single contribution of £10,000 would be recovered in full within ten years and five months (one month after payment, a lump sum of £2,500 is receivable, followed by a net monthly pension of £28.17 for ten years five months, assuming the man survived for that period). If his top rate of tax payable should fall below 40% after retirement, the net cost of the single contribution would be recouped more quickly.

3. The annual pension represents a return of 9.7% per annum on the net cash outlay of £3,500 (the gross contribution of £10,000 less the tax relief and the tax-free lump sum).

9:12   The employment of spouses

As mentioned in the previous chapter, it is often worthwhile for a self-employed individual to employ a spouse in his business and pay them a salary. As a result, he or she could then be provided with pension benefits in the same way as an employed person under a company arrangement. Moreover, if the salary was not greater than the amount at which national insurance contributions commence (currently £3,952 per annum), no liability for national insurance contributions would arise. In addition, the resulting pension would be free of income tax up to the amount of the spouse's personal allowance, subject to them having no other income.

The work performed for the business by the spouse must be such as to justify the salary paid. As an alternative to the spouse being an employee, it may be advantageous for them to be taken into partnership with similar results to the above except that higher remuneration can often be justified.

9:13   Personal pension term assurance

The provision of term assurance under a personal pension contract may, after tax relief, be cheaper than conventional life assurance contracts. The market for the latter is, however, far more competitive and this has driven premium levels down; for younger ages it is possible for a conventional policy to be cheaper than a pension term assurance, even allowing for the tax relief.

It should also be remembered that the contributions payable to provide term assurance under a personal pension contract have to be included within the overall contribution limits permitted. Therefore, if a person wishes to pay the maximum possible contributions for pension benefits, it is generally expedient for any term assurance to be obtained through a life assurance contract.

9:14   Loan facilities

Loan facilities are available in association with many personal pensions on the market. It must be stressed that pension funds are not being 'borrowed back' but that life companies are offering their policyholders the opportunity to borrow funds.

The following points should be noted

(a) there need not be any restrictions over the purpose of the loan and borrowing can be arranged as and when required;

(b) the company lending will normally require the loan to be secured on a property;

(c) life cover will probably be required;

(d) the loan will probably be 'interest only';

(e) the amount that can be borrowed will normally be limited to the value of the policy, excluding any Protected Rights element;

(f) the rate of interest attaching to the loan is likely to be several percentage points above the prevailing base rate.

It may be preferable to consider other sources of finance before resorting to this type of borrowing, particularly as it is likely that security will be required.

9:15   Regular or single contribution policies?

Where a person is eligible to pay personal pension contributions, it will be necessary to decide whether regular contribution or single contribution policies should be effected. The main advantages of regular contribution policies are as follows

(a) higher minimum guaranteed pensions are usually provided by with-profits investments;

(b) due to the ongoing nature of the contract, there may be a greater personal commitment to maintain the regular payment of contributions, thereby providing larger pension benefits;

(c) the need to shop around each year for a particular policy is avoided, with the consequent saving in time;

(d) the accumulation of a large number of policies is avoided;

(e) the following facilities are available under regular contribution policies (but not generally under single contribution policies)

   (i)   waiver of contribution option;

   (ii)   larger loans by way of a multiple of the annual contribution;

   (iii) pension mortgages (these are discussed in **Chapter 13**).

The principal advantages of single contribution policies are as follows

(a) Greater flexibility is provided. This is particularly important in the following cases

   (i)   since contributions cannot be carried forward for tax purposes, the risk of overpayment is reduced;

   (ii)   single contribution policies are very suitable for mopping up unused relief from earlier years, although this facility will end in April 2001;

(iii)   if a person suffers a reduction in earnings or ceases to be eligible to pay contributions, he can reduce or stop the payment of contributions without penalties being incurred. This is often not the case with a regular contribution policy if it is varied or made paid up;

(iv)   if adverse future legislation should be introduced, contributions can again cease without penalty.

(b)   A series of single contribution policies effected with one insurance company will usually produce superior results to a regular contribution policy arranged with the same company. This is mainly due to the higher initial charges of the latter contract, principally caused by the payment of larger introductory commissions and the longer investment term.

(c)   The individual has the ability to assess the market each year and choose investment managers likely to produce above-average returns. Contributions can also be avoided to managers whose investment performance is deteriorating.

9:16   Self-invested personal pensions

Joint Office Memorandum 101 introduced greater investment freedom for personal pension investors. Investors are now able to establish vehicles that allow them to select and control their investments rather than rely on the provider for investment management.

The permitted investments for self-invested personal pensions are

(a)   stocks and shares (including gilts and debentures) quoted on the UK Stock Exchange including securities traded on the Alternative Investment Market;

(b)   unit trusts, OEICs and investment trusts;

(c)   stocks and shares traded on a recognised overseas stock exchange;

(d)   insurance company managed funds and unit-linked funds;

(e)   deposit accounts;

(f)   commercial property; and

(g)   second-hand endowment policies.

Certain investments are prohibited

(a)   Scheme funds must not be used to provide loans to a member or any persons connected with a member.

(b) Schemes must not enter into any investment transactions with a member or any person connected with a member. This means that the transfer of an existing investment portfolio or commercial property is expressly prohibited. It also follows that a member cannot acquire scheme assets.

(c) Schemes must not hold residential property or land connected with such a property or chattels capable of personal use.

The one exception to the above is that once commercial property has been acquired within the regulations, it can be leased to a business or partnership connected with the member. The lease, including the rent payable, must be on commercial terms, supported by a professional valuation.

Self-invested personal pensions are likely to be most attractive to

(a) investment professionals who wish to manage their own funds;

(b) those with substantial transfer values;

(c) those hoping to acquire commercial property in future;

(d) those wishing to consolidate a number of different pension policies; and

(e) those whose funds are in income drawdown (see **8:9.3** above).

9:17 Personal pensions or company pension arrangements?

If a company director or executive is in non-pensionable employment, it may be that he or she has the option to effect their own personal pension or alternatively to be provided with pension benefits through the company. There are advantages to both options.

9:17.1 Advantages of personal pensions

(a) Personal pensions are simpler to set up. There is less documentation and no delay in obtaining Inland Revenue approval.

(b) Greater flexibility is provided, for example, the contributions paid can be varied more easily. In addition, it is unnecessary for personal contributions to be paid before the end of the current tax year due to the relating back and also possibly the unused relief provisions, although this facility will no longer be available from April 2001. It should be noted that employer's contributions cannot be carried forward or carried back.

(c) In certain circumstances, personal pensions may allow higher benefits. Unlike an arrangement made through a company where a minimum of 20 years' service by retirement is necessary in order to obtain maximum pension benefits, the benefits received under a personal pension are not affected by length of service or final remuneration.

(d) A personal pension may be preferable if the period of employment is likely to be relatively short. Contributions can continue if the investor moves to a new job.

9:17.2   Advantages of company arrangements

(a) It is normally possible for greater pension benefits to be obtained with the actual amounts receivable being based on final remuneration.

(b) The whole or a substantial part of the amount in the pension fund can, in some cases, be taken in the form of a tax-free cash sum.

Where an option is available between the two types of arrangement, all the circumstances need to be considered before a decision can be reached. However, in general, if large or maximum benefits are required or there is a substantial period until retirement, a company arrangement is likely to be more appropriate.

It will very rarely be appropriate for employees to opt out of their company pension schemes, unless an equivalent employer contribution is to be made to the personal pension. If this is offered, consideration needs to be given to whether it is worthwhile for an employee to opt out.

The main points are set out in **9:17.3** below.

9:17.3   Advantages of personal pensions for employees

(a) There is greater personal control and freedom of choice.

(b) If an employee is proposing to change jobs frequently, a higher ultimate pension is likely as transfer penalties will be avoided.

(c) It is easier for employees to take their pensions with them if they change jobs.

(d) Personal pensions will be preferable for those employees whose earnings will peak during their middle years of employment, rather than close to retirement.

9:17.4   Disadvantages of personal pensions for employees

(a) There may be no contributions from the employer.

(b) Any life assurance and disability benefits provided by the employer may cease.

(c) The final benefits are dependent on investment returns and are not related to final salary (this can also be an advantage).

(d) Economies of scale are not available as in a group pension scheme.

In addition, much will depend on

(a) the level of employer contributions to the pension scheme;

(b) whether the person concerned is likely to change jobs, and if so, the period remaining to retirement after the change;

(c) future salary increases and the impact of the earnings 'cap';

(d) future investment returns;

(e) the level of pension scheme benefits provided; and

(f) whether or not the employer will allow the employee to rejoin the company scheme in the future.

9:18   Section 226 retirement annuities

Prior to 1 July 1988, pension arrangements for the self-employed and those in non-pensionable employment were covered by section 226 of the Income and Corporation Taxes Act 1970 (which was consolidated as section 620 of the Income and Corporation Taxes Act 1988). Contracts in force before that date remain governed by this legislation and most allow for contributions to continue even where only single contribution contracts have been arranged.

Most of the personal pension details in this chapter apply equally to section 226 contracts, with the following exceptions

(a) The Finance Act 1989 earnings limit does not apply to section 226 contracts but the contribution limits have not been increased. The limits applying to section 226 contracts are as follows

Age at beginning of year of assessment	Maximum contributions (% of earnings)
Up to and including 50	17.5
51–55	20.0
56–60	22.5
61 or more	27.5

The limits for personal pension contributions will apply in place of these limits in any tax year in which the investor pays a contribution to a personal pension arrangement, including personal pension term assurance.

(b) The definition of relevant earnings for retirement annuities is different to that for personal pensions. A full definition can be found in section 623 of the Income and Corporation Taxes Act 1988. The main difference relates to the treatment of

(i)   share option proceeds;

(ii) golden handshakes and payments on removal from office; and

(iii) emoluments of controlling directors.

(c) The retirement pension cannot normally commence before age 60. As an alternative to a full pension, a tax-free lump sum on retirement may be taken together with a reduced pension. The maximum lump sum allowed is three times the amount of the remaining pension (it is permissible for the calculation to be on the basis that the pension is payable yearly in arrears with no guaranteed period, thus increasing the lump sum available). This formula normally produces a lump sum of between 25% and 40% of the fund. The precise figure is dependent on the level of interest rates and the age of the person at the time the benefits are taken.

(d) For each contract started on or after 17 March 1987, the maximum lump sum allowed is £150,000.

(e) A transfer payment can be received only from another section 226 contract.

(f) Complex calculations of the maximum contributions payable can arise where a person has section 226 contracts and personal pensions, especially where net relevant earnings are in excess of the earnings 'cap'. Generally, it is advantageous to ensure that contributions to only one type of contract (and not both) are paid in each tax year. Computations of available reliefs, where the carry forward of unused relief is combined with the payment of both personal pension and retirement annuity contributions, are also complex. Reference should be made to the Inland Revenue booklet IR76.

(g) A section 226 arrangement cannot be used to contract out of SERPS.

(h) The funds in a section 226 arrangement can be transferred to a personal pension plan. This is particularly useful if the investor wishes to draw his benefits between the ages of 50 and 60 or to defer the purchase of an annuity by using the income drawdown provisions.

(i) The ending of carry forward provisions for unused relief from 5 April 2001 does not apply to retirement annuity contracts.

10 Life assurance policies as investments

The principal purpose of this chapter is to discuss the two main types of regular premium investment policies which can be particularly useful in personal financial planning. These are with-profits endowment contracts and maximum investment plans. Also discussed are friendly society plans, some of the more usual methods of funding a life policy from capital and investment in second-hand endowment policies.

10:1   With-profits endowment policies

Under this type of policy, an insurance company promises to pay a fixed amount (the basic sum assured) on the maturity of the policy or on the death of the life assured, if earlier. To this reversionary bonuses are added, normally on an annual basis, with terminal bonuses also being paid by most insurance companies. A with-profits endowment policy is therefore likely to offer an individual a low-risk investment medium with capital appreciation and guarantees. However, the choice of the right life assurance company will be of the utmost importance in determining the benefits ultimately received. For example, for policies maturing on 1 February 2000, contracts with the best results over ten years and 25 years paid out 25% and 48% more respectively than the contracts with the worst results.

Before consideration can be given to the selection of a particular contract, certain basic information, such as the person's age and state of health and the date when the policy is required to mature, will be needed. It will then be possible to consider the particular company with which the contract should be taken out with careful attention being paid to

(a) past performance;

(b) surrender values;

(c) underwriting;

(d) other considerations.

10:1.1   Past performance

The following matters should be borne in mind when considering past performance

(a) It is normally worthwhile to select a life company which has produced consistently good returns over a reasonable period. However, it should be remembered that good past performance is no guarantee of good future results.

(b) The trend of past performance is very important, but it should be remembered that, with a long-term policy, the results could be largely based on earlier conditions which no longer apply. This could be due to changes in investment managers, investment policy or charging structure.

(c) The mutual offices have tended (with exceptions) to produce better results than the proprietary companies, as all profits of a mutual office are retained for the benefit of policyholders, whereas, in the case of proprietary companies, up to 10% of distributable profits are allocated to shareholders. However, if additional capital is required for future development, proprietary companies are likely to have greater flexibility.

(d) Large companies with greater financial strength have usually produced results superior to those of small companies.

(e) Terminal bonuses are much more volatile than reversionary bonuses, which are largely based on a company's investment income and, once declared, cannot be taken away. Terminal bonuses mainly reflect a company's investment surplus at the time policy benefits are paid. However, sometimes a proportion of terminal bonus is also paid when a policy is surrendered. Despite this, it should be remembered that bonuses reflect investment returns, with no absolute distinction between income and capital appreciation.

Some companies have regularly paid large terminal bonuses, while others have not paid any, or only small ones, or bonuses which have shown major fluctuations in accordance with market conditions at the time the policies have matured.

Recent industry trends have been, in general, to increase the proportion of total benefits paid via terminal bonuses and to weight reversionary bonuses towards longer dated policies. The combined effect of these trends has been to reduce yields on ten-year policies and increase them on longer-term policies.

(f) A company may have declared a special reversionary bonus out of successful investment operations which are not expected to recur. Such a bonus, unlike the terminal bonus, cannot be withdrawn once it has been declared and added to the policy. A special reversionary bonus is less of a burden to a life company than a reversionary bonus since there is no commitment to make the same ongoing payouts. Special bonuses have also been paid in recent years when a mutual company has been acquired by another company.

(g) The average results of ten-year with-profits endowment policies maturing on 1 February 2000 compare very favourably with the underlying rate of inflation over the same period and with other types of investment offering the same degree of security. In addition, life assurance cover is provided by the policy.

10:1.2 Surrender values

Although a life assurance policy would not normally be taken out as a short-term savings contract, unforeseen circumstances can occur which require the policy to be surrendered before its maturity date. It is for this reason that surrender values are important and, in order to provide some guide to the treatment by life companies of policies surrendered prematurely, the actual surrender values offered over different periods should be considered.

It should also be borne in mind that on surrendering a policy a charge to higher-rate tax could arise (the tax would be calculated in a similar way to the charge on investment bonds – see **Chapter 3**).

Due to the relatively low values normally offered on surrender, especially in the early years, a policy should be maintained to maturity if possible. This applies particularly to policies effected before 14 March 1984, whose premiums enjoyed a measure of income tax relief. Accordingly, where it is necessary to raise capital, a loan against the policy may be appropriate. Most companies will lend up to 90% of the surrender value, with interest rates normally in line with market rates.

Another possible alternative to surrendering a policy is to make it paid-up: no further contributions are payable and the benefits on maturity or death are reduced accordingly. However, if this course of action is taken, a charge to higher-rate tax may arise when the benefits are subsequently received.

Where a decision has been taken that a policy should be surrendered, it is useful to bear in mind that there are several organisations which specialise in arranging the sale of second-hand life policies. In these cases, the price fetched will often exceed the surrender value offered by the life company, with the taxation position being the same as if the policy was actually surrendered. This market is discussed in more detail at **10:5** below.

10:1.3 Underwriting

The degree or level of underwriting required by life assurance companies varies considerably. This can have an important bearing on the selection of a particular contract, as, generally, the more demanding companies have tended to produce the better results due to their more favourable mortality experience.

Therefore, before a particular policy is selected, details of the person's occupation, recreational pursuits and state of health, including smoking habits, should first be obtained and the information considered before proceeding further. If there are health problems, a medical examination can often be arranged for the use of more than one company.

In recent years, the medical information requested by life companies has generally been considerably reduced other than for larger proposals, mainly due to the expense and time involved. The main exception is in respect of individuals whose health or lifestyle might increase the chances of them being victims or carriers of AIDS. In these cases, blood tests or full medical examinations are usually required. An example of this is that many companies allow an endowment policy to be arranged within defined limits for the purpose of repaying a mortgage and seek only the minimum medical evidence.

10:1.4 Other considerations

In choosing a particular company, the following points are also important

(a) The financial strength of the life company. It should be remembered that bonuses will be paid from the surplus of a life company and this will largely depend on the investment performance, together with the level of the company's expenses. The stronger the company, the more flexibility it has to invest in equities and, therefore, the better its long-term returns are likely to be.

(b) The service provided by the life company.

(c) It is unlikely that policies taken out now will enjoy the returns produced by policies invested during the 1980s and 1990s. Policyholders therefore need to have realistic expectations of the sum that the endowment will ultimately produce.

10:1.5 Low cost endowment policies

Low cost endowment policies are a variation of the with-profits endowment policy and are usually a combination of a normal with-profits endowment and a decreasing term assurance (see **Chapter 11**). These policies are thus designed as endowment assurances which contain a guaranteed minimum death benefit at a level higher than that used for bonus purposes. They are often used as the repayment medium for mortgages, where the guaranteed minimum death benefit is equal to the amount of the mortgage outstanding.

10:2   Maximum investment plans

Maximum investment plans are unit-linked qualifying life assurance policies and thus incorporate the usual tax advantages. Therefore, income accruing within the life fund is taxed at a maximum rate of 20% and the policy proceeds are normally completely free of any personal liability to income tax and capital gains tax, provided that premiums have been paid for a minimum period of ten years (or three quarters of the term, if less, in the case of an endowment-type policy).

The main characteristic of these plans is that they are essentially investment vehicles which have the minimum amount of life cover necessary to retain qualifying life policy status. Part of each premium pays for the life assurance cover and the balance is invested in units in an investment fund. There is normally a higher allocation to units for larger premiums.

Although policy charges are important, it is the investment performance of the underlying fund that will normally determine whether a particular policy will prove to be good value.

10:2.1   Options available

To enable him to maximise investment performance, the policyholder is normally given the option to switch both the existing fund and/or future premiums between the different funds available. In order to provide maximum flexibility, virtually all life companies writing maximum investment plans permit a plan to be divided into a number of identical cluster policies.

At the end of ten years (or the agreed period, if longer), the following options are generally available to policyholders

(a) to take the accumulated fund as a tax-free lump sum;

(b) to stop paying premiums but leave the capital to accumulate within the policy;

(c) to continue paying the premiums in full for a further ten years (a higher investment allocation than that provided at the outset of the policy is generally given);

(d) to continue paying a nominal premium to maintain the policy and encash segments to provide a tax-free income.

The option to take a tax-free income after ten years can be particularly advantageous and is especially suitable in the following cases

(a) to increase the net spendable income of a higher rate taxpayer;

(b) to supplement a pension;

(c) to provide for school fees.

In the two latter cases, it is normally expedient that the policy should be linked to a stable fund rather than a volatile one.

By taking a tax-free income instead of a tax-free lump sum which is then reinvested, a higher rate taxpayer avoids the tax that would have been payable on the investment income, although the income arising within the life fund would still be taxed at life assurance company rates (20%). In the case of a husband and wife, a policy written on a joint life, last survivor basis should be considered. This has two advantages over a policy written on a single life basis

● the policy would continue until the second death – as a result, the tax-free income facility could continue after the first death;

● a higher investment allocation would usually be obtained, as the death benefit payable by the life company would normally be postponed.

It should be noted that, for many individuals who wish to invest on a regular basis in equities, a PEP savings plan directly into a unit or investment trust is likely to produce superior results to a unit-linked life policy. This is due to there being no tax payable either on capital gains or on dividend income.

10:3 Friendly society plans

Due to their advantageous tax treatment, these plans should generally produce satisfactory results, although the maximum premiums which can be paid are very low. Their main characteristics are as follows

(a) They are written as ten-year savings plans (sometimes for longer).

(b) Policyholders must be between the ages of 18 and 74 (although plans can be written for the benefit of children of any age).

(c) Investment income and capital gains accumulate within the friendly society investment fund free of all UK tax (this can be particularly advantageous where the main purpose of the fund is to produce a high income).

(d) The maximum annual premiums payable are £270 (£300 if premiums are payable more frequently than annually). However, some societies permit a lump sum to be paid at outset to cover the first premium and to purchase an annuity to fund all the premiums after the first. It is also possible to combine a friendly society plan with a conventional policy, which may provide a saving in expenses compared with two completely separate policies.

(e) The charges made on friendly society plans are frequently high in relation to the premiums paid.

(f) Although it is no longer necessary that a minimum of 50% of the underlying investments of the fund should be in narrower-range investments, some friendly societies have not changed their practice. This restriction can inhibit investment performance.

(g) At the end of ten years, the policyholder is usually provided with certain options (similar to those under maximum investment plans), but this will depend on the particular plan.

(h) If the plan is surrendered within seven and a half years when written as an endowment policy, or within ten years when written as a whole life policy, the penalties can be severe.

(i) Supervision of a friendly society rests with the Registrar of Friendly Societies and with the Personal Investment Authority if the society is engaged in long-term investment business. Although friendly societies are not covered by the Policyholders' Protection Act 1975, they are covered under the Friendly Societies Protection Scheme which provides policyholders with similar protection.

10:4   Funding a life policy from capital

In addition to paying premiums from income, a life policy can be funded from the investment of a capital sum by one or more of the following methods (these packages are generally known as capital conversion plans or, colloquially, 'back-to-back' schemes)

(a) Temporary annuities. These have the main advantages of guaranteeing returns and of simplicity and convenience. The disadvantages are that capital is locked in, the investment return is often not competitive and the annuity ceases on early death.

(b) A series of guaranteed growth bonds. Again, these have the advantages of having returns guaranteed and of convenience, but the disadvantage of an uncompetitive investment return in the early years.

(c) Investment bonds. The principal advantage of this method is that the return could be very competitive, as the underlying investments are not restricted to fixed-interest investments. In addition, some insurance packages are administratively easy to operate. The main disadvantage is the risk of the need to provide funds from other resources to pay the premiums if the value of the investment bond fails to show sufficient growth.

A further method would be to realise capital from existing investments on a regular basis to meet the premiums as they fall due.

The actual method selected would depend upon all circumstances of the case, including the return on the various investments at the particular time and the financial and tax position and age of the person concerned.

Capital conversion plans can also be used to generate an income for ten years with a subsequent return of capital at the end of that period. In this case, only part of the total amount arising each year from the capital sum is used to fund the life assurance premiums, with the balance being available as spendable income.

10:5   Second-hand endowment policies

Reference was made at **10:1.2** above to the facility which now exists for a with-profits endowment policyholder to sell his policy instead of surrendering it. There are two options

● to sell the policy at auction; or

● to sell the policy to a market-maker.

The proceeds of a sale at auction will depend upon the demand for the policy from those attending it. The seller can set a reserve price, but cannot be sure that it will be reached. A market-maker will offer a firm price, which the seller may accept or refuse.

The success of the second-hand (or traded) endowment policy market is the result of the appreciation by investors of the advantages of such policies. These are

(a) the fact that the heaviest expenses are borne by the policy during the first five years of its life; by buying the policy second-hand they avoid these expenses;

(b) much of the appreciation in the value of a policy arises at its maturity in the form of the terminal bonus;

(c) the risk of loss is limited to the difference between the purchase price and the surrender value, since the latter is the price which the insurance company would pay for the policy;

(d) endowment policies are low risk investments whose returns have historically been well in excess of the rate of inflation.

When a policyholder sells his policy it is assigned to the purchaser, who becomes responsible for paying the premiums. The original owner remains the life assured, however, and if he were to die before the maturity date of the policy, the life assurance company will, on presentation of his death certificate, pay the claim value to the purchaser. For this reason, market-makers arrange for referees to be appointed to whom the purchaser can refer, to ascertain whether or not the original policyholder is still alive.

Policies are priced by reference to a discount rate applied to the estimated maturity value of the policy. This value is calculated on the assumption that annual and terminal bonuses will continue at their present level – which, in view of the lower investment returns experienced in recent years and expected in the future, may not be the case. The market-makers will provide potential investors with a sensitivity chart showing the different returns which will be achieved on the basis of different assumptions about the level of bonuses.

Generally there is a 'turn' of about 6% (similar to the bid/offer spread of unit trust prices) between the price which a market-maker pays a seller and the price at which he sells to a new investor.

An alternative to direct investment in second-hand policies is the purchase of shares in one of the OEICs or investment trusts owning a portfolio of such policies.

The taxation position of the purchaser of a second-hand policy is as follows

● if the policy is a qualifying policy, he will be subject to capital gains tax on the maturity proceeds. He will be entitled to the indexation allowance on both the purchase price and on the premiums he has paid up to 6 April 1998 and to taper relief thereafter;

- if the policy is non-qualifying, he will be subject to income tax at the higher rate (if he is a higher rate taxpayer in the year the proceeds are paid). The calculation is similar to that for investment bonds in **Chapter 3**.

Not all endowment policies are 'tradeable' in this way. The market-makers do not accept all insurance companies' policies and require the policy to have been in force for at least five (in some cases seven) years and to have a minimum surrender value of £2,000. In addition to with-profits endowment policies, many market-makers will also deal in with-profits whole of life policies and guaranteed income bonds. One specialist area is 'viatical settlements' – the sale of life policies by those diagnosed as having a terminal illness. While it benefits them by providing funds to enable them to enjoy their last months, this practice requires great care and sensitivity.

11 Protection through life assurance

In the previous chapter, life assurance policies were considered as investments. However, their original purpose was to provide protection and it is this application that is now discussed. For most individuals, subject to their state of health, appropriate protection policies should be arranged in order to provide the required level of cover before investment is considered. These policies can normally be effected cheaply, with UK insurance companies offering amongst the most competitive rates in the world.

Although it is not always possible to distinguish completely between protection and investment policies (this can be seen later in this chapter when flexible unit-linked whole life policies are discussed), better results can often be achieved if the protection and investment needs are dealt with separately.

The amount of life cover required will vary depending on the individual circumstances. For example, a man approaching retirement would normally need less cover to protect his family than a younger person with dependent children, although it is more likely that he will wish to effect a policy for inheritance tax purposes. In any event, before a particular type of policy can be selected, the following matters should be considered

(a) the purpose of the policy and the exact needs of the individual's dependants;

(b) the ages of the individual and their dependants;

(c) the health of the individual, including their smoking habits;

(d) the resources to pay for the cover;

(e) the existing level of cover, if any, and to whom it is payable;

(f) the existing estate after inheritance tax which would be available to the dependants in the event of the life assured's death.

The two main broad categories of protection policies are term assurance and whole life. These policies can usually be effected in the following ways

(a) on a single life basis;

(b) on a joint life basis, payable on the first death;

(c) on a joint life, last survivor basis, payable on the second death.

Where a policy is arranged in order to provide protection for the family of the life assured, it is normally beneficial for it to be written in trust for the spouse or children or, alternatively, on a life of another basis. The particular method will depend on the precise circumstances.

11:1　Term assurance policies

Although there are several classes of term assurance, they all have the same principal purpose of providing a tax-free lump sum if death should occur within a preselected period. If the individual concerned survives until the end of that period, the policy automatically expires without value. There are no surrender values or paid-up values on term assurance policies. If premiums cease, the policy automatically lapses, with the insurance company having no further liability.

For each of the types of term assurance mentioned below, there is no personal liability to income tax or capital gains tax on the benefit payable from the policy. However, unless the policy is written under a suitably worded trust (see **Chapter 16**), the proceeds could form part of the deceased's estate for inheritance tax purposes. Therefore, it is advisable, in most cases, to write this type of policy under trust, in order to avoid the proceeds enhancing the deceased's estate, with the resulting adverse inheritance tax consequences. This also has the advantage that the proceeds can be paid to the trustees on production of the death certificate; they do not have to wait until probate has been granted to his executors.

The following are the most common types of term assurance policies (death-in-service benefits under company pension arrangements and personal pensions have already been considered in **Chapters 8** and **9** respectively)

(a) level term;

(b) decreasing term;

(c) mortgage protection;

(d) convertible term;

(e) convertible, renewable term;

(f) family income benefit.

11:1.1　Level term

This is the most straightforward type of term assurance, enabling a tax-free lump sum to be provided in the event of the death of the life assured within the preselected period. Apart from making provision for the death of the bread-winner, one of its most usual practical applications is in connection with a bank or other loan arranged on an interest-only basis, where the life of the borrower would be insured for the full amount of the loan. If the lender requires assignment of the policy, it cannot be placed in trust.

11:1.2 Decreasing term

Under this assurance, the amount of the life cover reduces each year (or lesser period) by predetermined amounts throughout the duration of the policy. Like level term assurance, decreasing term assurance is often effected in conjunction with a loan, but one whose principal is being repaid by equal instalments. The life cover provided then decreases in line with the amount of the loan outstanding.

Decreasing term assurance is also used to insure potentially exempt transfers between individuals which exceed the nil rate band where an inheritance tax (IHT) liability crystallises on the death of the donor. The cover reduces in such a way as to match the reducing tax liability over a seven-year period, namely

Years	Cover as a % of initial IHT liability
up to 3	100
3–4	80
4–5	60
5–6	40
6–7	20

11:1.3 Mortgage protection

This is a form of decreasing term assurance, where the amount of life cover is designed to be sufficient to repay the outstanding mortgage at death. Since the cover reduces more slowly in the early years than under a decreasing term assurance, the cost of a mortgage protection policy is normally greater.

Mortgage protection policies usually match the outstanding capital when a loan is being repaid by regular instalments of capital and interest. Any deviation from the original terms of the loan may upset the relationship between the capital outstanding and the cover provided.

Before a mortgage protection policy is arranged, it is worthwhile investigating the options available and particularly the position should mortgage interest rates rise substantially. If this were to happen and the policy lacked flexibility, the individual could find themselves under-insured.

Where the mortgage repayments depend upon the joint incomes of a husband and wife, it is often advantageous for two single life policies to be effected rather than one policy written on a joint life, first death basis, especially if the couple have dependent children. This then provides two sets of benefit if both parents should die within the term, usually at little extra cost. In addition, in the event of divorce or separation, matters are considerably simplified.

11:1.4   Convertible term

This type of policy is similar to level term assurance except that the policyholder has the option to convert to another type of life policy throughout the term, subject to conversion taking place before a maximum age of normally 60 or 65, regardless of the assured's state of health at the time the option is exercised. The premium rate applicable to the new policy is based on the individual's age at the time of conversion.

Before a person decides on a specific policy, it is important to consider whether they are likely to exercise the conversion option and, if so, into what type of policy. Policyholders will normally be allowed to convert into whole life or endowment contracts, while other options often include unit-linked or level term policies. Consequently, the competitiveness of the policy after conversion can be of greater significance than the initial cost of the term assurance itself. Convertible term assurance can be a particularly useful contract for a younger person who requires immediate life cover but cannot afford the cost of a more permanent policy at the time the convertible term assurance is effected. By subsequently being allowed to switch into, say, a whole life or endowment contract, irrespective of their state of health at that time, a very valuable option is offered at a relatively low cost.

11:1.5   Convertible, renewable term

These are usually short-term policies, typically of five years' duration, offering maximum flexibility but with minimum commitment. Two basic options are provided: to convert the policy into another contract and to renew the policy at the end of the original term.

The conversion option under this contract operates in a way similar to the option provided under a normal convertible term assurance policy. The conversion option can be taken up at any time during the term of the contract, with many insurance companies also allowing partial conversion. The renewal option allows the policyholder to renew the policy at the end of each term without further medical evidence normally until the age of 60 or 65. The premium will usually increase at renewal in line with the rates for their age at the time.

This policy therefore enables an individual to obtain guaranteed life cover in most cases until retirement age, at low cost. In addition, they are provided with the opportunity to convert the policy into a different contract more appropriate to their needs.

Due to the number of variations in the terms offered, it is important to compare like with like, as far as this is possible, when selecting a particular contract. The options which are likely to be exercised in the future should also be considered, bearing in mind that some contracts may offer very competitive rates at lower ages but uncompetitive rates at higher ages. Therefore, if the original intention is to renew the policy throughout, the cheapest contract at the outset may not necessarily be the most suitable.

11:1.6   Family income benefit

This policy is a form of term assurance where a tax-free income is provided from the date of death of the life assured to the expiry of the preselected term (an option is also often available to commute the future income payments into a cash lump sum). A family income benefit contract is therefore effectively a decreasing term assurance.

Although termed 'income', the payments are actually instalments of the sum assured under the policy, and therefore do not create any personal liability to income tax or capital gains tax. Policies which provide increasing payments to combat the effects of inflation are also available but these require higher premiums.

Although a family income policy may be effected on the joint lives of a husband and wife with the benefits payable on the first death, it is often preferable to take out two single life policies instead, especially where the couple have young children. If the husband should die before the children are financially independent, there could be considerable hardship for the rest of the family. Consequently, it is usually advisable that a policy should be effected at the time of the birth of a child for the period of likely dependence.

A husband and wife should also consider arranging a family income benefit policy on the life of the wife where she looks after the children or where he is dependent on her earnings. If the wife should die prematurely, the husband may need additional income, either to pay for home help and the supervision of the children while he is at work or to replace her lost earnings.

Due to the reducing nature of the life cover and to the death benefit only being paid in instalments (unless a cash lump sum is taken in commutation), this contract provides higher initial life cover for the same premium than other types of term assurance policy. Consequently, because of this and the important need it serves, a family income benefit policy is an essential requirement for many families.

The following example illustrates some of the more competitive rates for effecting the principal types of term assurance policies

Example 12

Two men aged 30 and 40 next birthday respectively, both in good health and non-smokers, arrange £100,000 initial life cover over a period of 20 years through the main types of term assurance policies. Premiums are to be paid annually

	Man aged 30 next birthday Annual premium	*Man aged 40 next birthday Annual premium*
	£	£
Level term	77	158
Decreasing term	120	190
Mortgage protection	66	112
Convertible term	135	280
Convertible renewable term	119	247
Family income benefit (see Note 1)	68	108

Notes

1. The family income benefit assurance provides a tax-free income of £5,000 per annum, payable monthly from the date of death to the end of the 20-year period.

11:2   Whole life policies

Unlike term assurance policies where the sum assured only becomes payable if death should occur within a predetermined period, the benefit from a whole life policy is payable whenever death occurs. In addition, a whole life policy acquires both a surrender value and a paid-up value, except generally in the first two years of the contract. Due to the certainty of eventual death, a whole life policy is usually considerably more expensive to arrange than a term assurance policy. The following are the more usual types of whole life policies

(a) whole life with-profits;

(b) low cost whole life;

(c) flexible unit-linked whole life.

Whole of life assurance also used to be written on a non-profit basis, i.e. with a fixed sum assured. This type of policy is no longer available.

11:2.1 Whole life with-profits

This type of policy provides a basic sum assured payable on death (similar to a non-profit policy). However, reversionary bonuses are also declared out of the surpluses on the company's life assurance fund and added to the sum assured, normally on an annual basis. In addition, terminal bonuses are paid by most insurance companies at the time of the death claim and sometimes on surrender.

11:2.2 Low cost whole life

This policy is usually a combination of a whole life with-profits policy and a decreasing term assurance policy. The principle behind a low cost whole life policy is that, for the period of the term assurance, the cover provided by the term assurance will decrease by the same amounts as the reversionary bonuses which are added to the whole life policy. In calculating the decreasing term assurance cover, reversionary bonus rates are generally taken to be at the same level throughout the duration of the policy. Terminal bonuses are disregarded for this purpose. Once the decreasing term assurance has expired, the amount of cover under the whole life policy will increase with the addition of further reversionary bonuses plus any terminal bonus. A low cost whole life policy can also be designed as a whole life with-profits policy containing a guaranteed death benefit at a level higher than that used for bonus purposes.

The main advantage of a low cost policy compared to a full with-profits policy is that it is much cheaper to effect, due to part of the initial cover being provided by term assurance. However, against this, the longer the life assured survives, the greater will be the difference between the amount of the death benefits of the two policies.

11:2.3 Flexible unit-linked whole life

This is a more modern type of whole life policy (often known as a flexible or universal life policy), which combines a mix of insurance and investment and is designed to cover an individual's life assurance needs throughout his or her life.

A wide degree of flexibility is offered as to the extent to which the emphasis can be varied between protection and investment during the term of the policy. There are normally at least three options – minimum, standard and maximum cover – for the specified level of premium. Minimum cover allows a high proportion of the premium to be invested, as only a small sum is required for the life cover. Most of a maximum cover premium will be spent on providing the life assurance, with only a small amount invested. Standard cover is the level of life assurance the company calculates it will be able to provide if the invested portion of the premiums grows at a reasonable rate; if this growth is achieved, it should not be necessary to increase the premiums. Maximum cover premiums, however, are reviewed after the first ten years and are then likely to be considerably increased, if the level of cover is to be maintained, in view of the policyholder's greater age; no further medical evidence is required.

A flexible unit-linked whole life policy works as follows

(a) Premiums are paid to the insurance company from which charges are deducted for the setting up and administration costs. The balance of each premium is then invested in units in one or more of the insurance company's unit-linked funds with the normal switching facility usually being available. This type of policy can also be effected on a single premium basis.

(b) Units are encashed each month to pay for the life cover, with the actual number depending on the value of the units allocated to the policy at the time, the amount of cover chosen and the age and sex of the policyholder. The units remaining provide the investment element of the policy; 'protection' cover is required for the difference between their value and the agreed sum assured.

(c) The insurance company sets the maximum amount of cover that can be chosen by assuming a growth rate for the value of the units, usually around 7.5% per annum. Some insurance companies base this maximum on the level of cover that could be maintained throughout the policyholder's life. Other companies call this maintainable level of cover 'standard cover', and offer a considerably higher maximum on the basis that it is maintained only for the first ten years of the policy, after which time the cover or premium may need to be adjusted.

(d) The premiums and life cover are reviewed at the end of the first ten years and at regular intervals thereafter (generally every five years, but usually more often for elderly policyholders). Between reviews, the insurance company agrees not to seek to change the amount of the premiums or life cover. However, the policyholder is still normally provided with the option to increase their cover each year without waiting for the next review date, although, in some cases, evidence of health may be required.

At each review, the insurance company looks at both the value of the remaining units and the current premium level in order to decide whether they are sufficient to maintain the chosen level of cover until the next review. If they are not sufficient, either the premiums have to be increased or the level of cover reduced.

If the value of the units has increased at a rate higher than that assumed, many insurance companies allow this to be used in order to obtain a greater level of cover, although medical evidence is generally required. However, only a small minority of companies permit a reduction in the amount of the premiums.

(e) On the death of the life assured, the policy will pay out the greater of the chosen amount of life cover and the value of the units.

(f) If the payment of premiums continues for a minimum period of ten years, similar options to those applicable with maximum investment plans will be available (these options have already been considered in **Chapter 10**). Alternatively, life cover can continue to be provided, subject to the value of the units being sufficient to meet the costs involved.

(g) Where premiums are paid for less than ten years, any value attaching to the policy can be used to take a lump sum, although a charge to higher rate tax may arise. As further options, the units can be left to accumulate or be utilised to pay for continued life cover, assuming they have sufficient value.

The main advantages of flexible unit-linked whole life policies are therefore as follows

(a) The convenience of having only one policy to serve both the protection and investment needs of an individual, together with the flexibility to make changes without excessive administration.

(b) Competitive premium rates. By regularly reviewing the progress of a policy and having the facility to make adjustments when considered appropriate, an insurance company need not use the same conservative actuarial basis as when a guaranteed sum assured is provided for a fixed premium over a very long period. As a result, it is possible for a less cautious approach to be adopted, with the consequent beneficial effect on premiums.

(c) A choice of funds and switching facilities are generally provided. If mortality trends improve, this can be taken into account when making reviews. Conversely, if the trends are worse than anticipated, this is likely to be a disadvantage.

Despite the above advantages, improved investment results may often be obtained if separate insurance policies are effected to provide the required life cover, with the balance of the funds available being used exclusively for investment in, for example, shares, ISAs, OEICs, unit or investment trusts.

Where an individual does decide to effect a flexible unit-linked whole life policy, its exact purpose should clearly be borne in mind before a specific contract is chosen, due to the varying terms and different options available. In addition, if the main purpose of the policy is to provide life cover, the investment link should be a relatively stable fund, such as a managed fund, rather than a volatile fund.

The following example illustrates some of the more competitive rates for effecting the principal types of whole life policies

Example 13

Two men aged 30 and 40 next birthday respectively, both in good health and non-smokers, arrange £100,000 initial life cover through the main types of whole life policies. Premiums are to be paid annually throughout life

	Man aged 30 next birthday Annual premium	*Man aged 40 next birthday Annual premium*
	£	£
Whole life with-profits	2,227	3,069
Low cost whole life (see Note 1)	691	1,123
Flexible unit-linked whole life (see Note 2)	688	1,227

Notes

1. Premiums payable in respect of the low cost whole life policy will reduce as follows

   • for the man aged 30 next birthday – to £443 after 48 years;

   • for the man aged 40 next birthday – to £731 after 41 years.

   These reductions are due to the expiry of the term assurance element of the policy.

2. Premiums for the flexible unit-linked whole life policy have been set to remain unaltered throughout life on the assumption that the price of the underlying units grows by 6% per annum.

11:3 Back-to-back arrangements

A further use of whole life policies has been in connection with back-to-back arrangements which combine purchased life annuities with regular premium whole life policies written under trust for named beneficiaries. The arrangements were mainly designed for elderly higher rate taxpayers in reasonable health, with their main purposes being to increase the net spendable income of the policyholder and the net estate available to the beneficiaries.

To ensure that the arrangements are not challenged by the Inland Revenue as 'associated operations', it is necessary that

● the life policy is issued after full medical underwriting of the life assured, following the normal requirements and limits set by the particular insurance company; and

● the terms on which the life policy is issued should have no regard to the purchase of the annuity. (It is therefore usually advisable to arrange for the two contracts to be effected with different life assurance companies.)

Generally, for the payment of annual premiums not to be subject to inheritance tax as gifts to the trustees of the life policy, they must fall within one of the specified exemptions. In order to qualify as 'normal expenditure out of income', the following conditions must be satisfied

(a) the payments must be part of normal expenditure, namely they must be habitual; in the case of a life assurance policy, it is accepted that this is covered by the nature of the contract to pay regular premiums;

(b) the payments must be made out of taxed income; the capital element of an annuity does not count as income for this purpose;

(c) after allowing for all payments forming part of normal expenditure, there must be sufficient income to maintain the usual standard of living.

If the normal expenditure exemption is not appropriate, the other annual exemptions could be utilised (see **Chapter 12**).

Due to the very low level of annuity rates at the current time, it is difficult to generate additional net spendable income by this method. However, should annuity rates improve in the future, this may again prove to be a viable option.

11:4   Other insurance contracts

Although not strictly life assurance policies, other insurance contracts can be arranged for protection purposes. The most usual of these contracts are as follows

(a) permanent health insurance;

(b) personal accident and sickness insurance;

(c) hospital insurance;

(d) private medical insurance;

(e) critical illness insurance;

(f) long-term care insurance.

11:4.1   Permanent health insurance

The purpose of permanent health insurance is to provide an income for an individual during prolonged disability following sickness or accident. Although far fewer permanent health insurance policies are arranged in comparison to many types of life assurance policies, they nevertheless serve a very important need. According to available statistics, a breakdown in health lasting more than six months before age 65 is ten times more likely than death before that age.

The following are some of the more important characteristics of individual permanent health insurance policies

(a) The contract cannot be cancelled by the insurance company after it has been effected (hence the word 'permanent') nor can the company refuse to renew the contract if the health of the policyholder should deteriorate.

(b) There are different definitions of disability. Some insurance companies are very harsh in their interpretation, while others take a more lenient approach. It is therefore very important to investigate a company's attitude to claims before effecting one of its policies.

(c) Some occupations are not normally acceptable to insurance companies, while others may attract special terms or restrictions.

(d) Benefits are not usually payable immediately from the time of disablement but after a deferred period (normally after a minimum of four weeks and a maximum of 52 weeks). The longer the deferment period, the lower the premiums will be. Policies are usually written to age 60 or 65. Benefits generally cease at the age selected even if disability continues.

(e) The maximum amount of benefit which can be received may be restricted, for example to 50%–60% of earnings less State Incapacity Benefit. Stricter limits are generally applied where the individual has a high level of earnings.

(f) The level of insured benefits may be arranged at outset to remain constant or increase on an annual basis by a fixed percentage or in line with the RPI. Where benefits increase, usually the premiums will also rise each year. Benefits following a claim can likewise be arranged to increase annually, usually by a fixed percentage of 5% or RPI.

(g) Benefits are not taxable.

11:4.2 Personal accident and sickness insurance

The purpose of this contract is to enable a person to insure against accident or sickness, the benefits being in the form of either a lump sum or an income. The lump sum could become payable on death, loss of sight or a limb or on permanent total disability.

The following are some of the more relevant features of personal accident and sickness insurance policies

(a) The contract is of an annual nature and subject to state of health each year. It can therefore be cancelled or special provisions made at the option of the insurance company at each renewal date.

(b) The amount of the premiums depends mainly on the level of benefits to be insured and the occupation and sex of the person concerned.

(c) In the case of sickness insurance, benefits are normally payable after one week. However, there is usually an option for the benefits to be deferred for a longer period, with a consequent reduction in premiums.

(d) The amount of benefit is usually restricted to a percentage of earnings, usually 50–60% thereof.

(e) Benefits are normally paid for a maximum of up to two years if the person is unable to work as a result of an accident or illness.

(f) Lump sum benefits are generally not taxable. The income benefits are not taxable.

Mainly due to the ability of the insurance company to cancel the policy each year, this type of contract is not generally of prime importance for many individuals. It is mainly encountered as part of a holiday insurance policy.

11:4.3 Hospital insurance

The purpose of hospital insurance is to provide the policyholder with funds to mitigate the loss of his earnings while he is in hospital and also to cover incidental expenses, such as the cost of relatives' travel to and from the hospital. In addition, the plans usually provide further benefits, such as a lump sum for a loss of a limb or eyesight.

Some of the more important aspects of hospital insurance plans are as follows

(a) The premiums on these policies are written on a renewable annual basis. Depending on the premiums, which are normally limited, the policyholder obtains a predetermined sum for each day or night that he stays in hospital.

(b) No medical evidence is required before a plan is effected. However, there may be problems when a claim is made as a result of the exclusion clauses in the policy.

(c) The policy conditions require careful consideration due to their varying terms; for example, most companies will not pay out the benefits during the first two years of the policy if the claim relates to a recurrence of an illness which the policyholder had before the policy was effected.

(d) Neither the lump sum nor income benefits are taxable.

Unless an individual thinks that he is likely to suffer ill-health, these policies are not normally a priority. The premiums paid could usually be better applied elsewhere to provide the additional funds which might be required to meet the costs of a stay in hospital.

11:4.4 Private medical insurance

The purpose of being a subscriber to a private health insurance scheme is to enable medical treatment to be arranged privately, rather than through the National Health Service, for an individual and their family. This will usually provide the following advantages

(a) there are effectively no waiting lists;

(b) the patient can choose the time for their treatment;

(c) the patient can select a hospital for their own convenience and often choose a particular surgeon;

(d) miscellaneous benefits are provided, such as a private room with better amenities and more flexible visiting hours;

(e) some health insurance schemes provide a daily cash benefit to pay for incidental expenses while in hospital, such as telephone calls.

Despite the benefits of being a subscriber to a private health insurance scheme, a material proportion of those who use private medicine in the UK still finance the costs out of their own funds without medical insurance. The view taken by many of these people is that it is less expensive to meet the costs of private medicine directly, as and when necessary, than it is to pay the subscription to an insurance scheme each year. They prefer to invest an amount equal to the cost of the premiums into other savings media. Whether this proves to be the right decision will depend on the extent of the private medical treatment required by the individual and his family.

In recent years, due to the mutual benefits provided, it has become increasingly common for private medical insurance to be arranged by a business for its staff and their families (it should be noted that this is regarded as a 'benefit in kind' and therefore a personal tax liability will almost always be incurred by the employees on the notional premium paid by the employer for their membership). The dramatically cheaper rates available for group schemes normally make this a much more attractive route than taking out cover personally.

11:4.5   Critical illness insurance

The purpose of this insurance is to provide a lump sum payment in the event of the insured person suffering a critical illness. The range of illnesses covered includes heart attack, cancer, stroke, conditions necessitating coronary by-pass surgery or major organ transplant, kidney failure, multiple sclerosis, paralysis, paraplegia, loss of sight or limbs, brain tumours, serious burns and motor neurone disease.

The critical illness cover can either be provided as an addition to a life assurance or permanent health insurance policy or as a stand-alone policy. The principal problem with this cover has been finding an industry-wide definition of critical illnesses. A broad consensus has now been found and the majority of companies now accept six standard definitions for the core critical illnesses, namely

(a) heart attack;

(b) cancer;

(c) stroke;

(d) coronary artery by-pass surgery;

(e) kidney failure; and

(f) major organ transplant.

There are no income or capital gains tax implications for critical illness policy claims. Payments made from life policies are not taxable as they fall outside the chargeable events legislation. The Inland Revenue has also confirmed that payments are not subject to capital gains tax.

The principal tax problems relating to critical illness cover are in connection with inheritance tax. A claimant's estate may be increased just before his death and it makes sense to try to mitigate the inheritance tax consequences. This is normally achieved by the use of trusts, but, to be effective, any trust requires the policyholder to be excluded from being a potential beneficiary. Where critical illness cover is provided as an addition to a life assurance policy, it may be difficult to draft appropriate trust wording for the separate benefits. An easier solution is to arrange critical illness and life assurance in separate policies.

11:4.6 Long-term care insurance

There is a growing need for contracts that assist in meeting the cost of professional care in later life. The statistics are persuasive. By 2020, the number of people over the age of 85 will have increased by 50%, whilst over the next 40 years, the number is expected to double. It is likely that the State will not be able to meet the full cost of care and individuals will be required to be responsible for a far greater level of private provision than they are currently.

There are two types of long-term care contracts. The first type are insurance policies. These insure the costs of long-term care for either a single lump sum or regular monthly premiums.

The second type of contract is arranged at the time care is needed. A lump sum purchases an annuity which provides the care costs. Because the individual is, by definition, in poor health, the rates are much better than for a healthy person.

Claims are paid when a level of incapacity, requiring long-term care, is reached. Most insurance companies measure this on the basis of the policyholder's ability to complete 'activities of daily living (ADLs)'. Typically, these are washing, dressing, feeding, toileting, mobility and transferring (from a wheelchair to a bed). A claim will normally be paid when two or three of these ADLs cannot be completed without assistance. Most policies will also pay out on cognitive impairment, such as senility or Alzheimer's disease.

All claims paid on long-term care policies are free from tax.

A variant on the two approaches outlined above involves an investment bond. Units are purchased in a gross investment bond fund and monthly premium deductions are made from the value of the bond. This approach enables the lump sum invested to continue providing an investment return. The investment fund is not subject to UK tax as it is based offshore.

When the policyholder makes a claim, premium deductions cease and care payments (made directly to the nursing home) begin. The policyholder must decide at the outset the extent to which the value of the bond is used to finance the payments. To the extent that there is value in the bond at death, it passes to the heirs.

The caveat of mixing insurance and investment obviously applies in this case. It is particularly important to quantify whether the investment vehicle is appropriate and whether growth will be sufficient to fund increasing care insurance premiums or whether capital erosion is likely.

11:5   Underwriting

Underwriting in connection with investment policies has already been discussed in **Chapter 10**. As far as protection policies are concerned, underwriting will generally be of greater relevance due to the extra risks involved, arising from the higher level and longer periods of life cover normally required. Consequently, life assurance companies are likely to take a more detailed approach to obtaining medical information.

A particular example of this concerns smoking. Many insurance companies now provide two different levels of premium rates for their protection policies, one for smokers and one for non-smokers (the definition of this can vary widely). The discount offered to non-smokers can be as much as one third off the rates for smokers.

Consideration of the risks of contracting AIDS and associated medical problems has had a much greater effect on protection policies than on investment contracts. Many insurance companies have ceased to write convertible or increasable contracts, or have made such options subject to fresh enquiry into the AIDS risk at the time of the options being exercised. Generally, premiums have increased substantially, particularly for the younger age groups.

New policies for permanent health insurance, personal accident and sickness, hospital insurance and private medical insurance generally exclude the AIDS risk (the possible exception to this is for group permanent health schemes, where greatly increased premium rates would usually be applied).

Where a medical examination is conducted as part of the underwriting process, the life assured has the right to see any medical report sent to the life company under the Access to Medical Reports Act 1988. If there are errors, the life assured has the right to request rectification.

11:6   Taxation position

Life assurance premium relief was abolished for all life policies effected after 13 March 1984. The position for policies arranged on or before 13 March 1984 which provide for the benefits to be increased or the term extended after that date, is as follows

(a) Where a policyholder exercises the option to increase or extend cover, such as in a convertible, renewable term assurance, the tax relief is lost on all subsequent premiums;

(b) where a policy has an in-built automatic increase for which the policyholder contracted at the outset, the premiums still qualify for tax relief;

(c) where the mix of insurance and investment within one policy can be altered without a change in the amount of the premiums, such as in a flexible unit-linked whole life policy, the policyholder continues to obtain life assurance premium relief, even if they choose to increase the life cover.

With effect from 6 April 1989, life assurance premium relief was reduced from 15% to 12.5%. Consequently, the net premium payable in respect of these policies is now 87.5% of the gross premium.

11:7   Some specific uses of protection policies

The following are some specific uses of life assurance protection policies

(a) funding for inheritance tax;

(b) partnership and share purchase assurance;

(c) keyman assurance.

11:7.1   Funding for inheritance tax

Life assurance protection policies written under trust for the benefit of nominated persons are often required in funding for inheritance tax liabilities.

The circumstances in which they may be used together with the appropriate type of policy are shown below

(a) To meet the inheritance tax payable on death – a whole life policy.

(b) To meet the inheritance tax payable on the death of a surviving spouse – a whole life policy written on a joint life, last survivor basis.

(c) To meet the inheritance tax payable if death should occur within seven years of a potentially exempt transfer (PET) when the nil rate IHT band has already been used – seven year decreasing term assurance.

(d) To meet the extra inheritance tax liability on a donor's death, resulting from adding back to their estate any PET, as reduced by taper relief (see **Chapter 12**), made in the seven years preceding death – seven-year level term assurance. This arises where the original PET was within the donor's nil rate IHT band.

(e) To meet any extra inheritance tax payable on death, which arises on a transfer that was chargeable during lifetime but the tax is recalculated as death occurs within seven years – a specially tailored decreasing term assurance.

11:7.2   Partnership and share purchase assurance

The purpose of partnership and private limited company share purchase life assurance arrangements is to assist in providing the funds required by the surviving partners to buy the share of a deceased partner or by the remaining shareholders to buy a deceased's shareholding. Partnership assurance enables the necessary funds to be received by the surviving partners, with the following advantages

(a) it removes the need for the surviving partners to borrow, liquidate assets or use existing funds already earmarked for other purposes to provide the money to buy the deceased's share;

(b) less attractive solutions, such as finding a new partner with capital or the widow becoming involved in the business, are avoided;

(c) those entitled to the deceased's estate will be able to benefit from readily available funds.

Since partnerships and companies can vary considerably in their constitution and organisation, each case should be considered on an individual basis. The following information should be ascertained before a life policy is effected

(a) the number of partners or directors, together with their ages, sex, state of health and smoking habits;

(b) the likelihood of future changes in the composition of the partnership or the shareholders;

(c) the current resources available;

(d) the value of the partnership shares or shareholdings;

(e) whether there are any relevant provisions in the partnership agreement or articles of association;

(f) whether there are any existing life assurance arrangements.

The main policies which can be suitably used in partnership or share purchase assurance to provide life cover for the appropriate period, normally up to the anticipated dates of retirement, are shown below

(a) level term assurance;

(b) convertible term assurance;

(c) convertible, renewable term assurance;

(d) term assurance provided under personal pension plans;

(e) flexible unit-linked whole life policies.

Following the abolition of life assurance premium relief, life policies effected by a partner or shareholder on his or her own life in trust for other partners or shareholders no longer have a tax advantage over policies written on a life of another basis (these policies were not eligible for tax relief even if effected before 14 March 1984). Consequently, it may be more appropriate to adopt the life of another basis so that the individuals paying the premiums can obtain direct benefit from them. This can considerably simplify matters both with regard to inheritance tax and also by ensuring that the cost of the arrangement is on an equitable basis. However, life of another arrangements can be very rigid. Therefore it may be preferable to use the own life route using a flexible trust wording, especially where frequent changes are a possibility.

11:7.3 'Keyman' assurance

The purpose of keyman assurance is to cover the loss of profits to an employer arising from the death of a key employee. This assurance could therefore be required where

(a) the owner has only provided the capital but the keyman has detailed knowledge of the business;

(b) the keyman has important personal and business connections;

(c) any other situation where the loss of the keyman's services will be critical to the business, and will result in a financial loss to the business or an extra burden, such as costs of recruiting a replacement or loss of orders.

The premiums payable will be allowed as a business expense providing the following conditions are met

(a) The sole relationship of the life assured to the company is that of employee to employer. The employee must not be a significant shareholder.

(b) The assurance is intended to meet the loss of profits resulting from the loss of the keyman's services. The Inland Revenue will accept a level of cover, normally up to a maximum of ten times the keyman's salary, but this will particularly depend on their status within the company and can be any amount actually justifiable in the given circumstances.

(c) The life policy is an annual or short-term assurance. This can normally be defined as not exceeding five years, although, in exceptional circumstances, terms of up to ten years or more may be acceptable.

The company should agree the tax position with the Inland Revenue at the outset. Each case will be considered on its own facts but, in principle, if the premiums are allowed as an expense for corporation tax, the proceeds will be taxed as income. If, on the other hand, the premiums are not allowed, the proceeds may not be taxed. The company does not have the option to select one alternative or the other. The Inland Revenue's ruling will need to be taken into account when arranging the policy (e.g. in determining the sum assured or arranging for the proceeds to be paid over a period of years rather than in a single amount).

Qualifying policies taken out by companies on or after 14 March 1989 are treated in the same way as non-qualifying policies for the taxation of policy gains. Consequently, in the case of a whole life policy, if the surrender value at the time of payment of any benefit is greater than the premiums paid, the gain is liable to corporation tax.

In addition to the benefits payable on the death of a keyman, it is also possible to arrange for them to be paid if they should become disabled. This will then provide the company with the resources to seek a replacement for the keyman or for any other required purpose. Again, if the critical illness or permanent health policy has a surrender value, a taxable policy gain could arise.

One particular consequence of arranging this type of assurance is that, where benefits are received on the keyman's death, the value of the business may be inflated by the cash received. Therefore, where the keyman is a shareholder, the value of their shares may be increased, with the result that their estate may be subject to a larger inheritance tax liability.

12   Tax planning

Tax plays an extremely important part in financial planning for an individual since the main objective of most people is to increase their capital and/or income after tax. However, saving tax should generally be of secondary importance to personal, practical and investment considerations. Many of the tax saving and planning aspects for individuals are discussed in the chapters to which they relate. The purpose of this chapter is to mention some of the other more important matters which have not been covered elsewhere. These can be shown under three main headings

(a) income tax;

(b) capital gains tax;

(c) inheritance tax.

12:1   Income tax

The following matters should be considered in relation to income tax

(a) All personal allowances and reliefs to which an individual is entitled should be claimed. Elections, where appropriate, should be made within the relevant time limits.

(b) A husband and wife are taxed independently for both income tax and capital gains tax purposes. For income tax, each has a separate personal allowance. The married couple's allowance has been abolished from 6 April 2000 onwards other than for taxpayers aged 65 or over.

Significant planning opportunities are, therefore, available to transfer assets between spouses to enable income to be taxed at lower rates. If one spouse is a higher rate taxpayer and the other is not, consideration should be given to transferring income-producing assets to the latter to enable him or her to use the personal allowance, lower and basic rate tax bands. This can be done free of capital gains tax (and also usually inheritance tax), but, to be effective, there must be an outright unconditional gift of the asset.

(c) If assets are held jointly, income is normally divided equally for tax purposes, irrespective of the actual division of ownership. If jointly held property is not held in equal shares a declaration may be made to the Inland Revenue so that each spouse is taxed on the income to which they are actually entitled, provided that this corresponds to their beneficial interest in the property. Such a declaration will lead to savings if the lower rate taxpayer or non-taxpayer is entitled to a greater share of the asset.

(d) Deductions such as annual payments should be paid by the spouse with the higher marginal tax rate.

(e) In any situation involving separation or divorce, there is from 6 April 2000 no relief for maintenance payments under arrangements set up on or after 15 March 1988 other than for taxpayers aged 65 or over. Consequently, the most tax-effective way of providing for a former spouse is now usually by way of a capital settlement, as the income from it will be taxed at a lower rate. However, this may not always be possible and, in any event, the payer does not obtain tax relief.

It should also be borne in mind that because maintenance payments are free from tax in the recipient's hands, it may be possible to settle on a lower annual payment to recognise the tax-free status of the payments.

(f) If it is desired to transfer income to a person with unused allowances, it is necessary to make an outright gift of a capital sum to generate sufficient income, or to create a settlement with a similar sum in favour of the individual concerned. This will not be effective in the case of a settlement by a parent in favour of a minor unmarried child. Before it is decided to set up a trust, it should be remembered that there may be both capital gains tax and inheritance tax consequences. Therefore, the total position must be considered.

(g) The 'accrued income scheme' is designed to combat 'bondwashing', which was the practice of converting income accruing on certain fixed-interest securities into capital so that it was exempt from tax as a capital gain rather than taxed as income. Broadly, the intention of the accrued income scheme is to treat interest on securities, such as gilts, local authority bonds and non-convertible company debentures and unsecured loan stocks, as accruing on a day-to-day basis between interest payment dates and separately from the capital value of the investment. Interest accrued at the date of sale is taxable as income and, in the case of a purchase, accrued income bought is offset for tax purposes against interest subsequently received. The accrued income scheme applies to all UK residents, except for those holding securities with a nominal value of £5,000 or less.

(h) Favourable income tax treatment can be obtained by individuals on certain transactions and investments. Shown below are some of those which are especially advantageous

(i)   National Savings Certificates (see **Chapter 2**);

(ii)   investments under the Enterprise Investment Scheme and investment in Venture Capital Trusts (see **Chapter 6**);

(iii)   individual savings accounts (see **Chapter 4**);

(iv)   additional voluntary contributions (see **Chapter 8**);

(v)   personal pension contributions (see **Chapter 9**);

(vi)   school fees composition schemes and educational trusts (see **Chapter 14**);

(vii)   covenants and gifts to charities where full tax relief is available;

(viii) Lloyd's Underwriters (see **Chapter 7**);

(ix)   purchase of an interest in an industrial or commercial building in an enterprise zone, either directly or through one of the property trusts set up for this purpose (see **Chapter 5**); and

(x)   in certain situations, income arising to an offshore trust where the settlor or his spouse is not a beneficiary can be free of UK income tax. These situations are rare, following law changes in 1991 and 1998;

(i) Investments in Enterprise Investment Scheme shares, Enterprise Zone property (and trusts and syndicates), venture capital trusts and individual savings accounts must all be made before 5 April to qualify for the reliefs or allowances for the current tax year. Where possible, it is sensible to make VCT and ISA investments early in the tax year in order to enjoy the potential for tax-free income and growth at the earliest opportunity.

(j) Non-taxpayers (i.e. those whose income is covered by their personal allowance) should invest in assets which pay gross income (including ISAs), to avoid the need for repayment claims. For example, interest on British Government stocks, National Savings Income Bonds and Pensioners' Income Bonds is paid gross and non-taxpayers can complete Inland Revenue form R85 to register for the payment of bank and building society interest without deduction of income tax.

(k) As well as enjoying capital gains tax exemptions (see **12:2**), a gift of shares or securities to a charity on or after 6 April 2000 qualifies for income tax relief. The value of the gift can be claimed as a deduction from income.

12:2   Capital gains tax

The following are main considerations for the planning of capital gains tax

(a) Timing of disposals is of the utmost importance

    (i)   if a disposal is postponed until shortly after 5 April, the payment of any capital gains tax is delayed for one year;

    (ii)   the Finance Act 1998 radically reformed CGT for individuals, trustees and personal representatives by freezing indexation allowance on the base cost and replacing it with taper relief. This treatment applies to disposals made by the aforementioned persons, on or after 6 April 1998. For these disposals, indexation allowance will be given in accordance with the increase in the Retail Prices Index up to April 1998 but not beyond. For disposals after 5 April 1998, the chargeable gain will be progressively reduced (tapered), according to the length of time the asset has been held after 5 April 1998, plus one extra year for assets held at 17 March 1998 in the case of non-business assets.

    The taper relief in respect of business assets was increased in the Finance Act 2000, and the table below relates to disposals on or after 6 April 2000.

    The maximum taper relief for non-business assets is 40% (60% of the gain being chargeable), when the holding period is ten years or more. The relief operates more rapidly and more generously for business assets. The following table provides details of all taper percentages

No. of complete years after 5 April 1998 for which asset held	Percentage of gain chargeable for business assets	Percentage of gain chargeable for non-business assets
0	100	100
1	87.5	100
2	75	100
3	50	95
4	25	90
5	25	85
6	25	80
7	25	75
8	25	70
9	25	65
10 or more	25	60

Thus, delaying the disposal so that an additional complete year of ownership is reached may considerably reduce the chargeable gain.

The effective rates of tax on gains realised by a higher rate taxpayer are, therefore, 10% (40% x 25%) after four years' ownership of a business asset and 24% (40% x 60%) after ten years' ownership of a non-business asset.

The distinction between business and non-business assets is therefore very important. From 6 April 2000 business assets are, broadly

(i)   assets used for the purposes of a trade;

(ii)   all shares and securities in unlisted trading companies;

(iii)   all shares and securities in a listed trading company where the investor is an employee or officer (including part-time employees); and

(iv)   all shares and securities in a company where the investor is able to exercise at least 5% of the voting rights.

Prior to 6 April 2000, more stringent rules applied and shares and securities only qualified if they were in trading companies and the individual could exercise at least 25% of the voting rights, reduced to 5% for a full-time working employee or officer of the company.

The following example demonstrates how chargeable gains are now calculated

Example 14

An asset was purchased in 1988 for £40,000 and sold on 31 July 2000 for £100,000. Indexation allowance for the period from 1988 to April 1998 is calculated at £12,000. The holding period for taper relief is three years for a non-business asset but two years for a business asset.

The chargeable gain is computed as follows

	£
Proceeds	100,000
Less: Cost	(40,000)
	60,000
Less: Indexation allowance	(12,000)
	£48,000

If the asset is non-business:

Percentage of gain taxable
95% x £48,000   £45,600

If the asset is a business asset throughout:

Percentage of gain taxable
75% x £48,000   £36,000

If an asset is partly a business asset and partly non-business during the period of ownership, complex time apportionment rules apply.

(iii) if disposals are spread over more than one tax year so that the realised gains in each year, after adjusting for indexation or taper relief, do not exceed the annual exemption (£7,200 for 2000/01), no capital gains tax liability arises (in the case of most trusts, the annual exemption is £3,600 for 2000/01);

(iv) if realised gains (as adjusted for indexation or taper relief) in excess of the annual exemption have been made in a tax year, consideration should be given to disposing of assets showing a loss. The losses can then be offset against the gains made, thereby reducing or eliminating the potential capital gains tax liability. Losses brought forward from previous years can also be used in a similar manner. In this instance, such losses will be used only to reduce realised gains before taper relief to £7,200, the exemption limit, with any unused balance being again carried forward. The interaction of losses and taper relief is complex, and careful consideration needs to be given to the time of disposal. Losses should be set against gains qualifying for the *lowest* rate of taper relief. Losses cannot be carried back to an earlier tax year; they can only be offset against chargeable gains realised in the current tax year or subsequent years.

Despite the availability of these timing opportunities, it should be borne in mind that disposals should first be considered from an investment viewpoint. As previously mentioned, a poor investment even with good tax planning is unlikely to produce a satisfactory result.

(b) Every person, including a minor, is entitled to his or her own exemption. Consideration should therefore be given to husbands and wives spreading the ownership of investments in a family so that each member is able to realise tax-free gains.

The income tax rule which treats a child's income from a parental gift as the parents' if it exceeds £100 per annum in total is not mirrored in the capital gains tax legislation. Parental gifts should therefore be invested in assets providing capital growth and no income, for example the capital shares or zero dividend preference shares of split capital investment trusts.

(c) Each spouse has an annual capital gains tax exemption. In order to make maximum use of this, it may be worthwhile for them to transfer shares to each other. In addition, as capital gains are aggregated with income to determine the rate of tax, gains should be crystallised by the spouse with the lower top rate of tax. For example, one spouse may have losses brought forward. These cannot be used directly to offset a gain to be made by the other spouse. However, if the asset to be realised is first transferred between the spouses, the necessary offset is achieved. No stamp duty would be payable on such gifts, but all the formalities of transfer of ownership should be carried out before any sale. Any such transfer must be unconditional.

(d) 'Bed and breakfasting' (the sale and subsequent repurchase of shares, generally on the following day) was widely used to crystallize capital gains or losses for set off purposes or to utilise the annual exemption.

This practice has been stopped for disposals made on or after 17 March 1998. Sales will now be identified with purchases made within 30 days of the disposal. Alternative techniques for avoiding being 'out of the market' with a particular share or collective investment could include

    (i) immediate repurchase of an identical holding by the spouse;

    (ii) immediate repurchase of a similar investment;

    (iii) repurchase within an ISA; or

    (iv) purchasing an option to protect against a price increase during the 30-day period (this will only be possible with shares and could be prohibitively complex and expensive).

(e) Gains and losses arising on the disposal of gilts and other qualifying corporate bonds (this includes local authority bonds and non-convertible company debentures and unsecured loan stocks) are completely exempt from capital gains tax. Consequently, investors are largely able to pursue a policy for such assets based entirely on investment criteria without being concerned with the tax consequences of any decision. The accrued income scheme (see **12:1(g)**) should, however, be considered.

(f) Since capital gains tax is not payable on death, it is often advisable for a person with a very short life expectancy to avoid realising substantial gains during the remainder of their lifetime, to benefit from the tax-free step up on death.

(g) Careful attention should also be paid to the effect of the taper relief rules on the capital gains tax position. In choosing which investments to sell, particular note should be taken of the holding period and the type of asset, to ensure that taper relief is maximised. Enhanced taper relief is available on business assets as defined above.

(h) If an individual wishes to make a large gift to a charity, it is usually beneficial, where it can be arranged, for the gift to be in the form of a chargeable asset showing a sizeable capital gain and not the equivalent cash value. Since gains arising on gifts to charities are completely exempt from capital gains tax, the potential tax liability would be avoided. From 6 April 2000, an income tax deduction is also available for the value of the shares, making such a gift extremely tax efficient.

(i) Where an individual becomes the owner of two homes, they should, within two years of acquiring the second home, make an election as to which home is to be treated as their main private residence. Since only one residence is exempt from capital gains tax, they should usually select the home likely to show the greater gain on sale (see **5:2** above).

(j) Where an individual owns an asset, such as shares, which becomes of negligible value, a claim can be made to have the loss treated as if it had been crystallised without an actual disposal being necessary. The loss can be used in any of the two tax years preceding the year of the claim, providing that the asset was also of negligible value at the earlier date.

(k) A capital loss on the disposal of subscriber shares in an unquoted company can be set against income in certain circumstances.

(l) Where a person is the owner of 5% or more of the shares in a trading company and works full-time in it as a director or employee, or is a sole trader, or a partner in a firm, he or she is entitled to capital gains tax retirement relief on all or part of a gain not exceeding £150,000 (for the year ending 5 April 2001) if the business is sold (or gifted), provided the individual is at least age 50, or has to retire earlier due to ill-health.

Retirement relief is being gradually phased out from 6 April 1999, and will not be available from 6 April 2003 onwards. However, taper relief will be available at increased rates for business assets, and a maximum of 75% of the gain will be exempted when a four-year holding period is reached.

The retirement relief exemption is reduced proportionately where the business or shares have not been owned for the whole of the previous ten years before the date of sale or, in the case of a company, where the director or employee has not been a full-time working director or employee for that period.

One-half of the gain in excess of £150,000 (or the proportionately reduced figure, if applicable) up to a maximum of £600,000 is also eligible for relief for the year ending 5 April 2001. In line with the phasing out of this relief, the exemption limits will be reduced for subsequent years. Effectively, the tax rate on this element of the gain is therefore reduced to a maximum of 20%. If the disposal is of shares in a company, the gain qualifying for relief would be in the proportion of the company's chargeable business assets to the total chargeable assets (chargeable assets are all assets on which a chargeable gain or allowable loss would arise if the company disposed of them). Thus, the holding of chargeable non business assets within a company should be minimised where possible.

In order to maximise retirement relief, it is usually worthwhile for the following action to be taken by an individual, when practicable

(i)   postpone the disposal of the business until age 50 and also, in the case of a company, continue to work in it until that time;

(ii)   postpone the disposal of the business until it has been owned for ten years; and

(iii)   arrange for the spouse to work full-time in the business and to own part of it. He or she will then also obtain retirement relief against their own gains on disposal of the business.

The replacement of retirement relief by taper relief has made it difficult to assess when overall relief would be maximised, as this would depend on the facts of each particular case.

In all cases, it is recommended that detailed professional advice is obtained, as the conditions which have to be satisfied can be complex.

(m) As capital gains may arise where a person becomes absolutely entitled to trust assets, consideration should be given to prolonging the life of the settlement if the beneficiary is prepared to receive the income but not the capital. This can be achieved by conferring on the beneficiary an interest in possession at age 25 instead of absolute entitlement. By this means, liability for capital gains tax is deferred, sometimes indefinitely.

(n) Capital gains can be deferred under the reinvestment relief rules or by an investment in EIS or VCT companies. Provided the sale proceeds are used to acquire shares in a qualifying unquoted trading company the capital gain can be deferred by the purchase of new shares, thereby deferring the gain until a subsequent disposal.

12:3   Other issues

There are two tax issues that are worthy of further explanation.

12:3.1   The taxation of savings income

From the year 1996/97 onwards, savings income of basic and lower rate taxpayers has generally been taxed at the 20% rate. This includes interest from banks and building societies, interest distributions from unit trusts, interest from gilts and other securities including corporate bonds, and purchased life annuities. It does not, however, include savings income from overseas taxed on a remittance basis for non-domiciled individuals.

The income tax implications are that

(a) those exempt from tax or not liable to tax may claim a refund of the tax credit or tax deducted at 20%;

(b) those liable to tax at 10% may claim a partial refund;

(c) those liable to income tax at the lower rate of 20% will have no further tax to pay;

(d) those liable to tax at the basic rate will not be required to pay further tax; and

(e) those who are liable to the higher rate of income tax will be taxed at 40% on the net income received grossed up at 20%.

For these purposes savings/dividend income is taken as the 'top slice' of an individual's income.

Different rules apply to dividend income, as the tax credit on dividends from UK companies was reduced to 10% from 6 April 1999. Lower and basic rate taxpayers have no further liability; higher rate taxpayers pay tax at 32.5% on such income, so that their effective rate of tax is the same as that on other savings income. Non-taxpayers will not be able to reclaim the tax credit.

As regards capital gains tax it is possible that receipt of dividend and savings income will cause difficulties in determining the rate at which capital gains are taxed. Professional advice should be sought in cases where

(a) capital gains are greater than the annual exemption (£7,200 in 2000/01);

(b) income other than dividends and savings income exceeds available allowances and the lower rate band; and

(c) dividend and savings income takes total income above the lower rate band.

12:3.2 Enhanced scrip dividends

As an alternative to the payment of a cash dividend, a number of UK companies have offered their shareholders the option of taking a dividend in the form of shares. In order to encourage the taking of such shares, the companies offered their shareholders an *enhanced scrip dividend* alternative, where the value of new shares received was greater than the cash dividend that would otherwise be paid. The tax position in respect of shares issued by a UK company under an enhanced scrip dividend alternative is as follows

(a) For income tax purposes, a shareholder who receives new shares instead of the cash dividend will be treated as having received gross income of an amount which, when reduced by the normal 10% dividend tax credit, is equal to the market value of those shares on the first day of dealing. For example, a shareholder taking new shares having a market value of £135 will be treated as having received gross income of £150 and as having paid income tax at 10% of £15 on the grossed-up amount.

Basic rate and lower rate taxpayers will have no further liability to tax as a result of receiving shares; however, shareholders who do not pay income tax will not be able to obtain a repayment of the tax they are deemed to have paid. Higher rate taxpayers will be liable to tax at an additional rate of 22.5% (32.5% less 10% credit).

(b) As regards capital gains tax, the issue of shares, as an alternative to the payment of a cash dividend, involves a reorganisation of the company's share capital. The new shares are treated as having been received at market value, £150 in this example, and will be added to the existing holding of shares and treated as though they had been acquired as and when the existing holding was acquired. Accordingly, the base cost for the new shares will be calculated by reference to the base cost of the shareholder's existing holding plus the amount given for the new shares. Taper relief (but not indexation allowance) will apply from the original date of purchase.

12:4 Inheritance tax

IHT is a tax on certain lifetime gifts and on an individual's estate on death. It operates on a cumulative basis and, subject to certain exemptions and reliefs, is chargeable on the cumulative total

(a) at death, on certain lifetime gifts made within the previous seven years;

(b) at death, on lifetime gifts with reservation (see **12:4.3** below);

(c) of gifts into discretionary trusts, whether in lifetime or on death;

(d) of the value of the assets passing on death.

For transfers made on or after 6 April 2000, the first £234,000 (for 2000/01) of cumulative chargeable transfers (the nil rate band) is exempt from IHT and any excess is taxed on death at a rate of 40%.

To some extent, IHT can be described as a voluntary tax due to the many exemptions and reliefs available. With early planning, it is often possible to reduce or eliminate potential IHT liabilities entirely, and this is helped by a husband and wife each having their own exemptions and rate bands. However, all assets are potentially liable to IHT on death, with only estates (including cumulative transfers) within the nil rate band not giving rise to a tax charge at all. Since an individual's house must be included in calculating the value of his assets, IHT may affect many individuals who otherwise have only relatively modest estates.

For the purpose of calculating the value of a lifetime transfer, it is the loss suffered by the donor on the transfer, rather than the benefit received by the donee, which is relevant for IHT.

12:4.1 Classes of transfer

Transfers can be broadly classified as follows

(a) exempt (see below);

(b) potentially exempt;

(c) chargeable.

A potentially exempt transfer (PET) is a lifetime gift made on or after 18 March 1986 by an individual to one of the recipients shown in **(a)**, **(b)** and **(d)** below – in the case of **(c)**, the relevant date is on or after 17 March 1987

(a) another individual;

(b) an accumulation and maintenance trust;

(c) an interest in possession trust;

(d) a disabled person's trust.

A PET is treated as an exempt transfer on which no IHT is payable at the time of the gift and, if the donor survives for seven years after the gift is made, no tax will be payable. If the donor dies within those seven years, the PET is treated as a chargeable transfer at the time it was made and IHT may become due at the date of death. However, a PET will still provide the benefits listed below

(a) Although the PET may have become chargeable, the amount on which the charge is based is the value at the time of the actual gift and not the value at the date of death when the charge arises. If the property gifted has increased in value, this 'freezing' of its value will often be advantageous. Where the value of the property has fallen since the gift, the lower value may be used in most circumstances.

(b) Payment of IHT is postponed until after the death of the donor, rather than becoming payable shortly after the gift is made.

(c) IHT is charged at the rates in force at the date of death, where they may be different to those applying at the time of the gift. If the gift is made more than three years before the date of death, the tax payable is subject to taper relief as shown below

Time between gift and death	% of full rate payable
Up to 3 years	100
3-4 years	80
4-5 years	60
5-6 years	40
6-7 years	20

It should be noted that it is the tax payable, not the value of the gift, which is tapered. If no tax is payable because the gift is covered by the annual exemption and the nil rate band, taper relief will not apply.

The IHT due on a PET is payable by the donee.

A lifetime gift which does not qualify as an exempt transfer or a PET (typically a gift to a discretionary trust) is regarded as a chargeable transfer at the time it is made, and, subject to the nil rate band, is immediately liable to IHT at one half of the death rates in force at the time. For this purpose, any chargeable transfers which have been made in the previous seven years are taken into account in calculating how much of the nil rate band remains unused. If the donor survives seven years, there are no further IHT consequences. However, if he or she does not, the tax charge is recalculated using the full rates in force at the date of death but reduced by any taper relief. If this produces a higher charge than the tax already paid on the lifetime transfer, a further liability arises. Where the calculation shows a lower charge, the difference is not repayable.

When making a chargeable transfer, the options below are normally available

(a) The donor pays the tax based on the value of the transfer plus the tax; or

(b) The donee pays the tax calculated on the transfer value only. In this case, the tax does not decrease the donor's estate and, consequently, both the amount of the transfer and the inheritance tax are lower.

12:4.2   Exemptions and reliefs

The following are the main IHT exemptions

(a) Transfers between husband and wife, whether made during lifetime or on death. The exception to this is where a husband or wife, domiciled in the UK, makes a transfer to a foreign domiciled spouse. In these circumstances, only the first £55,000 is exempt.

(b) Lifetime transfers in each tax year up to £3,000 (per donor). Any unused part of the exemption may be carried forward for one year only for use in the following tax year after the exemption for that following year has been utilised.

(c) Outright lifetime gifts to any one person not exceeding £250 in each tax year with no limit to the number of recipients. However, this exemption cannot be claimed in respect of gifts to a particular person where more than £250 is given to that person in a tax year.

(d) Normal expenditure out of income. This covers transfers of net income after tax, provided that they form part of normal (i.e. habitual) expenditure and leave sufficient income for the donor to maintain his usual standard of living. For this purpose, the capital element of a purchased life annuity is not treated as being part of the donor's income.

(e) Gifts in consideration of marriage. The following amounts are exempt

   (i)   £5,000 from each parent;

    (ii)   £2,500 from each grandparent;

    (iii) £2,500 from one party of the marriage to the other;

    (iv) £1,000 from any other person.

(f) Lifetime gifts for the support and maintenance of children and dependant relatives, including a former spouse.

(g) Gifts to charities both during lifetime and on death. This exemption can be of particular relevance to individuals with no relatives who prefer their favourite charities to benefit rather than the Crown.

Business property relief applies at 100% in respect of interests in unincorporated businesses and holdings of shares in unquoted trading companies, subject to certain conditions.

Similarly, relief of 100% is available against agricultural land and woodlands.

12:4.3   Gifts with reservation

Anti-avoidance provisions relating to gifts with reservation exist with the aim of counteracting 'have your cake and eat it' schemes such as inheritance trusts. The rules on gifts with reservation are essentially the same as the old estate duty provisions, with gifted property subject to a reservation if either the donee does not assume full possession and enjoyment of the property at the time it is gifted or at least seven years before the donor's death; or if the donor retains a benefit or enjoyment from the property at any time in the last seven years of his or her life.

The consequences of a gift with reservation depend on whether or not the reservation ceases during the donor's lifetime, or whether it is still in existence at the time of death. If the donor releases the reservation before death, he or she is treated as having made a PET of the gifted property at the time the reservation is released. Where the donor dies without releasing the reservation, the gifted property is treated as part of the estate at death. IHT is charged according to the value of the property at that time. The original gift may also be charged as a lifetime gift in certain circumstances.

The gift with reservation provisions particularly affect many individuals with medium-sized estates who may now feel unable to pass on their property before death.

12:5   Inheritance tax planning

The following matters are of the utmost importance in IHT planning

(a) Subject to the individual circumstances, it is often beneficial from an IHT viewpoint for the assets of a husband and wife to be divided between them so that they are both able to take advantage of the various exemptions and the nil rate band. However, care should be taken to ensure as far as possible that the 'associated operations' rules do not apply, in order to avoid the transfer between the husband and wife, and the subsequent transfer from the recipient, being treated as one transaction.

In practice, the Inland Revenue is unlikely to use the associated operations provisions where a husband shares capital with his wife who then chooses to make gifts out of the money she has received. The exception to this is where there is a blatant case of a husband's gift to his wife (or vice versa) being made on condition that she should at once use the money to make gifts to others.

A further advantage to a married couple of dividing their estates could accrue if a wealth tax were to be introduced. Since it seems likely that this would be calculated on the separate estates of a husband and wife at progressive rates, less tax would be payable on two smaller estates than on one larger one.

(b) Maximum advantage should be taken of the opportunity to make gifts within the various exemptions available. In this way, a considerable amount can be transferred from an estate over a period of years without any IHT liability.

(c) In addition to exempt gifts, an individual with a large estate should consider making further outright lifetime gifts, rather than waiting until death, for the following reasons

   (i)   cumulative chargeable lifetime gifts may be made within the IHT nil rate band (£234,000 for transfers made on or after 6 April 2000). Gifts made more than seven years previously drop out and, consequently, further gifts can be made within the nil rate band without attracting IHT;

   (ii) if the gifts were treated as PETs, the benefits mentioned earlier in this chapter would apply. Accordingly, it will often be particularly advantageous to gift those assets which are likely to increase in value. In particular, the spouse with the longer life expectancy should make PETs and this may involve transferring assets from one spouse to the other prior to making a PET, subject to the associated operation rules set out above.

However, as capital gains tax holdover is now only available for gifts of business assets, the capital gains tax implications of such gifts must also be considered.

Any tax payable by the donee if death occurs within seven years should be covered by decreasing term assurance (see **11:1.2**).

(d) In appropriate circumstances, it may be beneficial to 'skip' a generation and make gifts (or legacies) to grandchildren rather than to children. There will then be no charge to inheritance tax on the children's deaths. The grandchildren's interests could be held in an accumulation and maintenance trust.

(e) An inheritance tax saving will be made if an amount equal to the nil rate band is left away from the spouse, so that this exemption is not wasted. In order to avoid redrafting a will each time the nil rate band changes, the will can bc drawn up on the basis that an amount equivalent to the current nil rate band, less any chargeable gifts made within the previous seven years, is left in this way. A common provision is for a discretionary trust for the widow(er) and children, thus enabling the whole of the surviving family to benefit from this gift (see **Chapter 16**). Care should be taken, however, to ensure that a share in the family home does not become an asset of the trust. If the surviving spouse continues to live there, he or she is likely to be regarded as having an interest in possession in the whole property, with the result that its value will be included as part of their estate on their death.

(f) As previously mentioned, it is the loss suffered by a donor on a transfer, rather than the benefit received by the donee, which is relevant for IHT purposes. Therefore, an individual should be aware of the circumstances where a gift providing a small benefit for the donee can give rise to a large potential IHT liability, for example, a gift of 2% out of a 51% family company shareholding. Although, in this case, the gift may be of little value to the recipient, the donor would lose control of the company, with the result that a large reduction in the value of the estate would be likely. Under current legislation, 100% business property relief would be available on such a transfer.

(g) If appropriate, advantage should be taken of business property relief and/or agricultural property relief. Where relief is available, the transfer will be assessed for IHT purposes at a nil, or reduced value. It must be borne in mind, however, that the donee will not qualify for the relief until he or she has owned the property for two years. In connection with agricultural property relief, it is very important that ownership of a farmhouse should not be retained without some of the farmland, otherwise it will not enjoy agricultural property relief. For transfers after 9 March 1992, relief may be as high as 100%.

(h) If a loan is obtained, it should be secured against non-business assets where possible. A loan secured against business property will reduce the amount of business property relief available.

(i) The setting up of a trust may be especially useful to pass capital to children, grandchildren or other dependants, but at the same time enabling some flexibility and control over the assets to be retained. The particular type of trust would depend on the exact circumstances, although a typical arrangement might be a discretionary trust up to the amount of the nil rate band.

(j) Funding for IHT through life assurance policies (see **Chapter 11**) is now likely to play an even greater role in IHT planning, due to the treatment of gifts with reservation and the changes to capital gains hold-over relief for gifts.

(k) Where a life or pension policy is arranged in order to provide protection for the family of the life assured, it is often advisable for it to be written in trust or under nomination to pass free of IHT to the dependant concerned.

(l) Even after death, a variation of a will or a disclaimer may be effected. These can produce considerable IHT savings (see **Chapter 15**).

(m) On certain assets, an option is provided to pay an IHT liability by interest-free instalments over ten years. Where this is permitted, it is usually beneficial to exercise the option. In other cases, the IHT liability may also be paid by instalments but interest would be payable. In this connection, the order of gifts made in a lifetime can be critical. If a PET becomes chargeable, it is important that, where it is a gift of an asset on which tax can be paid by instalments, it is not the part of the estate which is within the nil rate band.

12:6 Overriding considerations for tax planning

Although this chapter has been written from a tax planning viewpoint, the following overriding considerations should be borne in mind

(a) Personal and family happiness is of greater importance than saving tax. The possibility of the children being financially immature or having unsatisfactory marriages should be taken into account.

(b) Although tax considerations are often vital in making a financial decision, the investment aspects will normally be paramount – the tax tail must not wag the investment dog.

(c) Advice which may be suitable for most people will need to be adapted to the practical circumstances of the particular case. For example, in IHT planning, assets should generally only be passed to children or grandchildren provided the surviving spouse has been left with sufficient capital and/or income on which to live. It may also be unwise to pass assets of high value to relatively young children until they are more responsible. It might also be unwise to split the ownership of the family home on the death of the first spouse as this may severely affect the future well-being and lifestyle of the surviving spouse.

(d) In the light of court cases and Inland Revenue statements in recent years, considerable caution should be exercised before proceeding with certain tax mitigation schemes.

(e) It is usually advisable to keep matters simple and for any scheme to be as flexible as possible. It should be remembered that not only do individuals' family and financial circumstances change, but also governments and tax legislation.

(f) Income and capital should not be considered separately for tax planning purposes. Frequently, a higher net return can be obtained by making capital gains than by creating income.

(g) A course of action should be considered from the viewpoint of all forms of tax and not just one tax in isolation. For example, while a lifetime gift may be advantageous for IHT purposes, the benefit could be outweighed by the capital gains tax payable.

(h) Tax planning can be very complicated. It is therefore generally worthwhile for an individual to obtain professional advice before entering into any arrangement where a large sum of money is involved.

13   Mortgages

Apart from the personal satisfaction and enjoyment of owning one's home, it has, in many periods, been one of the best investments an individual could make. In order to finance the purchase, it is quite usual for a mortgage to be obtained from a building society, bank or other lender.

13:1   Guidelines on the amount which can be borrowed

The maximum loan which can be obtained will normally be limited by reference to the size of the borrower's income and the value of the property. This is discussed below.

13:1.1   The size of the borrower's income

(a) Lenders usually base their loans on a multiple of income. For a single person, the multiple normally varies from $2^1/2$ times to $3^1/4$ times income.

(b) In the case of couples, both of whom are earning, the basis of the loan would often be the greater of

(i)   three times the main income plus the second income; or

(ii) $2^1/2$ times the joint income.

(c) Some lenders operate low start schemes (usually for first-time buyers), whereby a higher multiple of income is accepted. However, such schemes usually result in larger repayments being made over the total term of the mortgage.

(d) The definition of 'income' varies between lenders. Some allow overtime, bonuses, commission and profit-related pay, while others automatically exclude them.

(e) For the self-employed, the loan is usually based on the income of the previous year. The lender will also normally wish to examine audited accounts for the last three years.

13:1.2   The value of the property

(a) The normal maximum amount that a building society or bank will lend varies between 85% and 100% of the agreed purchase price or valuation, whichever is the lower. Since the property is used as security for the loan, the lender will wish to ensure that its value is adequate and will appoint its own valuer for this purpose.

(b) If the loan required is very large or it is to be used to purchase an older or less common type of property, there may be a further restriction on the percentage offered.

13:2   Taxation position

In order to encourage private home ownership, successive governments provided assistance to individuals in the form of tax relief on mortgage interest and an exemption from capital gains tax on the profit made from the sale of the main home. The latter continues but interest relief was ended on 5 April 2000 (for the exception, see **13:8** below).

Prior to that date income tax relief was given on interest paid in respect of loans up to £30,000, or the first £30,000 of larger loans, used to buy the only or main residence. It was also allowed (subject to the overall loan limit of £30,000)

(a) Where a property was purchased before 6 April 1988 for a former or separated spouse or a dependent relative (this includes a widowed, divorced or separated mother, whether dependent or not).

(b) Where an employee living in accommodation provided by his employer was purchasing a separate house to occupy at a later date, for example, at retirement.

(c) On interest on a bridging loan of up to £30,000.

The tax relief was normally given under the mortgage interest relief at source (MIRAS) system. The relief at the prevailing rate was automatically deducted at source from the amounts charged to borrowers. The non-taxpayer gained considerable benefit from this since the tax deducted was not subsequently recovered by the Inland Revenue. For loans larger than £30,000, tax relief was deducted at source only up to that figure.

13:3   Main types of mortgage

The method selected to repay a mortgage will depend on the exact circumstances of the individual, including his age, state of health and tax position. The main types of mortgage are

(a) repayment mortgages;

(b) endowment mortgages;

(c) pension mortgages;

(d) PEP mortgages; and

(e) flexible mortgages.

13:3.1   Repayment mortgages

Under this method, both interest and part of the capital of the outstanding loan are paid to the lender monthly. In addition to the monthly loan repayments, most lenders insist that the borrower pays premiums to a mortgage protection policy or other term assurance in order to provide life cover for the outstanding mortgage.

With this type of mortgage, an increasing proportion of the regular payments is applied each year to reduce the capital outstanding. Most lenders offer 'constant net repayment' mortgages. These mortgages are costed so that, if interest rates and tax relief remain static throughout the mortgage term, the monthly repayments remain the same.

13:3.2   Endowment mortgages

Payments made under an endowment mortgage consist of two separate parts: interest to the lender (in most cases, this will be at the same rate as for a repayment mortgage) and life assurance premiums to an insurance company. The interest is payable throughout the term of the mortgage and will only vary with movements in interest rates and any change in the rate of tax relief.

The proceeds from the life policy are used to repay the mortgage at the end of the term, with any surplus arising being available to the borrower. Both unit-linked and with-profits policies can be taken out to repay a mortgage. Although unit-linked endowments are offered by almost all life companies, with-profits policies are normally more appropriate because of the greater certainty provided.

The main type of with-profits policy which is used to repay a mortgage is a low-cost endowment policy. Occasionally, a full with-profits endowment policy may also be suitable (these policies were considered in **Chapter 10**).

Most low-cost endowment policies are effectively a combination of with-profits endowment assurance and decreasing term assurance, but, since future bonus rates are not known, the life cover from the term assurance is not defined. In reality, these policies are endowment assurances with a guaranteed death benefit which is higher than the amount on which bonuses are declared. A low-cost endowment policy can also be a combination of a with-profits endowment policy and a level term assurance.

Since the total death benefit from the low cost endowment policy is normally set equal to the amount of the mortgage, the policy should provide sufficient cover to repay the loan in the event of the death of the borrower while the loan is still outstanding.

During the 1990s, competition in the mortgage market led to a reasonably relaxed approach by many lenders to the growth rate assumed for a low-cost endowment taken out to repay an interest only mortgage at the end of the term. This and the reductions that all life companies have had to make to their bonus rates has resulted in some borrowers being told by their life assurance companies that the projected maturity proceeds of their policies will be insufficient to repay their loans. They have, therefore, had to increase their premiums or start a new savings plan to fund for the shortfall. Policyholders who are a considerable way into their policies should not be concerned as they will have enjoyed the excellent returns of the 1980s. Premiums for new policies now reflect the companies' expectation that future investment returns will be lower than in the recent past.

The main advantage of a low-cost endowment policy, when compared to a full with-profits policy, is that it is much cheaper, due to part of the initial cover being provided by term assurance. Against this, the longer the period, the greater will be the difference in the amount of the proceeds of the two policies.

However, even where an individual has sufficient resources to be able to afford to repay a mortgage by way of a full with-profits endowment policy, it is not usually advisable to do so. Instead, it would normally be advantageous to effect a low-cost endowment to repay the mortgage and arrange an additional savings plan, such as an ISA for the uncommitted funds. In this way, the additional plan will not be charged to the lender and can be stopped at any time and the proceeds used for other purposes. It will also be more tax-efficient.

It should be noted that the high charges and lack of flexibility inherent in endowment policies has recently caused them to lose favour with borrowers as a means of repaying a mortgage.

13:3.3   Pension mortgages

These mortgages, which are usually arranged by the self-employed or employees not in an occupational pension scheme, have similarities to endowment mortgages. A personal pension policy is effected instead of a life assurance policy and the tax-free cash lump sum is used to repay the mortgage. However, while an endowment policy can be assigned to a lender, this is not possible with a personal pension policy providing retirement benefits. Consequently, the lender will normally require a separate term assurance policy, which can be written under personal pension rules, to be assigned to it to cover the borrower's death before the loan is repaid. It is also possible for a pension mortgage to be taken out by a director, executive or other person through a company pension arrangement.

The main advantage of a pension mortgage, compared with the other methods, is the favourable tax position in respect of both the contributions paid and the pension fund itself. As mentioned in **Chapter 9**, contributions up to the maximum permitted are effectively allowed against the highest income tax rates payable by the individual. The pension fund grows free from capital gains tax, and attracts no additional income tax charge, although since 2 July 1997 pension funds are no longer able to reclaim the tax credit on UK dividend income. As a result, pension mortgages are particularly advantageous for higher rate taxpayers.

However, against these advantages, only a proportion of the amount in the pension fund at retirement can be taken in the form of cash, with the balance being taken by way of pension. Despite the attractions of a pension mortgage, the following matters should be considered before a decision is taken to use this method to repay a loan

(a) it will not normally be possible to repay the mortgage or receive the pension and any surplus cash before age 50 (access to retirement annuity funds can be obtained through switching to personal pensions);

(b) by using the tax-free cash to repay the mortgage, the cash benefit available for retirement purposes is reduced (this is particularly important where maximum contributions are already being paid);

(c) if earnings are volatile, there may be a restriction in poor years on the level of contributions which can be paid;

(d) if the person concerned should cease to be self-employed or become a member of an occupational pension scheme, he would be ineligible to pay contributions into the existing contract and, consequently, would have to make alternative arrangements.

Pension mortgages are mainly suitable for those who are able to predict their future with a reasonable degree of certainty. These will largely be high-earning, self-employed professional people who are unlikely to work for an employer in the future, or directors and executives who are able to utilise their potential benefits under a company pension scheme or individual pension arrangement. In any event, before the pension method is decided upon, consideration should be given to the position which would arise if, at a future date, contributions cannot be maintained. It is also important to remember that legislation could be introduced to reduce the tax advantages of a pension mortgage, perhaps restricting or taxing the lump sum available when benefits are taken.

13:3.4   PEP and ISA mortgages

These mortgages are similar to pension mortgages, except that a PEP or ISA is used as the repayment medium. Although the plans (see **Chapter 4**) do not enjoy tax relief on subscriptions, the funds currently roll up tax-free. In addition, all of the accumulated funds can be used to repay the loan. Surrender penalties do not apply on the cessation or reduction of a PEP or ISA investment and this may be attractive if the intention is to reduce the mortgage before the end of the term.

Separate term assurance will be required to cover the possibility of the borrower's death before repayment. Borrowers taking out ISAs should be prepared for volatility in the value of their investments; however, over a 25-year period this should not be of great concern. To an extent, volatility can be reduced by opting for an OEIC or unit or investment trust ISA.

The fact that (apart from the period from 6 April 1999 to 5 April 2001) the maximum annual subscription to an ISA is £5,000 per annum rather than the £6,000 per annum allowed for a general PEP, could cause problems for borrowers with large mortgages who previously used their full general PEP allowance.

The following example illustrates various ways of repaying a mortgage

Example 15

A man aged 40 next birthday, paying tax at 40%, takes out a £50,000 mortgage repayable over 25 years. He is in good health and a non-smoker. The gross interest rate charged under each type of mortgage is 7.75%

	Repayment mortgage	Low cost endowment mortgage	Pension mortgage	ISA mortgage
	£	£	£	£
Net monthly payments				
To lender	382	323	323	323
To insurance company:				
term assurance premiums	10		8*	11
endowment premiums		93		
pension premiums			196*	
To ISA provider				85
	£392	£416	£527	£419

Net of tax relief at 40%

Illustrative benefits at end of mortgage term

Assumed growth rate	–	6%	7%	7%
		£	£	£
Illustrated value of life policy/ pension fund/ISA	–	50,000	50,000	50,000
Annual gross pension	–	–	9,630	–

Notes

1. The illustrated values of the life policy, pension fund and ISA fund are based on the rules laid down by the Financial Services Authority (FSA) and assume that contributions, after allowing for a deduction for expenses and the cost of life cover (in the case of the life policy), will be invested to earn 6% per annum net of tax, 7% and 7% respectively. For the purpose of calculating the annual gross pension, immediate annuity rates are based on an interest rate of 6% per annum, 3% escalation and a 50% spouse's benefit.

2. The term assurance premiums relate to a mortgage protection policy in respect of the repayment mortgage, a level term assurance effected under a personal pension policy in respect of the pension mortgage and level term assurance for the ISA mortgage. The pension policy would also repay the accumulated value of the fund in the event of death before retirement.

3. Comparisons between the different house purchase methods will vary with the age of the person concerned and the level of interest rates.

13:3.5 Flexible mortgages

A recent development in the mortgage market is flexible mortgages. These are available on an 'interest only' basis and the repayment medium is left to the borrower's choice. This enables a 'cocktail' of different repayment media to be used. These flexible mortgages also permit 'payment holidays', lump sum repayment at any time and often carry a cheque book facility which permits borrowers to re-access funds repaid (up to the original amount borrowed).

13:4 Early repayment of a mortgage

From a financial viewpoint, it can be advantageous to repay a mortgage if a lump sum should become available to do so. However, it is sometimes possible to obtain a greater return by investing the lump sum than the net saving which could be achieved by repaying the mortgage. A further factor is that, once a borrower has made an early repayment, the capital so used cannot be applied for other purposes, with the result that liquidity and flexibility are lost. It should also be borne in mind that interest rates on most other forms of finance are higher than those on mortgages.

However, following the abolition of mortgage interest relief, early or partial repayment of a mortgage is generally worthwhile in the circumstances below

(a) Where both spouses are fully utilising their personal allowances, with income generated from sources other than the cash sums being considered for the repayment.

(b) Where a building society mortgage is near the end of its term. In these circumstances, the effective rate of interest charged can be very high if it is based on the amount of capital outstanding at the beginning of a year with no account being taken of the capital subsequently repaid during that year.

Even if it is not financially expedient to repay a mortgage early, many people prefer to do so from an emotional viewpoint. If this is the situation, it should be remembered that an individual's personal requirements are generally of prime importance, even to the point where financial returns are not maximised.

If it is proposed to make a significant partial repayment, the lender should be asked the optimum date for this to take place. This is because interest is sometimes calculated only on periodic balances, and there could be some time before the repayment is taken into account for the calculation of future interest.

Before the final payment on a mortgage is made to a building society, whether by early repayment or otherwise, it should be remembered that it is often worthwhile to leave a nominal amount unpaid, for the following reasons

(a) the building society will continue to store the title deeds free of charge;

(b) if a further advance is required, the individual may not incur further legal fees; and

(c) in the event that the society is taken over or converts to a public limited company, mortgage holders are likely to benefit from a cash bonus or an allotment of shares.

However, against these advantages, a higher rate of interest is often charged for further advances.

13:5   General principles in choosing a mortgage

The following general principles will often apply in choosing a particular type of mortgage

(a) If the individual's main requirement is to keep the monthly outgoings to a minimum, a repayment mortgage is often most appropriate.

(b) A repayment mortgage is normally more flexible than the other types of mortgage. However, against this, if a person sells a property in the early years of a mortgage, only a small proportion of the capital will have been repaid. Many new mortgages are taken out with the same term as the previous repayment mortgage, which may mean that the final repayment is delayed beyond the date originally anticipated.

In the case of endowment, pension and ISA mortgages, the investments can usually be continued if a new loan is subsequently arranged. Consequently, the mortgage will be repaid within the original term selected.

(c) If a person is in poor health, he may not be able to arrange an endowment mortgage since underwriting will generally be required.

(d) Endowment mortgages may not be available to older borrowers and, in the case of a pension mortgage, the amount of the loan may be restricted because of the limits on contributions.

(e) For a self-employed person or an employed person not in an occupational pension scheme, a pension mortgage is likely to produce the best results, although it requires the highest contributions.

(f) As ISAs are generally equity-based, they are prone to short-term volatility. If markets fall, their value will be reduced, which may mean that they are not adequate to repay the mortgage at the desired time.

13:6   Other mortgage considerations

The following are other matters which should be borne in mind

(a) The type of property may restrict the choice of lender or method of repayment. This includes timber-framed houses and older or listed buildings.

(b) The Consumer Credit Act 1974 does not apply to any loan, regardless of size, if it is used to finance house purchase. However, the Act is applicable in all other cases of loans of £15,000 or less, except where the loan is required for property improvements or repairs and there is an existing mortgage which was originally taken out with the same lender to buy the property.

(c) All lenders are required to show the annual percentage rate (APR) of interest in all advertisements and personal quotations. This rate is calculated according to a statutory formula and is designed to show in a single figure all of the different elements of the cost of a mortgage. It is therefore important to compare APRs rather than the quoted interest rates when considering a mortgage, as this is likely to provide a more reliable indication of the total costs involved.

(d) It is often possible to arrange a remortgage. This can then be used to repay an existing mortgage and provide additional capital for home improvements, perhaps at a lower interest rate. However, the amount used for purposes other than repaying the existing mortgage might be treated as a further advance and consequently may attract a higher rate of interest. Some building societies charge a higher rate of interest on the entire amount of the remortgage.

(e) If an individual has financial problems in meeting his mortgage repayments, it is generally advisable to inform the lender as soon as possible. Very often, a temporary arrangement can be made to assist the borrower over a difficult period.

13:7   Mortgage variations

The following are types of mortgage which have been recently developed and are generally variations of those previously mentioned

(a) A fixed interest mortgage can be arranged where the rate of interest charged remains constant for the first few years of the mortgage term, regardless of movements in the general level of interest rates. This type of mortgage can be suitable where a borrower considers that interest rates are likely to rise on average over the term for which the rate of interest is fixed or requires certainty of the level of monthly payments.

(b) Low start or deferred payment mortgages provide for deferment of part of the interest or capital payments in the early years, the payments rising either in steps or at the end of an agreed period. Unpaid interest is added to the debt so that the overall cost will be higher. Another form of low start mortgage involves an endowment or low-cost endowment policy on which the premiums rise in steps over a five-year period. This type of scheme is now rare.

(c) LIBOR mortgages have their interest rate linked to the London Inter-Bank Offered Rate for three-month loans between the major banks. Due to the short-term nature of the rate, the interest on the mortgage is likely to fluctuate more than with a building society loan, although, in most cases, interest is only adjusted quarterly.

(d) Discounted mortgage rates are offered by a number of banks and building societies. The discount usually runs for between one and five years and is relative to the provider's normal variable rate. These rates are offered to attract new borrowers or remortgage business and can offer very competitive short-term rates.

With many discounted rate mortgages, there is a redemption period which may extend several years beyond the discounted period. This effectively ties the borrower into the provider's standard variable rate for a number of years because if the loan is repaid before the end of the redemption period, a penalty (often substantial) will be charged.

(e) Another method used by providers to attract new business is to offer a 'cash-back' lump sum to the borrower when the mortgage is first taken out. As with discounted rate mortgages, there will usually be a redemption period to prevent the borrower repaying the mortgage for a number of years without a substantial penalty.

(f) 'Caps' and 'Collars' limit the borrower's exposure to mortgage rate movements. With a cap, the mortgage rate cannot move higher than the capped level during the period to which the cap applies. With a collar, there is a limit below which the rate cannot fall, as well as an upper limit.

The lower limit is clearly of no direct benefit to the borrower but may enable the lender to provide a more attractive upper limit by sharing some of the benefit of a fall in rates with the borrower.

(g) Unit-linked mortgages are endowment-based, but instead of being on a with-profits basis, growth in the policy is linked to the performance of one or more selected investment funds (see **Chapter 10**). The policy is reviewed at intervals to check the performance of the fund. If it falls short of the value deemed necessary to produce the required amount, the level of premiums will be increased. However, in this case, care must be exercised to avoid the policy becoming non-qualifying, otherwise a tax charge may arise when the proceeds are received.

(h) Unit trust mortgages provide for repayment through the accumulation of units in a regular unit trust savings plan (see **Chapter 3**). Interest only is paid on the loan during the mortgage term, together with monthly contributions to the regular savings plan. The plan will be reviewed at intervals to check that the savings rate is adequate, or to release capital if the performance of the underlying funds is greater than that assumed at the time the mortgage was arranged. This type of mortgage should only be considered if borrowers are already taking advantage of their full ISA allowance. OEICs or investment trusts could be used in a similar way.

(i) Foreign currency mortgages are simply loans in a foreign currency such as Swiss francs or euros. Interest is payable at the rate applicable to that currency. Such loans are often superficially appealing, as interest rates in many countries are lower than those in the UK. This usually reflects the fact that their currencies are regarded as stronger than sterling and the risk of currency loss should not be overlooked. The exchange rate between the selected currency and the pound sterling will vary, so that the sterling value of the debt will increase if the pound weakens, and vice versa. The sterling value of the interest payments will also vary to the same extent.

In view of the possibility that adverse currency movements could dramatically increase the size of the mortgage, these loans are only for the most sophisticated investor. This type of mortgage could be of use to borrowers whose earnings are not in sterling, and who will be able to borrow in that currency to hedge their position against adverse fluctuations.

A further variation of this form of lending is the managed currency loan, which represents a basket of currencies. As a result, the risk from exchange rate fluctuations in a single currency is reduced.

It should be remembered that unit-linked, unit trust, ISA and foreign currency mortgages carry a greater risk that the capital accumulated at the end of the mortgage term may not be sufficient to repay the loan. However, if the underlying investments perform well, then either the overall cost will be less or the return at the end of the mortgage term will be greater than originally projected.

13:8   Raising income from the home

Various schemes are available to help older homeowners to raise capital or generate income through the mortgage or deferred sale of their property. The development of these schemes reflects the plight in which some elderly homeowners find themselves, having little by way of realisable assets and inadequate income. In many cases, their largest asset is their house, the real value of which can only be unlocked by the upheaval and cost of a move to less expensive property, with any balance of the sale proceeds being invested to generate income. These schemes enable elderly homeowners to continue to live in their homes, whilst realising at least a proportion of the value, which can be used to generate income.

Apart from raising capital or generating income, these schemes can often be advantageous in inheritance tax planning. This is because the mortgage or deferred sale causes a reduction in the estate.

Whether or not it is worthwhile to arrange one of these schemes can only be decided after all circumstances have been considered. These will include the health and age of the person or couple, whether there are any close relatives and whether other resources are available. In any event, before an arrangement is made, professional advice should be obtained on both the financial and legal consequences.

13:8.1   Home income plans

The basis of these schemes is for the homeowner to be granted a mortgage on their home and the loan used to purchase an annuity. This will provide a monthly income for the remainder of their life or, in the case of married couples, until the death of the survivor. At that time, the mortgage will be repaid either from the sale proceeds of the property or other sources. Consequently, the benefit of any capital appreciation on the home will be retained.

Before income payments are made to the homeowner, two deductions are normally made. These are interest payments on the mortgage and lower rate tax on the income element of the annuity. The operation of these schemes is considerably simplified when the MIRAS system applies, as the deduction for mortgage interest is made net of basic rate tax.

In order to obtain tax relief on interest on loans up to £30,000 arranged under a home income plan, the following conditions must be satisfied

(a) the loan must have been made before 9 March 1999;

(b) the homeowner must have attained the age of 65 or, in the case of a joint scheme, both annuitants must have reached a combined age of 140;

(c) a minimum of 90% of the loan must be applied to purchase an annuity, only the remaining 10% being retained by the borrower;

(d) the loan must be secured on property in the UK or Eire;

(e) the property on which the loan is secured must be the only or main residence at the time the interest is paid.

The rate of income tax relief on the interest paid was not reduced, and then abolished, as was relief on mortgages to purchase a main residence. It was given at the basic rate from 6 April 1991 to 5 April 2000 and, when the basic rate was set at 22% for 2000/01, it continued at 23%. The income element of the annuity is normally paid after deduction of lower rate tax. However, it is possible for a non-taxpayer to arrange for the annuity payments to be paid gross without this deduction being made.

There are other considerations to be taken into account

(a) The home must be a freehold or long leasehold, have no tenancies and be in reasonable condition.

(b) It is preferable for the property to be free of all mortgages. Consequently, any existing mortgages should be repaid before a home income plan is arranged.

(c) Like the annuity, the loan interest rate is normally fixed, with the result that the homeowner will usually know the amount of income which will be provided by the plan throughout their lifetime, subject to changes in tax rates and allowances.

(d) Apart from any contribution made by the company offering the home income plan, the homeowner is responsible for the legal and valuation costs involved in arranging the scheme.

The income produced by arranging a home income plan will mainly depend on the following factors

(a) the amount of the annuity purchased;

(b) the age of the homeowner when the plan is taken out (the older the person or persons concerned, the greater will be the annuity);

(c) the tax position of the homeowner;

(d) whether the annuity is arranged on a single life or joint life basis;

(e) the level of interest rates at the time the plan is effected;

(f) whether the whole amount of the loan is used to purchase an annuity or whether a part is taken in cash;

(g) whether the annuity is taken out on a capital-protected basis in order to reduce the loss in the event of early death.

The following example shows the increase in net spendable income that can be obtained by arranging a home income plan

Example 16

A woman aged 75 obtains a mortgage of £30,000 (50% on a house valued at £60,000) with an interest rate of 8.25%. No cash is being taken, and the annuity is on a non-capital protected basis

Income tax rate	Nil %	23%	40%
	£	£	£
Annual gross annuity	3,413	3,413	3,413
Less: lower rate tax on income element	–	223	223
Net annuity	3,413	3,190	3,190
Less: mortgage interest	2,475	2,475	2,475
Less: higher rate tax on income element of annuity	–	–	223
Increase in net spendable income	£938	£715	£492

The combination of the removal of tax relief for new plans, a relatively high interest rate and low annuity rates has made this type of contract much less beneficial than in the past. A better return than that shown in the example may be obtained by agreeing to surrender a percentage of the future appreciation of the property's value in exchange for a lower interest rate on the loan.

Before making a final decision to proceed with a home income plan, the following matters should be borne in mind

(a) Where there are no capital resources other than the home itself, it will be necessary for the property to be sold on the death of the individual (or individuals, in the case of a joint life plan) in order for the outstanding loan to be repaid. Therefore, the home cannot be left to children or other dependants.

(b) Once the contract has been established, there is no scope for an individual to change his mind and encash the annuity.

(c) When the individual dies, the annuity ceases. Consequently, if death occurs immediately after effecting the contract, the beneficiaries are just left with an outstanding loan and no compensating benefit. As a result, a home income plan is not normally suitable for those in poor health. Despite this, if the homeowner is prepared to receive a lower net income, they can choose a capital-protected annuity so that, in the event of early death, some of its cost is repaid.

(d) The annuity payments can affect eligibility for means-tested benefits, such as housing benefit and income support (age allowance, however, is not reduced as the interest paid on the mortgage will exceed the taxable income received).

Consequently, the advantage of increased income from a home income plan can partially be lost by a reduction in other benefits.

13:8.2 Home reversion schemes

A further method for a homeowner to raise capital from their home is to enter into a reversion scheme. Under these contracts, the property is sold for approximately half its value, depending on the age and sex of the person concerned, with the homeowner normally being allowed to live in the home at no cost for the remainder of his or her life. The property then reverts to the buyer on the death of the occupant (or occupants). Usually, it is required that the capital raised be invested in an annuity for life, either on a single or joint life basis. A major disadvantage of these schemes is that the homeowner loses the benefit of any future capital appreciation on the home.

Variations on the home reversion scheme include

● instalment reversion, where the property is sold in stages over a ten-year period;

● a 50% reversion where the owner retains a half-share in the equity of the property.

As with home income plans, the annuity payments can affect eligibility for means-tested benefits but, in addition, may affect age allowance.

13:9　Other factors

Some lenders offer roll-up plans to elderly homeowners, where loans are made without interest or capital repayments being needed. Interest is rolled up and added to the loan, with the final debt being satisfied by the sale of the property on the death of the occupant (or occupants). As interest is chargeable on both the capital and accrued interest, the debt can escalate rapidly, outpacing the increase in value of the house and leaving the borrower vulnerable. Consequently, these schemes should be regarded with great caution.

There is no question that home income plans properly used have a valuable role to play in financial planning for the elderly. Potential borrowers should restrict themselves to plans offered by SHIP (Safe Home Income Plans), an association of the leading companies in this market.

14 Providing for school fees

Next to purchasing a house, the cost of educating children privately is likely to be a family's largest financial commitment. Fees at an independent school can currently be as much as £13,000 per annum for one child, with further expenses for other activities. In many cases, provision for the costs of university education is a growing concern, and references to 'school fees' in this chapter will apply equally to university costs.

There is no magic formula in providing for school fees. The most successful planning is a combination of early recognition and careful identification of the most practical and cost-effective method. Each case must be considered individually, with the purpose of making the necessary monies available on the required dates in order to pay the fees. School fees provision is therefore very much an investment problem, but with due regard being given to the taxation consequences of any plan and the commitment being undertaken.

Before a school fees scheme can be properly considered, the individual's asset and income position should be assessed, together with the overall situation.

14:1 Assessing the situation

Before embarking on private education, a proper evaluation should be undertaken to decide whether this is possible at all. A detailed schedule should be produced to show the estimated funds required to pay the school fees, together with the dates when they fall due, with allowance being made for extras and future increases (these usually exceed the rate of retail price inflation). After this schedule has been prepared, it will be necessary to consider the possible sources of funds from which the school fees can be paid. These sources may be broadly classified as

(a) capital;

(b) income; and

(c) other (such as grandparents' gifts).

In practice, it will often be necessary to draw upon more than one source to provide the funds required.

If a decision is then taken to educate a child privately, the following matters should be considered before a school fees scheme is implemented

(a) the choice of school;

(b) the possibility of the child not attending the chosen school or any other private school;

(c) whether the child will be a day pupil or a boarder;

(d) the possibility of the child changing to a different school mid-stream;

(e) the possible death or incapacity of the child;

(f) possible increases in costs due to inflation or government action;

(g) the possibility of the abolition of private education;

(h) a deterioration in the parents' financial circumstances;

(i) the possible death of the parents;

(j) the availability of scholarships and bursaries;

(k) possible special needs if the child is gifted (academically or artistically) or handicapped; and

(l) eligibility for grants and allowances.

If it is intended that the child will attend university or other further education, provision should also be made for parental contributions to tuition fees and to augment student maintenance grants to cover living costs during term-time (the annual contribution payable would mainly depend on where the student lives and the income of the parents, unless the student is classed as independent). The student loan scheme is an additional source of finance, but leaves the student in debt at the conclusion of his or her course. Further education is likely to prove increasingly costly for the family from now on. Many students get no grant at all.

14:2   Funding from capital

Apart from paying school fees directly out of capital as and when they fall due, the following are the five principal methods by which capital can be applied for school fees purposes

(a) investment portfolios;

(b) family trusts;

(c) school fees composition schemes;

(d) educational trusts;

(e) back-to-back arrangements; and

(f) loan arrangements.

14:2.1 Investment portfolios

Establishing an investment portfolio, using unit and investment trusts, personal equity plans, government stocks, the zero dividend preference shares of investment trusts, National Savings products, investment bonds and/or building society accounts, is often the easiest, and certainly the most flexible, way of providing for school fees from capital. This approach has the following advantages

(a) maximum advantage can be taken of all tax-efficient investment opportunities;

(b) the funds can be used for other purposes, if necessary, without penalty;

(c) the funds need only be realised when there is a shortfall in the income providing the fees.

A single premium investment bond may in some circumstances be an appropriate vehicle. For a higher rate taxpayer, the facility to withdraw 5% per annum of the initial premium, with no immediate charge to income tax, may be attractive. This fixed limit may, however, be exceeded in time by the amount of the fees, which are likely to increase each year. For larger withdrawals, a multi-segmented policy would enable an appropriate number of segments to be encashed each year. This would avoid the problems which can arise from partial withdrawals and a basic rate taxpayer would have no additional income tax liability, unless the gain on the bond took his total income for the year over the threshold for higher rate tax (see **3:13.1**).

14:2.2 Family trusts

If the student or one of his parents is a beneficiary of a family trust, it may be appropriate for the trustees to release capital or income to assist with the payment of the student's educational fees. The trustees should consider the tax and legal implications of such a distribution, particularly if the trust is located offshore.

If the family's finances permit, it may be particularly beneficial for grandparents to create an accumulation and maintenance settlement (see **Chapter 16**) with a view to providing for their grandchildren's educational costs. The transfer of assets into the trust is a potentially exempt transfer which will reduce the settlors' estates (although not completely for seven years) and bypass the parents' estates. When income is applied for a child's benefit, the child will, if his or her gross taxable income is less than the personal allowance, be able to reclaim some or all of the income tax paid by the trustees.

Grandparents may, alternatively, place assets in a bare trust for the student, perhaps administered by the parents. Again, the child may be able to reclaim income tax deducted at source; preferably investments should be made in assets which pay income gross.

14:2.3   School fees composition schemes

School fees composition schemes are essentially deferred annuity contracts, allowing a lump sum to be paid in advance at a discount to the total fees to be funded. The following are the main characteristics of school fees composition schemes

(a) The terms which the school will offer largely depend on the length of time before the fees become due and interest rates prevailing when the lump sum is paid.

(b) As the school has the status of an educational charity, the scheme is particularly attractive to a higher rate taxpayer, since there would be no liability to either income or capital gains tax on the investment of the lump sum by the school. Furthermore, if the lump sum is paid by a parent or guardian and a trust is declared under section 11 of the Inheritance Tax Act 1984, this is exempt from inheritance tax. A section 11 trust enables parents and (in restricted circumstances) other donors to make dispositions for the education, maintenance or training of a child, without liability to inheritance tax. The practical implications of declaring a section 11 trust are considered in **14:2.4**.

However, if the payment was made by a person not covered by the restrictions, a chargeable transfer arises, although this may be within their annual or other inheritance tax exemptions or the nil rate band (£234,000 for 2000/01).

(c) One of the main advantages of school fees composition schemes is that they are simple and convenient. Against this, a major disadvantage is that they are often inflexible. The following matters, which may be open to negotiation, should be investigated before a scheme is arranged to see what would happen if

(i)   the child does not attend the school (normally, a repayment is made, but on unattractive terms);

(ii)   the child leaves the school or dies before completing his education;

(iii)   the tax advantages relating to educational charities are abolished.

(d) The competitiveness of a school fees composition scheme will depend, to a large extent, on the rates offered at the particular time. Consequently, a quotation specifying individual requirements should be obtained and the investment return in percentage terms compared with possible alternatives.

(e) It should be noted that a payment to a school fees composition scheme does not necessarily guarantee a place at the chosen school.

14:2.4   Educational trusts

Educational trusts are effectively independent versions of the fees composition schemes operated by schools and therefore many of the above comments will also generally apply to educational trusts. Until 1997, such trusts had charitable status, but following a review by the Charity Commission, only trusts then in existence continue to enjoy this benefit, provided they are not significantly amended. All new trusts are subject to tax on their income and gains, with the result that these vehicles are no longer available in their previous form.

As far as the basic operation is concerned, it was the trust rather than the school which purchased the annuity from an insurance company. The annuity instalments are made payable to the school by the trust and sent via the parents or donors (with a top-up payment by the parents if necessary) to meet the school fees for the child concerned (these payments are provided on a level basis or increase each year at a fixed rate to allow for fee inflation).

The following are some of the more important practical differences between school fees composition schemes and educational trusts

(a) Although school fees plans arranged through educational trusts still lack complete flexibility, this is less so than with composition schemes due to the factors listed below

(i)   The school to which the fees are to be paid need not be nominated until shortly (normally about one month) before the first payment becomes due. As a result, the problem of the child not attending a school previously nominated is largely overcome. Payments can also be switched easily from one school to another.

(ii)   There is usually a facility to switch funds from the benefit of one child to another, subject to there being at least one other child undergoing private education.

(iii) If the child should die before the termination of the school fees plan, the amount paid into the plan, less any school fee payments already made, is usually guaranteed to be repaid under the trust deed. However, although the repayment is generally made with interest, this interest is normally below market rates.

(iv)   It is possible to surrender plans, unless a section 11 trust has been established. Different providers have various formulae for calculating surrender values. The income tax consequences of surrender must also be considered.

(b) The inheritance tax position of school fees plans using educational trusts may also be different from school fees composition schemes and will depend on whether the lump sum payment is made by the parent, and, if so, whether he or she declares a section 11 trust, and also on whether the right to surrender the plan is retained.

If payment was made by a parent or guardian who does not wish to use their annual exemptions for school fees purposes, they could declare a section 11 trust, in which case the payment would be exempt for inheritance tax purposes. However, under the trust, the benefits of the plan are held for a specified child and consequently cannot be used for another child or returned for the parent's own use. Therefore, even where the right to surrender the plan has been retained, the amount payable on surrender would be required under the terms of the trust to be applied for the education, maintenance or training of the child concerned.

If a section 11 trust is not declared, the payments arising under the plan can normally be used for the benefit of a different child, providing sufficient notice is given (usually a minimum of one month).

In the case of any payer other than a parent or guardian, a chargeable transfer of value for inheritance tax will arise. If the right of surrender was waived at the outset, the liability would arise at the start of the plan. However, if the right to surrender was retained, the chargeable transfer would not be deemed to arise until the first term's payment of school fees is made (the amount of the transfer would be equivalent to the surrender value of the plan at that time).

Where a donor gives the money unconditionally to the parent, who then takes out the plan as bare trustee for the child, the gift would be treated as a potentially exempt transfer.

14:2.5 Back-to-back arrangements

Capital may be applied to purchase a temporary annuity or other suitable funding medium which will provide the required premiums for appropriate life assurance policies. The maturity proceeds from the life policies can then be used to pay the school fees.

14:3 Funding from income

Unless the school fees are paid directly out of net income as they fall due, it will usually be necessary for the payments to be spread over a period longer than the period of education. It is therefore worthwhile, wherever practicable, for appropriate action to be taken at the earliest possible date, not only to prevent the payment period extending beyond the time the child leaves school or university, but also to minimise the cost involved.

Consideration should also be given to the position should the provider's main source of income cease. This could arise if he or she was to die early, become disabled or be made redundant. Adequate life assurance and permanent health insurance should always be in place to cover the first two eventualities.

The following are the principal methods of funding school fees out of income

(a) life assurance schemes;

(b) unit trust, OEIC and investment trust regular savings plans;

(c) a series of individual savings accounts; and

(d) deferred annuities through an educational trust.

14:3.1 Life assurance schemes

Although there are several different types of qualifying life assurance policies available, they all enable the proceeds to be received with no personal liability to income tax and capital gains tax provided that premiums are payable for a minimum period of ten years (or three quarters of the term, if less, in the case of an endowment-type policy). Accordingly, where premiums are started in sufficient time for them to be paid for this period before the school fees commence, the policies outlined below would normally be most suitable

(a) A series of with-profits endowment policies maturing in successive years over the period of the child's education at a senior school. This method has the advantage of generally providing a competitive and relatively secure return, particularly for higher rate taxpayers, with scope to receive increasing maturity proceeds each year in order to cover the higher education costs caused by inflation.

(b) Flexible endowment policies where the parent can choose the date when the policy proceeds are received. However, this flexibility does not come without cost and therefore these policies are in general less attractive than the more usual with-profits endowment policies.

(c) Unit-linked policies (such as maximum investment plans) offering a tax-free income facility after ten years. Where a policy is issued for school fees purposes, it is usually expedient that it should be linked to a stable fund rather than to a volatile one.

(d) Friendly society policies (see **Chapter 10:3**).

(e) Non-qualifying life policies, such as five-year endowments, can, for basic rate taxpayers, provide a shorter-term alternative to qualifying endowments.

If there are any existing life assurance policies, it is possible that these could also be used for school fees provision.

Using life policies as a method of providing for school fees offers a number of advantages

(a) The regular premiums are spread over a long period.

(b) If circumstances change, the policy proceeds can be applied for other purposes without any penalty being suffered.

(c) The death benefits provided would normally be available to pay the school fees should the parents die prematurely.

(d) The policyholder can borrow against the policy once it has acquired a surrender value.

The recent trend towards weighting with-profits bonuses more in favour of longer term policies has made the returns on the 10–15 year policies suitable for school fees planning less attractive. The greater emphasis on terminal bonuses also means that the maturity values are less predictable than in the past.

14:3.2   Unit trust, OEIC and investment trust regular savings plans

These plans, which were considered in **Chapter 3:20**, represent direct investments into unit trusts, OEICs and investment trusts on a regular (usually monthly) basis. They have many of the characteristics of unit-linked life policies investing in equities, although the taxation position is different. As no life cover is provided, consideration should be given to effecting a separate term assurance policy in order to safeguard the future provision of fees in the event of the early death of the parents.

Unit trust, OEIC and investment trust savings plans provide even greater flexibility than unit-linked life policies and may be terminated at any time without penalty. This is particularly important for parents whose disposable income fluctuates. Such plans are also likely, in many cases, to produce results superior to those of a life policy investing in the same fund (see **Chapter 10**). It is generally desirable for the savings plan to be linked to a broadly based fund rather than to a more volatile one to reduce the risk of the plan having a low value at the time the proceeds are required to pay the school fees. Index-tracking trusts may be particularly appropriate.

Capital gains tax may arise on the sale of the units or investment trust shares, although, if these are being sold gradually, they will usually fall within the annual capital gains tax exemption unless substantial funds are realised. If the holdings are in the names of both parents, then both their annual exemptions will be available.

14:3.3   A series of individual savings accounts

As stated in **Chapter 4**, a UK resident aged 18 or over may invest up to £5,000 per tax year (£7,000 in 1999/2000 and 2000/01) into an individual savings account. Like unit-linked life policies and unit trust, OEIC and investment trust regular savings plans, the choice of underlying investments should be conservative, to reduce the risk of the ISA having a low value at the time the school fees become due. A separate term assurance policy should be considered, as life cover is not provided by the ISA.

A series of ISAs is a very tax-efficient method of providing for school fees, since there is no tax to pay either on capital gains or on dividend income. Consequently, if an individual decides to arrange a unit trust, OEIC or investment trust regular savings plan, this is likely to be more advantageous within, rather than outside, an ISA. However, as previously mentioned, any account should be regarded as a medium- to long-term investment.

14:4   Funding from loan arrangements

There are several methods by which borrowings can be made to pay for school fees, but the interest on the loan is not allowed as an expense for tax purposes. This course may be the only one available where earlier planning was not possible, but the cost of the interest can increase the overall cost considerably.

The following ways of raising funds may be particularly suitable in appropriate circumstances

(a) a parent who owns their own business may be able to increase their drawings and then arrange a loan to replenish working capital, so tax relief is then obtained indirectly on the amounts withdrawn to meet the school fees;

(b) if the parent cannot afford the cost of both personal pension contributions and school fees, it may be worthwhile to pay the contributions and then arrange a loan under the pension policy, so tax relief would effectively be allowed on the premiums against the parent's highest income tax rates, even though relief would not be obtained on the loan interest paid;

(c) if the parent lives in a house with no mortgage or only a relatively small mortgage, it may be possible to obtain a larger mortgage, either by moving house, or remortgaging, or under an 'equity release' scheme offered by some banks. Again, no tax relief would be given on the interest paid and provision would have to be made to repay the loan at some future date;

(d) where there is insufficient time for premiums to be paid to a life assurance policy for the minimum qualifying period before the school fees fall due, it may be worthwhile to obtain loans from the insurance company against the surrender value of the policy in order to pay the school fees. The loans are then repaid out of the policy proceeds at maturity. It is therefore important at outset to obtain a positive commitment from the insurance company that loans will be available together with the relevant terms and conditions. The rate of interest on policy loans is often lower than a bank would charge.

14:5   Funding for university costs

With the phasing out of maintenance grants and the introduction of parental contributions to tuition fees, the need to provide for the costs of a student's three or four years at university affects a growing number of parents. The costs will vary considerably, but an annual budget could be around £6,500. This can partly be financed by a student loan, which carries a low rate of interest and is repayable only when the student starts earning a reasonable income.

Where parents are funding a minor child's education, the planning should take into account the fact that, if the child's income from parental gifts exceeds £100 a year, that income is aggregated with the parents'. This does not apply once the child reaches 18, however, so that the capital from parental gifts can be invested to produce an income after that age which will be taxable on the child and, in all probability, covered by his or her personal allowance. (Many students these days do, however, have part-time jobs, and the amount of their earnings must be taken into account.)

One investment where the tax treatment is beneficial for this situation is the offshore roll-up fund (see **2:3.4**). If investments are made for the benefit of the child during his minority, no income tax is payable on the accumulated income. Gains ('offshore income gains') realised on encashments after the child reaches 18 will be subject to income tax but can be arranged so as to be covered by the child's personal allowance and thus be tax-free.

The child will also have the use of his own annual exemption for capital gains tax to cover gains realised from capital growth investments.

14:6   Conclusion

For many parents, considerable sacrifices will have to be made in order to send their children to private schools. These sacrifices, however, can often be mitigated by making the best use of the facilities that exist in the circumstances. In particular, it should be remembered that

(a) while the best results are generally achieved by early action, taken as soon as possible after the child is born, even a late contribution is usually worthwhile;

(b) a well designed scheme will have a considerable amount of in-built flexibility – this is of the utmost importance in view of the uncertainties that may lie ahead.

15 Wills

15:1 Intestacy

Although many people delay making a will, the consequences of this can be very serious. If a person dies without having made a will, their estate will be distributed according to the laws of intestacy (see **Appendix 4**), subject to any post-death variation. The main disadvantages of dying intestate are listed below

(a) The estate may not necessarily be distributed in accordance with the individual's wishes. In particular, the surviving spouse is likely to be disadvantaged; if there are children the widow(er)'s entitlement is limited.

(b) The appointed administrators may not be those whom the individual would have chosen.

(c) It may take longer for the estate to be distributed. When a will has been made, an executor can take up his duties immediately after death occurs.

(d) The costs may be greater.

(e) There may be an unnecessary inheritance tax liability.

(f) Children will receive capital automatically at the age of 18; it may be the individual's wish that capital should be paid at a later age. Furthermore, assets such as the family home may have to be sold in order to raise the capital.

(g) A testamentary guardian is not appointed for young children.

(h) Trusts may arise under an intestacy which can produce complications, including statutory restrictions on the trustees' power to invest and advance capital. These restraints might be particularly onerous where the estate wishes to hold shares in private companies.

15:2 The need for professional advice

In order to avoid the danger of having a will which is uncertain as to the intentions of the testator, or having a will which proves to be invalid, it is essential that its wording should be clear and precise and that the wording and execution of the will should conform with various formalities. Consequently, it is generally advisable that the will should be drawn up by a solicitor and that other professional advice obtained where appropriate, for example, to minimise inheritance tax. In this way, the following common mistakes should be avoided

(a) failure to dispose of all the estate, resulting in partial intestacy;

(b) specific gifts that are free of tax could dissolve the residuary estate unintentionally;

(c) uncertainty as to where the burden of tax should lie where the residuary estate is left to a tax-exempt beneficiary (such as a UK spouse) and a non-exempt beneficiary (such as a child) in equal shares;

(d) gifts being made to witnesses or their spouses (as a general rule, these are legally ineffective and therefore the person concerned would not be able to receive his or her legacy);

(e) alterations being made to the will at or before the time it is signed without being sufficiently authenticated and therefore having uncertain validity;

(f) no consideration being given to the possibility of a beneficiary dying before the testator or not surviving long enough to enjoy any real benefit;

(g) failure to consider the effects of the testator's divorce and/or remarriage;

(h) being unaware of the rights of certain family members and dependants to make a claim against the estate if reasonable financial provision has not been made for them;

(i) failure to appreciate that the word 'children' includes legitimate, illegitimate and adopted children but not normally stepchildren.

15:3   Important matters before drawing up a will

The following are some important matters which should be attended to before a will is drawn up

(a) Consideration should be given to the disposal of the body on death, including bequests for scientific research.

(b) Agreement should be obtained from the persons to act as executors and trustees.

(c) If there are young children, consideration should be given to the appointment of a guardian (and his or her consent obtained) to cover the event of the testator's early death. This is particularly important if only one parent is still alive.

(d) An estimate must be made of the value of the estate by calculating the market value of assets and deducting any liabilities. A list of these assets would also be desirable. (**Appendix 5** is a detailed 'dying tidily' log which should be completed and filed with the individual's private papers.)

(e) A list of the persons (including charities) to benefit under the will should be compiled, showing any particular assets to be passed to specific beneficiaries.

(f) Trust provisions, including the powers given to the trustees, should be specified.

(g) Consideration should be given as to whom the assets should pass if a beneficiary dies before the testator.

(h) Where a testator owns property overseas, in general it is preferable that this should be dealt with by a will drawn up under the terms of the local law. Care is required that it should not inadvertently be revoked when making a new UK will and that the provisions are consistent.

15:4   Executors

The responsibility of an executor is to collect in the estate of the deceased and deal with the distribution of the estate according to law. This can involve arranging the funeral and generally taking over the deceased's affairs, including being responsible for the payment of all taxes due in respect of the estate. In order to preserve the estate, the executor should consider taking immediate possession of any valuables in order to secure their safety and should arrange insurance where appropriate. Although an executor's responsibility commences from the time the deceased dies, it will still be necessary for the will to be proved and the appointment confirmed by a grant of probate.

The choice of an executor, who may also be a beneficiary, is very important as a considerable amount of work and responsibility may be involved. The following matters should be borne in mind before an appointment is made

(a) It is often advantageous for co-executors to act, such as the spouse (or if not alive, a friend or relative), together with a person in professional practice, such as an accountant or solicitor.

(b) An executor should preferably be younger than the testator, though a minor cannot obtain probate.

(c) It is often worthwhile to include a substitute executor, in the event of the appointed executor dying before the testator or being unwilling or unable to act.

(d) If the will includes a trust, it will usually be expedient for the trustees to be the same as the executors. A testator should endeavour to ensure that the executors know his or her wishes and can be relied upon to carry them out.

(e) The will can be written so that the final decision over the distribution of some or all of the estate is postponed until after death. The executors can then make a decision as to how to distribute that property based on all the circumstances. This can be achieved by including what are known as discretionary trust provisions in the will. This will only be suitable if a testator is confident of the executors' judgement.

15:5 Variations and disclaimers

At the present time, a beneficiary can tax-efficiently redirect certain property to another person within two years of the deceased's death. This is effected by means of a written variation, with an election being made to the Inspector of Taxes for capital gains tax purposes or the Capital Taxes Office for inheritance tax purposes within six months of the date of the variation. A beneficiary can also, within the same two year period, disclaim an inheritance, which has not previously been accepted.

Variation of a will can be particularly appropriate where a deceased may for instance have gifted the entire estate to his widow without having made use of the inheritance tax nil rate band, or where the beneficiary does not wish to receive the inheritance. A variation is also possible under an intestacy.

While similar in many respects to a variation, a disclaimer has several important differences, which are set out below

(a) Under a disclaimer, the beneficiary can merely disclaim or waive their entitlement without making any election to the Inspector of Taxes or Capital Taxes Office.

(b) The terms of the will or intestacy should be examined in order to discover who benefits in lieu, whereas, in the case of a variation, the assets can pass as agreed; for example, a widow who has benefited under her husband's will can effectively rewrite it to benefit the children.

(c) A disclaimer will normally relate to the whole gift, whereas a variation can be made either in respect of the whole or only part of it.

(d) In the case of a disclaimer, the beneficiary must not have received any previous benefit from the gift, such as receipt of income.

Variations and disclaimers can be very helpful in both capital gains tax and inheritance tax planning, mainly due to changing circumstances, especially tax, and the testator not always being aware of the wishes of the various beneficiaries. However, their use would arise less often if wills were properly prepared at the outset. They should also not be regarded as a substitute for proper estate planning. Infants cannot consent to a variation; if the will has made gifts to infants, a variation may not be possible or its effect may be limited.

One further point is that a variation must genuinely vary the inheritance made under the will. For example, if on a father's death his entire estate passes to the children who, by variation, re-route their inheritance to their mother, the mother could subsequently make a potentially exempt transfer of the property back to her children. In such a case, the Inspector of Taxes and/or Capital Taxes Office will enquire as to whether the variation was genuine or artificial.

15:6   Other matters

The following are other matters relating to wills which should be borne in mind

(a) The will should be kept in a safe place, such as in a bank or with a solicitor or accountant, and the executors advised of its location.

(b) Marriage (or remarriage) will automatically revoke a will unless it states that it was made in expectation of that particular marriage.

(c) Divorce (decree absolute) or annulment of marriage (unless the will states otherwise) automatically disinherits the spouse from receiving any defined interest under the will and prevents the spouse from acting as an executor or trustee of the will. The will takes effect as if the spouse died on the divorce or annulment.

(d) The will should be reviewed at regular intervals (say, not less than every five years) in order to take into account changes in the testator's circumstances and in tax legislation.

(e) If a person wishes to alter their will, this is usually possible by way of a codicil. However, in almost all cases it is preferable for a new will to be made which reflects the required changes.

Note

This chapter has been written based on the law in England and Wales. It must be remembered that the position may be different in Scotland and Northern Ireland.

16   Trusts

Trusts, in various forms, have been in existence for centuries. However, their concept is strange to many people and their uses, particularly following recent changes in tax legislation, are not widely appreciated. The principal purpose of this chapter is to discuss some of the terms of English trust law, the differences between the various types of trust, and the uses to which the more common forms of trust can be put.

16:1   What is a trust?

A trust is a separate legal entity, usually set up with a formal document or under a will. Trusts are often referred to as 'settlements' and for all practical purposes the two words are interchangeable. There are five main constituents of a trust

(a) *the settlor* – the person who sets up the trust, usually by passing assets to the trustees;

(b) *the trustees* – the people (usually two, three or four in number) in whose name the assets are registered and who control them in accordance with the terms of the trust deed;

(c) *the trust deed* – the legal document which instructs the trustees how to administer and distribute the trust fund;

(d) *the trust fund* – the assets of the trust, including the original property given to the trustees, and assets transferred to the trustees subsequently, the capital growth on the assets, and any income retained by the trustees on behalf of the beneficiaries;

(e) *the beneficiaries* – the people, whether specifically named or not (but who must be identifiable with reasonable certainty), who can benefit from the trust fund under the terms of the trust document.

Thus, although the trustees have legal ownership of the trust assets, they have no personal interest in them, unless they are also beneficiaries of the trust. Trusts are used in a wide variety of situations, including charities, employees' pension schemes, life assurance policies and the maintenance of historic buildings. However, this chapter is limited to the use of trusts for the financial benefit of an individual's family, relatives and friends.

243

16:1.1   The settlor

The settlor often wishes to dispose of capital for the benefit of members of his or her family, but for practical reasons, may not wish to give them outright control of the capital. For instance

(a) the settlor might not wish to lose effective control of the capital;

(b) the beneficiaries may be children or young adults;

(c) the settlor may not know specifically whom he or she wants to benefit;

(d) the beneficiaries may not have the experience, time or ability to look after the capital;

(e) the settlor may wish to protect the capital in the event of a bad marriage, a death or a bankruptcy.

The settlor can himself be a beneficiary of a trust, but there are no tax benefits in this case. Indeed, there can be tax disadvantages, particularly in connection with the reservation of benefit rule.

16:1.2   The trustees

Although the trustees have to administer and distribute the trust fund in accordance with the terms of the trust deed, in modern trusts they are usually given very wide discretionary powers. It is therefore important that trustees are chosen carefully. Settlors cannot directly impose their wishes on the trustees, but, in practice, they can strongly influence them by

(a) making themselves a trustee (normally the first-named);

(b) writing a 'letter of wishes' to the trustees at the time of setting up the trust;

(c) reserving the power to appoint new trustees and remove existing trustees.

Although trustees have to act unanimously, where votes on a company's shares are concerned, these are exercisable only by the first-named trustee.

The role of a trustee can sometimes be onerous, particularly in the cases of larger complex trusts or where trustees might have to make difficult choices in dealing with beneficiaries who are close members of the family. For this reason, the appointment of an independent professional trustee can often be advantageous. It is also important to explain the responsibilities involved to a lay trustee before they accept appointment.

16:1.3   The trust deed

Trusts can be set up either during the settlor's lifetime or under the terms of a will on death. Trusts set up during a lifetime are often referred to as 'settlements', those under a will as 'trusts', but these are not set in stone.

It is not essential to have a written trust deed. However, without this, the trustees are extremely limited in the way they can act, and doubts can arise in later years as to what the settlor intended. For maximum flexibility, it is advisable to have a modern form of trust deed drafted by a solicitor who has a good working knowledge of trusts.

Trust deeds tend to be lengthy and are often difficult to understand. Much of the text is of a technical nature and deals with the various powers given to the trustees. As a guide, the legal costs involved in setting up a trust range from £750 to £2,000, depending on complexity and the variations required from standard precedents.

Depending on the type of trust (see below), a good modern trust deed will generally give the trustees wide discretionary powers, including

(a) the extent to which a beneficiary will benefit from the trust, if at all;

(b) the age at which a beneficiary will benefit;

(c) the power to invest the trust fund in any form of investment, whether or not producing income, including the purchase of a house for a beneficiary;

(d) the power to set up subsidiary trusts for beneficiaries;

(e) the power to borrow and lend.

Unless the trustees act fraudulently, they are usually protected from any personal financial liability.

16:1.4   The trust fund

A trust is often set up with a nominal amount of, say £100 and further capital is usually gifted subsequently. The trust fund consists of two elements

- *Capital* – the original and subsequent gifts, plus any growth in the value of the assets.

- *Income* – arising on the capital assets. Except in the case of interest in possession trusts (see below), if income is not distributed to beneficiaries, it is accumulated in the fund, usually by way of a transfer to capital.

As mentioned above, the trustees are usually given extremely wide powers to invest in any form of asset. These can include land, life assurance policies, shares in family companies, paintings and overseas assets. In some cases, there may be restrictions on the particular type of asset in which an investment can be made.

16:1.5 The beneficiaries

Other than in specific types of trust, such as those set up under the Married Women's Property Act 1882, there is no restriction on who can be a beneficiary of a trust. The person does not need to be specifically named in the trust document, but does need to be in a specified class of beneficiary, such as grandchildren. However, in some cases, it is possible to add a beneficiary where he was not originally included. Many trust documents provide for substitution, so that, in the event of a beneficiary dying, his children acquire his interest in the trust fund.

Depending on the type of trust, trustees are often given the maximum flexibility in deciding to what extent, if at all, a beneficiary should benefit from the trust fund, in terms of both annual income and capital.

Where appropriate, children can benefit from trusts from the day they are born, often with significant income and capital gains tax advantages.

16:2 Tax position of trusts

16:2.1 Setting up a trust

Changes in tax legislation have made it extremely cheap, in terms of tax, to set up a trust. It may not be necessary for capital gains tax to be paid on the transfer of certain assets to a trust (see **Chapter 12**) as the trustees would, in these cases, be deemed to acquire the assets at the original cost to the settlor. Stamp duty on gifts has been abolished (apart from a nominal 50p in some cases). The present inheritance tax legislation is comparatively liberal and the exemptions reasonable. In larger cases, where tax liabilities do arise, they are likely to be substantially less than they would ultimately be if no action was taken.

Provided gifts are not deferred until too late in life (at least seven years before death), a husband and wife can dispose of substantial amounts of capital, even more so where business assets are concerned, without paying large amounts of inheritance tax. By the use of trusts, they can often at the same time keep effective control over the assets.

16:2.2 The trust

(a) *Inheritance tax.* The extent to which there is a liability to inheritance tax on creation or during the life of a trust depends upon the particular type of trust (see **16:3** below).

(b) *Income tax.* Generally, when a trust has been created, income which arises from the assets put into trust is treated for all purposes as the income of the trustees. This is completely separate and independent of their own personal tax affairs and those of the settlor. The main exceptions to this rule are where the settlor has included himself or his spouse as a beneficiary, or where income is distributed to the settlor's children while they are under 18 and unmarried. In such cases, the income is treated as that of the settlor for tax purposes.

The tax liability on the income of the trust again depends upon the type of trust. However, where a beneficiary has a right to income, the trust will pay tax at the Schedule F rate (10% in 2000/01) on dividends, at the lower rate (20% in 2000/01) on savings income and at the basic rate (22% in 2000/01) on certain other types of income such as property or trading income. If a beneficiary is liable to tax at the higher rate (40% in 2000/01), he will be responsible personally for the extra tax on the trust income.

If the beneficiary has no right to income, but its amount is determined at the discretion of the trustees, the trust pays tax on its income at a rate broadly equivalent to 34% for 2000/01. However, because the 10% dividend tax credit is not repayable, trustees who distribute all the trust income may have to pay a further amount of tax (see **16:3** below). Where income is distributed, it is deemed to have suffered tax at 34%, and if the beneficiary is personally liable to tax at below 34%, he or she can recover the excess. Thus, a child who does not have any other income can recover the whole of the tax suffered by the trust on the income distributed to them to the extent of the single person's tax allowance (£4,385 in 2000/01). If the beneficiary pays higher rate tax, further tax is payable on the income received.

(c) *Capital gains tax.* Trustees are liable to capital gains tax at 34% on realised gains (less losses), subject to both indexation allowances and/or taper relief and an annual exemption (£3,600 in 2000/01, which in appropriate circumstances may have to be divided between all the settlements made by the same settlor). However, as with the income tax rules, gains made by trustees will be charged to tax upon settlors who retain or give their spouse any interest in the trust. As mentioned earlier in this chapter, it may be possible for a gain arising on the transfer of specific assets into a trust to be deferred. Similarly, it may be possible for a gain arising on specific assets leaving a trust, which are also subject to a tax charge, to be deferred.

16:3   Types of trusts

There are five main types of trust which are described below

(a) interest in possession trusts;

(b) voluntary trusts;

(c) accumulation and maintenance trusts;

(d) discretionary trusts;

(e) bare trusts.

16:3.1   Interest in possession trusts (also known as life interest or fixed interest trusts)

16:3.1.1   *General description*

In broad terms, an 'interest in possession' is defined as a right to receive the income arising from the trust assets. Thus, an interest in possession trust is where the income arising on the trust capital is payable to a named beneficiary, the life tenant, usually for his or her lifetime. The beneficiary may also have the use of the property within the trust if, for example, a house was settled upon trust giving the beneficiary the right to occupy it for life. The capital remains under the trustees' control and, on the death of the life tenant (or early termination of their interest), the capital can pass to other beneficiaries (the remaindermen) as specified in the trust document (or, if the trust document permits, to those nominated by the life tenant).

The trustees are often given a discretionary power to advance capital to the life tenant.

16:3.1.2   *Uses*

Interest in possession trusts are most suited where beneficiaries are over the age of 25 and a settlor does not wish to pass outright ownership of assets to them, but wishes the beneficiaries to enjoy the income generated by the assets. Such trusts are particularly useful where

(a) shares in family companies are involved, since any voting rights remain with the trustees;

(b) the settlor considers the beneficiary might not want the responsibility or be able to look after the capital;

(c) the settlor wishes to protect the capital in the event of, say, a bad marriage or the premature death of a son or daughter;

(d) the settlor wishes to remove an asset from his or her estate and yet does not wish the beneficiary to be entitled to the capital until their (the settlor's) death;

(e) the settlor wishes to create an inheritance tax-free fund payable on death, which can be used by the beneficiaries to pay the inheritance tax due or to replace the inheritance tax paid from the estate.

16:3.1.3   Tax position

(a) *Inheritance tax.* Transfers by an individual into an interest in possession trust qualify as a potentially exempt transfer (PET) and do not attract a charge to inheritance tax, provided that the settlor survives seven years from the time of the transfer. Similarly, on most transfers from interest in possession trusts (such as the life tenant surrendering their interest in favour of another individual), no charge arises if the transferor survives seven years.

On the death of a life tenant, a charge to inheritance tax arises, as the life tenant is deemed to own the underlying trust assets on which they have been receiving income. On such occasion, tax is chargeable at the full rate.

(b) *Income tax.* The trustees pay income tax at the basic rate, either direct to the Inland Revenue (for example, on rental income), or by deduction at source (for example, on interest from government stocks). As with individuals, most savings income is taxed at the 20% lower rate. Dividends are taxed at the 10% Schedule F ordinary rate. After deducting expenses (which are set off in the first instance against the income with the lowest tax credits), the trust income is added to the beneficiary's other income and, if liable to the higher rate of tax, the beneficiary pays the extra tax. If the beneficiary does not have sufficient income to cover his or her personal tax allowance, a tax repayment can be obtained.

(c) *Capital gains tax.* Capital gains are taxed at 34%, after the deduction of the appropriate annual exemption (see **16:2.2(c)**).

16:3.2   Voluntary trusts

16:3.2.1   General description

This is any trust made without consideration, including a trust which an individual makes for his or her own benefit by transferring assets to trustees, who then pay the income to the settlor during his or her lifetime, with the capital remaining in trust, normally for the settlor's children.

16:3.2.2   Uses

Voluntary trusts are used when the individual wishes to protect himself from wasting their own capital or where they do not want the responsibility of managing it. Voluntary trusts can be particularly useful if the settlor is non-resident for a period.

16:3.2.3   Tax position

There are no tax advantages during the lifetime of such trusts. Although no inheritance tax liability arises on the transfer of funds to the trustees, or from the trustees to the settlor, capital gains tax could be payable on such transfers depending on the asset transferred. A settlor is assessed to tax on the trust income and gains as if they continued to own the trust assets. In addition, the settled property remains part of the settlor's estate for inheritance tax purposes.

16:3.3   Accumulation and maintenance trusts

16:3.3.1   General description

Accumulation and maintenance trusts are normally established for the maintenance, education and benefit of children under the age of 25, including those not yet born. While the children are under that age, the trustees may be able to accumulate income (i.e. add it to trust capital) or it can be used to pay the children's living expenses (such payments would normally be made to a beneficiary's parents or guardian while the children are minors). Capital may also be advanced to a beneficiary at the discretion of the trustees. Trustees can be given complete discretion over the allocation of both capital and income between beneficiaries while they are under the age of 25. Thereafter, trustees can retain control of the capital, paying only income to a beneficiary, but reserving the right to advance capital to him or her at any time.

16:3.3.2   Uses

These trusts are mainly of use to a parent or grandparent who wishes to benefit their issue under the age of 25, both during minority and in later years. They are also very beneficial in tax planning, for example, where a grandparent wishes to provide funds to meet school fees, or where a parent wants to give children shares in the family company, but does not know at the time which children will take an active interest in the company. Accumulation and maintenance trusts provide flexibility, without the inheritance tax charge normally associated with discretionary trusts.

16:3.3.3 Tax position

(a) *Inheritance tax.* A gift by an individual into an accumulation and maintenance trust is treated in the same way as an outright gift to another individual and qualifies as a potentially exempt transfer (no inheritance tax is chargeable on the gift if the settlor survives for seven years). These trusts are also not liable to tax when a beneficiary becomes entitled to capital or income and are not subject to a ten year charge as in the case of discretionary trusts (see below).

(b) *Income tax.* Income (other than dividends) is subject to tax at the trust rate (34% for 2000/01) in the trustees' hands. Dividends are taxed in the trustees' hands at the Schedule F trust rate (25% for 2000/01). When income is distributed to beneficiaries at the trustees' discretion, it carries a tax credit of 34% which, depending on the tax position of the beneficiary, may be recoverable, either in whole or part, or further tax may be payable if the beneficiary is liable to the higher rate of tax. However, because the 10% dividend tax credit suffered by the trustees is not repayable, it is not available to frank the 34% tax credit carried by the income distributions. The effect of this is to reduce the maximum possible distribution of dividend income to beneficiaries by 20% although, in practice, the problem may be alleviated in the short to medium term if full distributions of income have not been made prior to 6 April 1999.

Where income is distributed to the settlor's children while they are under the age of 18 and unmarried, the income is treated as that of the settlor for tax purposes. Where a beneficiary is specifically entitled to income, for example, where they are over the age of 25, the income tax treatment is the same as for an interest in possession trust (see above).

(c) *Capital gains tax.* The rate of capital gains tax for this type of trust is 34% after deduction of the appropriate annual exemption (see **16:2.2(c)**).

16:3.4   Discretionary trusts

16:3.4.1   General description

A discretionary trust is one set up for a number of designated beneficiaries or classes of beneficiaries, in which distributions of capital and income during the trust period are entirely at the discretion of the trustees. The trustees have no obligation to distribute income to all beneficiaries and, subject to certain restrictions, any income not distributed can be retained in the trust fund.

16:3.4.2   Uses

Discretionary trusts are very flexible and can be used in a number of different situations, including the following

(a) where a settlor wishes to give away capital to his or her family but does not know at the time whom they want to benefit;

(b) where the settlor wishes one class of beneficiary to receive income, but another class to receive capital;

(c) where one spouse wishes to pass capital to the next generation, but wants the surviving spouse to have the opportunity of receiving income and/or capital if required.

16:3.4.3   Tax position

(a) *Inheritance tax.* Although discretionary trusts are the most flexible type of trust, they are the least favourable for inheritance tax purposes. The creation of a discretionary trust attracts a charge to inheritance tax if the value of the assets gifted, together with the value of any other gifts that were not PETs made within the seven preceding years, exceeds the amount of the nil rate band (£234,000 for 2000/01). This charge is at one-half of the normal rate, so it is 20% in 2000/01. A further charge, generally at very low rates of tax, may be made on capital distributions from such trusts or on each tenth anniversary of their existence. The latter (generally known as the 'periodic charge') is subject to a maximum of 6% of the capital value of the trust. This should be compared, however, to the rate of 40% which would apply to assets held at death, either personally or in an interest in possession trust.

(b) *Income tax.* Income (other than dividends) is subject to tax at the trust rate (34% for 2000/01) in the trustees' hands. Dividends are taxed in the trustees' hands at the Schedule F trust rate (25% for 2000/01). When income is distributed to beneficiaries at the trustees' discretion, it carries a tax credit of 34% which, depending on the tax position of the beneficiary, may be recoverable, either in whole or part, or further tax may be payable if the beneficiary is liable to the higher rate of tax. However, because the 10% dividend tax credit suffered by the trustees is not repayable, it is not available to frank the 34% tax credit carried by the income distributions. The effect of this is to reduce the maximum possible distribution of dividend income to beneficiaries by 20% although, in practice, the problem may be alleviated in the short to medium term if full distributions of income have not been made prior to 6 April 1999.

(c) *Capital gains tax.* On the creation of a discretionary trust, the settlor and the trustees may elect that the capital gains on the assets transferred are 'held over', so that they pass to the trustees. The trustees, therefore, take the assets at their base cost when acquired by the settlor. The rate of capital gains tax for discretionary trusts is 34% after the appropriate annual exemption (see **16:2.2(c)**).

16:3.5   Bare trusts

16:3.5.1   General description

Assets transferred to a bare trust are held by trustees for a named beneficiary who has an absolute and unconditional title to both the capital and the income. In effect, the transfer is an outright gift with the trustees holding assets in name only; the beneficiary can insist at any time that the assets are transferred to him or her.

16:3.5.2   Uses

Generally, a bare trust is used when an individual wishes to make a gift to a minor, an overseas beneficiary or an elderly beneficiary who has difficulty in managing his own affairs.

16:3.5.3   Tax position

(a) *Inheritance tax.* Assets held on bare trusts are deemed for inheritance tax purposes to belong to the beneficiary and offer no additional tax advantages over outright gifts.

(b) *Income tax.* The income on the assets is assessed on the beneficiary and taxed at his or her appropriate rate of tax. Where, however, a parent transfers assets into a bare trust for their own children, who are under the age of 18 and unmarried, the income is treated as the parent's if it exceeds £100 in a tax year.

(c) *Capital gains tax.* Gains of trustees will be assessed on the beneficiary and taxed at his or her appropriate rate of tax.

16:4   Non-resident trusts

Prior to the Finance Act 1991, a popular way of holding investments was via a non-resident trust. A trust created since 19 March 1991, or an existing trust which has received additional capital since that date, is subject to a special tax regime, where the settlor is domiciled in the UK and either resident or ordinarily resident in the UK. Briefly, if the settlor, or his wife, or his children (including adult children), can benefit from the trust, all income (see below) and capital gains are taxed on the settlor. There is, therefore, no income tax or capital gains tax advantage. For all other trusts, mainly those created before 19 March 1991, there were, until the 1998 Finance Act, still capital gains tax and income tax advantages. Those advantages have now largely been removed.

16:4.1   Tax position

(a) *Inheritance tax.* For a trust made by a UK-domiciled settlor, the inheritance tax treatment is the same as for a resident trust. For a settlor who establishes a settlement whilst he is not either domiciled or deemed domiciled for inheritance tax purposes, non-UK situs assets held within the trust will not form part of his UK estate for inheritance tax purposes.

(b) *Income tax.* If the settlor or their spouse cannot benefit from the trust, foreign income can be accumulated free of UK income tax by the trust. However, UK-resident beneficiaries will be taxable on any income distributed to them, or on the value of any benefits provided out of trust assets.

(c) *Capital gains tax.* For capital gains tax purposes, a trust will be non-resident if the trustees, or a majority of them, are not resident in the UK and the administration of the trust is carried out abroad. The effect of such non-residence is that the trustees are not liable to capital gains tax and trust gains are only taxed if they are paid to a UK resident beneficiary, or benefits are provided to the beneficiary out of trust assets. For example, if non-resident trustees make capital gains of £8,000 and a beneficiary receives a capital payment of £12,000, that beneficiary would be liable to capital gains tax on £8,000. Therefore, if the trustees reinvest such gains, whether in UK or overseas assets, it is possible to defer capital gains tax indefinitely (it is also possible entirely to avoid capital gains tax if the beneficiary whom it is desired to benefit ceases to be resident *and* ordinarily resident in the UK (to the satisfaction of the Inland Revenue) and then receives such payments of capital out of the trust). However, the rate of tax payable by a beneficiary depends on the number of years that have elapsed since the gain was made and can be as high as 64%.

The 1998 Finance Act introduced a number of further restrictions on the use of non-resident trusts for the purposes of capital gains tax planning

(i)   gains of pre-19 March 1991 settlements made by a UK domiciled settlor from which the settlor, his spouse and his children can benefit will be taxed on the settlor as they arise for tax years 1999/2000 onwards, unless the only beneficiaries are children of the settlor aged under 18 at the start of a tax year;

(ii)   gains of trusts set up by a UK domiciled settlor on or after 17 March 1998 from which the settlor's grandchildren can also benefit will be taxed on the settlor. Existing trusts which receive additional capital after 17 March 1998 will also fall within the charge.

(iii) prior to 17 March 1998, UK-resident and domiciled beneficiaries were only taxable on capital payments received from a settlement with a UK-resident and domiciled settlor. For capital gains arising and capital payments received on or after 17 March 1998, the status of the settlor will be irrelevant.

It is seldom advisable to set up a non-resident trust, unless substantial tax savings can be achieved, as its administration must be in a tax haven in order to avoid local tax. Management expenses can also be very high.

16:5   Trusts and life assurance policies

Life assurance policies are frequently subjected to trusts in order to provide a fund outside the estate of the settlor to pay inheritance tax on death. Usually, the settlor will pay all premiums. If the premiums are large, to ensure they are PETs where they are paid to an accumulation and maintenance trust or interest in possession trust, the cash should be gifted to the trustees who should pay the premiums. Where the assured is the settlor, a fund can be built up outside their estate with no tax payable on death. At that time, the fund can be used by the beneficiaries to pay inheritance tax, allowing the assets of the estate to be distributed intact.

Where the trust is in the form of an interest in possession trust, it will often provide that any proceeds can be advanced to the beneficiaries absolutely to enable the tax to be paid. If the trust is in the form of an accumulation and maintenance trust, the power to advance capital, before or after the beneficiaries attain the age of 25, will generally provide sufficient flexibility to enable any policy proceeds to be used to fund the payment of inheritance tax. However, the trustees of neither trust can compel the beneficiaries to use the monies to pay inheritance tax, nor can the trustees pay it on behalf of such beneficiaries.

The 1998 Finance Act introduced measures to ensure that where the settlor is either dead or not UK-resident at the time of encashment, the gains arising can be taxed on either any UK-resident trustees or UK-resident beneficiaries. This applies to chargeable events on or after 6 April 1998.

16:6   Modern day use of trusts

Modern trusts are normally very flexible and are used for a wide variety of purposes. A large proportion of the country's wealth is held upon trust, for example, pension funds. Family trusts have played an important part in personal financial planning for a considerable time and, with today's complex tax legislation, they are now even more useful.

Family trusts are used for many purposes in tax planning, but their principal purpose is not in tax mitigation, but the retention of wealth within the family and the management of capital and income for beneficiaries. However, significant tax advantages are usually available. There is generally a trust suitable for most situations but, before creating a trust, it is essential to seek professional advice from an adviser who is experienced in current trust law and taxation.

Appendix 1

Bodies that regulate investment business

FSA
Financial Services Authority
25 The North Colonnade
Canary Wharf
London E14 5HS
Tel: 020 7676 1000

Note: The following self-regulatory organisations (SROs) are now care of the Financial Services Authority at the address above:

- Investment Management Regulatory Organisation (IMRO)

- Personal Investment Authority (PIA)

- The Securities and Futures Authority (SFA)

Recognised professional bodies (RPBs)

ACCA
Chartered Association of
  Certified Accountants
29 Lincoln's Inn Fields
London WC2A 3EE
Tel: 020 7242 6855

Institute of Actuaries
Staple Inn Hall
High Holborn
London WC1V 7QJ
Tel: 020 7632 2100

**Institute of Chartered Accountants
  in England and Wales**
PO Box 433
Chartered Accountants' Hall
Moorgate Place
London EC2P 2BJ
Tel: 020 7920 8100

**Institute of Chartered Accountants
  in Ireland**
87-89 Pembroke Road
Dublin 4
Ireland
Tel: 00 353 1 668 0400

IBRC
Insurance Brokers' Registration
  Council
Higham Business Centre
Midland Road
Higham Ferrers
Northamptonshire NN10 8DW
Tel: 01933 359083

**Institute of Chartered Accountants
  of Scotland**
27 Queen Street
Edinburgh EH2 1LA
Tel: 0131 225 5673

**The Law Society of England and
  Wales**
The Law Society's Hall
113 Chancery Lane
London WC2A 1PL
Tel: 020 7242 1222

**The Law Society of Northern
  Ireland**
Law Society House
98 Victoria Street
Belfast BT1 3JZ
Tel: 01232 231614

The Law Society of Scotland
26 Drumsheugh Gardens
Edinburgh EH3 7YR
Tel: 0131 226 7411

Ombudsman schemes

Certain investment sectors, such as banking, building societies, insurance and pensions, operated ombudsman schemes which allowed anyone who had a grievance against a particular financial institution to make a complaint to the Ombudsman of that financial sector. All of these are now to be combined into a single Ombudsmen scheme for financial services at

The Financial Services Ombudsman
South Quay Plaza
183 Marsh Wall
London E14 9SR

At July 2000, the telephone numbers for the individual Ombudsman schemes were still in force, as follows

Banking Ombudsman	020 7404 9944
Building Societies' Ombudsman	020 7931 0044
Insurance Ombudsman Bureau	020 7964 1483
Investment Ombudsman	020 7796 3065
Pensions Ombudsman	020 7834 9144
PIA Ombudsman	020 7216 0016

Other useful addresses include

Inland Revenue, Customs and Excise, and Contributions Agency Adjudicator's Office

3rd Floor
Haymarket House
28 Haymarket
London SW1Y 4SP
Tel: 020 7930 2292

Registrar of Friendly Societies
25 The North Colonnade
Canary Wharf
London E14 5HS
Tel: 020 7676 1000

Appendix 2

Personal financial planning questionnaire

1. Personal and family details

Self

Name	Title Surname
	Forenames

Address	Home	Correspondence (*if different*)
	Postcode	Postcode

Date and place of birth

Telephone numbers	Home	Business

Fax numbers	Home	Business

Business details	Occupation	Employer

Spouse

Name	Title Surname
	Forenames

Date and place of birth

Business details	Occupation	Employer

Children and other dependants

Full name	Relationship	Date of birth	Financially dependent on you? Yes/No

2. Residence and domicile

	Self	Spouse
Country of residence (*for tax purposes*)		
Country of domicile (*country you regard as your permanent home*)		
Nationality		
Nationality of children (*if different from parents*)		

3. Income details

Please attach a copy of your most recent tax return or give details below of your spouse's income.

Earned income	Self	Spouse
Basic salary	£	£ ....
Bonuses	£	£ ....
Taxable benefits (*for example company car or private medical insurance*)	£	£ ....
Pensions – state	£	£ ....
– other	£	£ ....
Investment income		
Dividends etc	£	£ ....
Bank/building society interest	£	£ ....
Trust income	£	£ ....

Income from other sources (*please specify below*)

	Self	Spouse
	£	£ ....
	£	£ ....
	£	£ ....

Please give details below of any substantial changes in your or your spouse's income in the foreseeable future.

4. Value of assets

Please give below the approximate values of assets held by you, your spouse and your dependants. Where appropriate please include copies of valuations of investments.

	Self	Spouse
Principal residence (*If jointly held specify whether joint tenants or tenants in common*)	£	£ ....
Other properties	£	£ ....
Agricultural land	£	£ ....
House contents and valuables	£	£ ....
Quoted stocks and shares	£	£ ....
Share options	£	£ ....
Lloyd's funds	£	£ ....
Insurance bonds	£	£ ....
Unit trusts	£	£ ....
BES, EIS, VCT and Enterprise Zone property	£	£ ....
Personal Equity Plans, ISAs and TESSAs	£	£ ....
National Savings	£	£ ....
Other savings plans	£	£ ....
Building society deposits	£	£ ....
Bank accounts: Current	£	£ ....
Deposit	£	£ ....
Other assets – please specify (*see note below*)		
	£	£ ....
	£	£ ....
	£	£ ....

Dependants' assets

Name	Type of asset	Value

Note: Business interests, pensions and life assurance are covered in sections 5, 8 and 9.

5. Business interests

Please give below details of your business interests. If you do not have any please ignore this section.

Nature of the business

Are you a: sole trader?   yes ☐   no ☐

partner?   yes ☐   no ☐

director?   yes ☐   no ☐

shareholder?   yes ☐   no ☐

If sole trader or partner please give estimated value of your share of the business   £

Do you own shares in a private company?   yes ☐   no ☐

Name of company

Number of shares held and percentage of the total shares issued   %

Annual turnover and accounting year end

Please give details below of the principal directors, shareholders, partners or other key people in the business.

Name	Position	% Shareholding

What provision has been made for the death of controlling shareholder(s) or partner(s)?

If you hold any other directorships, please state the name of the company and the size of your shareholding.

6. Liabilities

	Self	Spouse
Net payments made under deed of covenant per annum	£	£
Contributions to saving schemes per month	£	£

Please give details of your current liabilities, for example mortgages, overdrafts, loans, hire purchase and other debts.

Date incurred	Lender	Purpose	Original term	Amount outstanding	Interest rate	Final repayment date

Outstanding taxes

Date payable	Amount	Type of tax	Self/spouse

Please give details of any substantial capital expenditure you or your spouse expect to incur in the foreseeable future.

7. Educational fees

Please complete this section if you wish to provide or are already providing fees for your children's or grandchildren's schooling or further education costs.

Child's name	Start date	Educational establishment	Current termly fees (if known)	Number of years fees required

8. Pension arrangements

If you do not have sufficient information available to complete the specific details about your pensions, please provide any relevant records such as a scheme members' handbook or pension policy documents.

	Self	**Spouse**
Your anticipated retirement age		
Are you currently contributing to a company pension scheme?	yes ☐ no ☐	yes ☐ no ☐
Have you made any other pension arrangements?	yes ☐ no ☐	yes ☐ no ☐

Company pension scheme – current

Please complete the following section only if you or your spouse are currently contributing to a company pension scheme or if you belong to a non-contributory scheme.

	Self	**Spouse**
Date started		
Your gross annual contribution (amount or percentage of your salary)		
Additional voluntary contributions		
Does your employer contribute to the scheme?	yes ☐ no ☐	yes ☐ no ☐
Is the scheme contracted out of SERPS?	yes ☐ no ☐	yes ☐ no ☐
Retirement age under the scheme		
Basis on which pension is earned (*for example, 1/60th, 1/80th or other*)		
What life cover is provided on death before retirement? (*please show this as a multiple of your salary, for example 3 X salary*)		
In whose favour have you nominated this lump sum?		
Dependant's pension on your death (as a fraction of your pension)		
– before retirement		
– after retirement		

8. Pension arrangements (*continued*)

Pension benefits from previous employments

	Self	Spouse
Are you entitled to pension benefits from previous employments?	yes ☐ no ☐	yes ☐ no ☐

If yes, please give details

Name of company	Years of employment	Amount of pension	Transfer value

Other pension arrangements

Please give details of any other pension arrangements made by yourself or your spouse.

Self

Name of company	Policy number	Type of policy	Contributions	Start date	If written in trust, beneficiary's name

Spouse

Name of company	Policy number	Type of policy	Contributions	Start date	If written in trust, beneficiary's name

	Self	Spouse
Is the scheme contracted out of SERPS?	yes ☐ no ☐	yes ☐ no ☐

9. Insurance

Please give details of any insurance policies in which you and your spouse have an interest.

Life assurance and endowment policies

Life assured*	Type of policy	Company	Policy number	Sum assured	Premium	Date started	Maturity date

*Please mark with an asterisk if the policy has been written in trust for someone else, and give details below.

Other insurance

Do you or your spouse have permanent health, critical illness or private medical insurance? If yes, please give details below.

Self/spouse	Company	Premium	Benefits

10. Wills and gifts

Wills

Please attach a copy of your will or, if this is not convenient, give brief details of your will. If you have not made a will, briefly describe your wishes for the distribution of your estate in the event of death, including any specific bequests you intend to make.

Self

Date made

Details of the will

Executors

Spouse

Date made

Details of the will

Executors

Gifts

Please give details of any substantial gifts including transfers into trust made by you or your spouse within the last seven years.

Self/spouse	Date	Description of asset	Value	Donee

10. Wills and gifts (*continued*)

Trusts

Also list the names of the trusts of which you are a trustee. If you or your spouse are entitled to benefit from a trust please give details.

11. General

Please give any other relevant information, such as early retirement or possible relocation.

	Self	**Spouse**
National insurance number		
Tax district and reference		
Are you a smoker?	yes ☐ no ☐	yes ☐ no ☐
Are you in good health?	yes ☐ no ☐	yes ☐ no ☐

12. Financial objectives

Please indicate below which of the following financial objectives are most important to you. Please state your priority on a scale of 1 to 5 (1 least important and 5 most important).

Objectives	Priority	Objectives	Priority
Creating or increasing capital	☐	Inheritance tax planning	☐
Increasing net income	☐	Provision for children's or grandchildren's education	☐
Planning for retirement	☐		
Reducing income tax	☐	Financial security for your family	☐
		Overall financial planning review	☐

Please give details below of any other specific financial objectives you wish to achieve.

Investment risk profile

The answers to the following questions will help us to decide what type of investment to recommend to you. They will be regarded as a general guide rather than absolute criteria.

Please indicate below your attitude to investment.

Conservative ☐   Balanced ☐   Speculative ☐

(The degree of risk you can accept will vary with different investments and in different circumstances. We will discuss this with you each time we advise on a particular investment).

Please tick the appropriate box to indicate your main investment objective.

Maximum capital growth ☐

A reasonable balance between growth and income ☐

High income subject to protection of capital value ☐

Maximum income, accepting possible erosion of capital ☐

Other (please specify) ☐

Please state any restrictions you wish to impose on particular areas of investment.

13. Your advisers

Accountant

Name
Address
Telephone no.   Fax no.

**Stockbroker/
Investment
manager**

Name
Address
Telephone no.   Fax no.

Solicitor

Name
Address
Telephone no.   Fax no.

Client's signature   **Date**

Thank you very much for completing this client information form.

Appendix 3

Minimum retirement ages for certain occupations

Retirement ages have been agreed by the Inland Revenue for self-employed persons or persons not in an occupational pension scheme in respect of the following professions and occupations

Profession or occupation	Retirement age
Athletes	35
Badminton players	35
Boxers	35
Cricketers	40
Cyclists	35
Dancers	35
Divers (saturation, deep sea and free swimming)	40
Footballers	35
Golfers	40
Ice hockey players	35
Jockeys – flat racing	45
– national hunt	35
Members of the reserve forces	45
Models	35
Motorcycle riders (motocross or road racing)	40
Motor racing drivers	40
Rugby League and Union players	35
Skiers (downhill)	30
Snooker and billiards players	40
Speedway riders	40
Squash players	35
Table tennis players	35
Tennis players (including real tennis)	35
Trapeze artistes	40
Wrestlers	35

Note

The concession to take pension benefits at an early retirement age may be withdrawn if the individual changes occupation but continues to contribute to the same policy. Therefore, when a change of occupation arises before benefits are taken, it may be worthwhile for the old policy to be made paid-up and a new policy effected for subsequent contributions.

Appendix 4

Distribution of an estate under an intestacy

A summary of the position in respect of the distribution of an estate under the laws of intestacy in England and Wales is shown below. Since 1 January 1996, a spouse must survive for 28 days to become entitled under these rules. It should be noted that the position in England and Wales differs in some respects from that in Northern Ireland and considerably from that in Scotland.

England and Wales

If deceased dies leaving	*Persons who benefit*
1. Spouse, but no issue, parent, brother or sister, nephew or niece	1. Spouse takes everything absolutely.
2. Spouse and issue	2. (a) Spouse takes £125,000 absolutely, plus personal chattels (car, furniture, pictures, clothing, jewellery, etc.), plus life interest (income only) in half of residue. (b) Issue take half residue on reaching age 18 or marrying before that age, plus, on death of spouse, the half residue in which the spouse had a life interest.
3. Spouse, no issue, but parent(s) or brother(s) or sister(s) of the whole blood or their issue	3. (a) Spouse takes £200,000 absolutely, plus personal chattels, plus half residue absolutely. (b) Parents, but, if none, then brothers and sisters (nephews and nieces step into their parents' shoes if the latter are dead) take half residue.

If deceased dies leaving	*Persons who benefit*
4. No spouse	4. Everything is taken by:

    (a) Issue on reaching 18 or marrying under that age; but if none

    (b) Parents; but if none

    (c) Brothers and sisters of the whole blood (nephews and nieces step into their parents' shoes); but if none

    (d) Half brothers and sisters (or failing them, their own respective issue); but if none

    (e) Grandparents; but if none

    (f) Uncles and aunts of the whole blood (cousins step into their parents' shoes); but if none

    (g) Half uncles and aunts (or failing them, their own respective issue); but if none

    (h) The Crown.

Notes

(a) 'Issue' is defined as children (including illegitimate and adopted children), grandchildren and so on. However, it does not include stepchildren.

(b) Where part of the residuary estate includes a dwelling-house in which the surviving spouse resided at the date of death, the spouse has the right to have the dwelling-house as part of the absolute interest or towards the capital value of the life interest under **2(a)** and **3(a)** above.

Appendix 5

Dying tidily log

This log should be completed and filed with your private papers. Your next of kin should be informed of its contents and location. This should assist considerably with the administration of your estate when the need arises.

Information about estate and assets of:

Name	
Address	
Date of birth	
National Health number	
National Insurance number	

1. Will

Date	
Location	
Executors – names, addresses, telephone numbers	

Funeral wishes (burial, cremation, name of cemetery and plot number)

2. Professional advisers, etc.

(state name, address and
telephone number)
Doctor

Dentist

Solicitor

Accountant

Bank

Stockbroker

Insurance broker

HM Inspector of Taxes

District

Reference number

Others

3. Assets

Main residence

Address

Ownership (sole, joint, tenants in common)	
Subject to or free from mortgage	
Mortgagee or lender	
Address	
Reference number	

Other properties

Address	
Ownership (sole, joint, tenants in common)	
Subject to or free from mortgage	
Mortgagee or lender	
Address	
Reference number	

Business or share of partnership	

Investments (please state if held jointly)

(a)	Bank accounts and building society accounts	
	Name and address of bank/building society	
	Type of account	
	Account number	
(b)	National Savings	
(c)	Guaranteed income bonds/ guaranteed growth bonds	
(d)	Fixed interest securities	
(e)	Ordinary stocks and shares (equities)	
(f)	Unit trusts	
(g)	Investment bonds	

(h)   Private companies

(state approximate %
holdings, including related
holdings)

(i)   Other investments

(j)   Assets held in trust

4. Liabilities

Bank overdraft arrangements

Loans

Other liabilities

5. Gifts

Details, values and dates of all
material gifts made within the
last seven years.

6. Pension and life assurance policies

Name of company	Policy number	Type of policy	On whose life	Sum assured	Name of beneficiaries (if applicable)	Names of trustees (if the policy is written subject to a trust)

7. Location of valuables

(a) Property deeds

(b) Stock and share certificates, unit trust certificates, National Savings Certificates, building society passbooks, etc.

(c) Pension and life assurance policies

(d) Contracts (hire purchase agreements, loan agreements, general insurance policies, etc.)

(e) Safe deposit box (if any)

(f) Safe deposit key (if any)

(g) Personal papers (birth certificates, marriage certificate, partnership agreement, etc.)

(h) Passports

(i) Bank statements

(j) Others (please specify)

8. Notifications required

(in addition to those mentioned in earlier section)

(a) Employer (name, address and telephone number)

(b) Membership of occupational pension schemes (including former employers)

(c) Department of Social Security

(d) Deeds of covenant ceasing on death

(e) Standing orders and direct debits

(f) Credit cards/charge cards (name and number)

(g) Trusteeships, executorships and guardianships held

(h) Memberships of associations (name, address, membership number, etc.)

Professional/trade associations

Clubs

Other organisations (AA, RAC, etc.)

(i) Honorary offices held

(j) Contracts (with whom held, renewal date, where kept)

Hire purchase or loan

General insurance

House

Contents

Car

Other insurances

Other contracts

(k)   Licences

Road fund licence
(registration number
and date of expiry)

MOT certificate
(registration number
and date of expiry)

Driving licence
(serial number)

TV licence
(date of expiry)

Other licences

(l)   Others

9. Other information

Relevant information not
already stated in this log.

INDEX

This index is in alphabetical, word by word order. Location references refer to chapter number (bold type), followed by a colon and the relevant section number. For example:

Accident insurance.........**11**:4.2

indicates that information on accident insurance can be found in Chapter **11**, section 4.2.